PRACTICAL TRUTHS

FROM
JUDGES

PRACTICAL TRUTHS
FROM
JUDGES

by
Luke H. Wiseman

KREGEL PUBLICATIONS
Grand Rapids, Michigan 49501

Practical Truths From Judges by Luke H. Wiseman
Copyright ©1985 by Kregel Publications, a division of
Kregel, Inc. all rights reserved.

Library of Congress Cataloging in Publication Data

Wiseman, Luke H., 1821-1875.

   Practical Truths From Judges.

  Reprint. Originally published: Men of faith. London:
Hodder & Stoughton, 1874.
  1. Bible. O.T. Judges—History of Biblical events. I.
Title.
BS1305.W56 1985   222'.3209   85-8096
ISBN 0-8254-4034-3

Printed in the United States of America

CONTENTS

6 **CONTENTS**

PREFACE

THE design contemplated in this book may be described as threefold. In the first place, I have endeavoured to present a general view of that important period in the history of the Hebrew people, intervening between the death of Joshua and the anointing of their first king, during which, to use the language of St. Stephen, "the Lord gave them Judges." Then, selecting the four most eminent persons whom the sacred narrative presents to our view during that period—Barak, Gideon, Jephthah, and Samson—men who are specially mentioned by the author of the Epistle to the Hebrews as men of faith; the results of a careful study of the history of each of them are submitted to the reader. Lastly, I have wished to render the whole subservient to purposes of edification, and have therefore introduced practical remarks and reflections.

The Book of Judges is perhaps less studied and quoted from than most other historical books of Scripture. Indeed, it is surprising how scanty, comparatively, are references to it in the writings of our standard English preachers and divines. But even the most neglected parts of the Lord's garden will be found to yield flowers of heavenly fragrance; and I am not without hope that the present attempt, which has been on the writer's part a labour of love, may be the means of awakening in some minds a deeper interest in this part of the history of God's ancient Church.

L. H. W.

Part 1

THE PERIOD
OF THE JUDGES

1

EARLY VICTORIES

THE last recorded scene in the life of Joshua is invested with singular grandeur. He "called for the elders of Israel, and for their heads, and for their judges, and for their officers," to meet him in solemn assembly. The spot selected for their meeting was calculated, by its historical associations, to confirm their faith in the God of their fathers. As they "presented themselves before God" in the most wildly beautiful of all the plains of Ephraim, the plain of Shechem, they could scarcely fail to remember how their ancestor, Abraham, who had left his country and his father's house five centuries before, had rested there, and had built in Shechem the first altar to the living God which the Holy Land had known; how the same spot, almost two hundred years afterwards, became the first possession of their race in the Land of Promise ; how Jacob, finding a home after his long wandering, bought the parcel of the field where he had spread his tent, at the hand of the children of Hamor, Shechem's father ; how Moses, not long before his death, and almost within sight of Canaan, had ordered them, as soon as they should have passed over Jordan, to build an altar upon that very mount Ebal, which now bounded their horizon toward the west ; and how Joshua, their venerable captain, had built the altar soon after the tribes had crossed the Jordan.*

These associations of the place must have lent additional impressiveness to the parting words of their chief, as he recited once more God's gracious dealings with them and with their fathers, and adjured them, three times in succession, to choose Jehovah for their God. It was not Abraham's own choice, but God's decree, which had separated him from his idolatrous kindred "on the other side of the flood," and given him the Land of Promise. It was Jehovah's arm which had chastised the Egyptians and divided the waters and set Pharaoh's bondmen free. It was not by their own sword or their own bow that they had got the land in possession ; it was the Lord, "who had sent the hornet before" them, had driven out the kings of the Amorites, and had given His people the land, a

---

* Gen. xii. 6 ;   xxxiii. 18, 19 ;   Deut. xxvii. 4, 5 ;   Josh. viii. 30 ;
xxiv. 1.

land for which they did not labour, and cities which they had not built." The descendants of him who all his life had " dwelt in tabernacles"* as a stranger, had at length become possessors of the country. The promises made to Abraham had been fulfilled. His life-long faith had been justified. The men, who now for the last time surrounded Joshua, remembered these things. Moved, perhaps, by the aspect of their veteran chief, and by the historical associations of the place whereon they stood, they bound themselves anew, in vows thrice repeated,—" *The Lord our God will we serve, and His voice will we obey.*"†

The men of that generation remained faithful to their engagements. In the supplementary paragraph appended to the book of Joshua, it is stated that "Israel served the Lord," not only during "all the days of Joshua," but also, " all the days of the elders that overlived Joshua." These men, who had themselves "known all the works of the Lord that he had done for Israel," ‡ in bringing them into Canaan and in subduing the hostile nations, never forsook His worship for the worship of the idols of the land, of whose boasted power they had witnessed so signal a discomfiture. The character and admonitions of Joshua were not forgotten. His disinterestedness, his energy, his singleness of purpose, his faith, had left a track of glory behind, as the sun, after he has sunk below the horizon, flings gorgeous hues and

---

* Heb. xi. 9. † Josh. xxiv. 24. ‡ Josh. xxiv. 31.

golden light over all the western sky. The men who had themselves seen the conquests of Joshua would have been doubly inexcusable if they had forsaken the worship of Jehovah. Like the disciple, Thomas, because they had seen they had believed. How indeed could it have been otherwise? How could they, standing there in Shechem,—the site of Abraham's altar, of Jacob's well, of Joseph's tomb, of Joshua's victories,—refuse to believe in the Divine calling of the people Israel?

The length of time which elapsed between the death of Joshua and the circumstance related in the first verse of the Book of Judges, has not been precisely ascertained. The Israelites "asked the Lord," apparently as the act of a solemn assembly, which of the tribes should be the first to "go up against the Canaanites, to fight against them." * From this it would appear that the Canaanites had now assumed a threatening attitude. They had in some measure recovered their strength after the blows which had been inflicted on them by Joshua. Their king Adoni-bezek, under whose table seventy kings,† dishonoured and mutilated, had picked up the falling crumbs, was able to raise a powerful force, and is spoken of as a great public enemy. It seems scarcely credible that

---

* Jud. i. 1.

† Stüder (*Buch der Richter*, p. 12), suggests that "seventy," like "forty" elsewhere, may be a round number. In this way we speak in English of a "score," or a "thousand." Probably they were not all there together, but at different times.

such a prince, if in force during the lifetime of Joshua, should not have been attacked by him ; and the inference is, that at the time when the Lord is said to have "given rest unto Israel from all their enemies round about,"* previous to Joshua's death, the power of Adoni-bezek had not yet become considerable. A short period, however, may have sufficed for the growth of this power. The heathen would take heart as soon as they heard that the mighty captain of the Israelites was no more. It is not improbable that during the years of Joshua's decline, the Canaanites were biding their time and nursing their strength, so as to be able, as soon as the Israelites were deprived of a leader by his death, to burst upon them unawares.

The condition of Israel, on this irruption of the Canaanites, was critical indeed. They had no leader, for Joshua had named no successor ; and who would dare to face the enemy without him ? In this their earliest trouble they betook themselves to the Lord their God. They did not inquire whether or not they were to go to war. On this point there was no room for doubt or debate. The enemy was at their gates. The man who had led captive seventy kings was close upon them. Fight they must, to preserve themselves from destruction. The question was, who should undertake the work ? None were willing to begin uncalled ; therefore *"the children of Israel,"*—all their tribes, assembled by their representatives,—" *asked*

---

* Josh. xxiii. 1.

the Lord, saying, Who shall go up for us against the Canaanites first, to fight against them?" *

An answer was returned which could not be mistaken. "Phinehas prophesied"—so Josephus explains the circumstance—"that they should commit the government to the tribe of Judah." † The Divine will, he says, was intimated to the high-priest, through the Urim and Thummim. By whatever means conveyed to the chiefs, the command of Israel was clear and decisive; and it was accompanied with a promise of success: *" Judah shall go up: behold, I have delivered the land into his hand."* ‡

May we not pause here for a moment to allow this oracular response to sink into the heart? How full it is in its manifold meaning! It asserts the sovereignty of God in disposing and ordering the work which His servants have to perform. It reminds us that every one is not to attempt everything; for Judah is to fight the enemy, and the other tribes are to remain at home. It promises victory, not to every ardent soldier who might volunteer to take the field, but to the tribe whom the Lord shall order to the battle. It disturbs all rule-of-three calculations of success in proportion to the number of agents men may induce to go to work; success is for those whom the Lord shall send. It allows of no objection, no plea of incompetency, no deceitful humility, on the part of the called soldier: *Judah shall go up;* it is the word

---

* Jud. i. 1.   † Antiquities, book v. chap. 2.   ‡ Jud. i. 2.

of a king. It hides pride from man, by declaring
that although Judah would conquer, it would be only
through Divine ordination and help.

The men of Judah therefore went up to meet the
enemy. But they did not go alone. The inheritance
of the tribe of Simeon lay within that of the tribe of
Judah, or rather formed a part of it; * and the two
tribes agreed to assist each other. The fierce and
wild sons of Simeon would prove valuable auxiliaries
to the more disciplined bands of Judah, and they
marched together in pursuit of the Canaanites. It
was not for the defence of their own particular territory that they were now taking the sword, but in the
common cause of Israel. A great public enemy, a
conqueror of seventy kings, had arisen, and he must
be attacked and subdued in order to secure the
general safety.

We have few details of the march, or of the battle,
beyond the brief statement that " *the Lord delivered
the Canaanites and the Perizzites into their hand.*" †
They fell in with the enemy in Bezek. In a decisive
encounter at that place, the locality of which is
uncertain, ten thousand were slain; and Adoni-bezek
(*lord of Bezek*) himself was captured after a vain
attempt to escape by flight. It appears that this
heathen chief had not been a stranger to the name
and power of the God of Israel; nor did he complain
of his punishment as unjust. When his toes and his

---

* Josh. xix. 9.   † Jud. i. 4–7.

thumbs were cut off by the men of Judah, he exclaimed, " *Threescore and ten kings, having their thumbs and their great toes cut off, gathered their meat under my table : as I have done, so God hath requited me.*" Such mutilations were not uncommon among the ancients, nor are they unusual among barbarous nations of this day. The loss of the thumbs incapacitates for military service ; and so common among the Romans was voluntary mutilation of this kind, in order to escape conscription, that their historian, Ammianus, adduces, as a singular instance of martial spirit, the fact that among the Gauls no man was to be found who had lost his thumbs. It would be easy to multiply illustrative instances ; but it may be sufficient to mention that our own English language retains a trace of this once prevalent practice, in the word *poltroon*, which is no other than the old Italian *poltrone*, or " *thumbless* "—signifying a soldier who is a coward.

Seventy kings thus incapacitated for future resistance had been yet further degraded by being compelled to lie under Adoni-bezek's table and subsist upon the broken morsels which fell from it. This custom of heaping insult upon a vanquished enemy was in accordance with the spirit and practice of most ancient nations, even of those which boasted a far higher civilization than the Canaanites. Many instances might be cited, such as that of Sesostris, king of Egypt, who harnessed the kings whom he had conquered to his chariot, and compelled them to

draw it ; or that of Sapor, king of Persia, who compelled the Roman emperor Valerian to stoop down, so
that he might use his back as a block from which to
mount his horse ; or that of the Assyrian monarchs,
who are represented in the Nineveh sculptures drag-
ging along royal captives whom they had taken in
war, by means of a cord attached to a kind of fish-
hook, which was thrust through the lower lip, or
through the cartilage of the nose,* and by which the
prisoner was pulled along. It appears that the
Israelites did not inflict upon Adoni-bezek all the
ignominy which he had himself inflicted on others.
They spared him the disgrace of being fed like a dog
under the conqueror's table; and contented themselves,
having incapacitated him for further resistance, with
taking him a captive to Jerusalem.†

His notions of justice and of retribution open an
interesting glimpse into a heathen's breast. "*As I
have done*," he exclaimed, "*so God hath requited me.*"
Thus Adoni-bezek illustrates the statements of St.
Paul concerning "the Gentiles who have not the law."
He shows evidently "the work," or substance, "of the
law written on his heart, his conscience accusing him."
He "knows the judgment of God, that they which
commit such things are worthy of death." ‡   He

---

* To this practice Isaiah xxxvii. 29 refers.

† Jerusalem was at this time already reckoned, though the
strongest part of it was not yet in possession, as one of the
twenty-six cities belonging to the tribe of Benjamin (Josh
·xv. 8, xviii. 28).

‡ Jud. i. 7 ; Rom. ii. 15, i. 32.

exemplifies the force of that natural conscience which is a gift of God's grace not lost through the fall, or if lost, restored through that "free gift which has come upon all men." *   And his humble and public confession may perhaps be viewed as an evidence of his repentance, according to the light which he possessed. His penitence may have been the reason why he was not put to death, like the other kings who were vanquished, but was allowed to live. How long he survived his defeat and disgrace cannot now be known ; the historian has only informed us that he was brought from Bezek to Jerusalem, where he ended his days in captivity.†

The great public enemy having been effectually dealt with, the two tribes next turned their attention to the work of destroying such of the heathen as dwelt within their own borders, and along the great

---

* Rom. v. 18.

† The occurrence of the name Jerusalem appears to have led the compiler of the book of Judges into a digression, which commences at the eighth verse of the first chapter, the regular narrative resuming at the beginning of the seventeenth verse. The digression relates to the first taking of Jerusalem and places adjacent during Joshua's lifetime ; and the account of Othniel, who won by his valour the daughter of the mighty Caleb, is repeated *verbatim* from the book of Joshua. (a) A brief notice of the Kenites is also added ; perhaps because, as their tents were now pitched within the territory of Judah, some of the warriors of that tribe accompanied the men of Judah and Simeon in their expedition against the Canaanites. Passing by the facts narrated in that paragraph, as belonging to an earlier period of the history, we continue our review of the progress of Judah's army.   [(a) Jud. i. 8–16 ; Josh. xv. 14–19, xv. 63.]

sandy plain toward their west and north, upon the
Mediterranean shore.* The city of Zephath,—or
Hormah, as it had been called by Moses, who had
approached within a short distance of it during the
early part of the sojourn in the wilderness,—appears
to have been situated on that undulating and arid
frontier, where a few wild and scanty shrubs, and a
few distant and uncertain wells, mark the transition
from the desert to the vegetation of Palestine. Hormah, which was included in the inheritance of Simeon,
had been devoted to destruction by the vow of the
Israelites while yet in the wilderness, and its king
had been afterwards reduced to subjection by Joshua;†
but its destruction had not hitherto been complete.
Its complete destruction was now effected. It is only
mentioned subsequently as one of the places "where
David and his men were wont to haunt" in the days
of the minstrel king's adversity, and as a city inhabited
by sons of the foul-tongued Shimei.‡ "In the midst
of this wild frontier," says Stanley, "ruins still appear
on the rising grounds as if of ancient cities; such as
may have been Arad, the abode of the southernmost
Canaanite king;"§ and we may add, with perhaps
equal probability, Zephath, or Hormah,—the earliest

---

* Jud. i. 17.

† Num. xxi. 1–3 ; ver. 3, except the last clause, may have
been added to the original text by a later writer, to mark the
completion of the Israelites' vow.

‡ 1 Sam. xxx. 30 ; 1 Chron. iv. 30.

§ "Syria and Palestine," p. 161.

reward of the faith and valour of the men of Judah and Simeon.

From the border of the wilderness there is ready access to the sandy plain which lies between the mountains of Judah and the sea, the country of the Philistines.   To this maritime region the two victorious tribes next directed their steps.   They went at the Divine command, and they went in faith ; and the strong holds of Philistia could not resist them. Their course, from south to north, is accurately marked by the sacred writer.   Up to this time, however remote may have been the period when the seafaring Philistines first landed from Asia Minor, or from Crete, they had probably enjoyed undisturbed possession of their coast, their plains, and their cornfields.   Even the mighty Joshua had not taken Gaza, the southernmost city of the plain ; but the Anakims remained there after he had cut them off " from all the mountains of Judah, and from all the mountains of Israel."*   Already, perhaps, the men of Gaza had raised a stately temple in honour of Dagon, the fish-god ; their city, protected both by its eminence and by the sandy tract reaching up to the base of the hill on which it stands, had remained untouched by the invader.   It surrendered, however, to the wild and impetuous men of Simeon and the disciplined bands of Judah ; they " *took Gaza with the coast thereof.*" †

---

* Josh. xi. 21, 22.   † Jud. i. 18.

From Gaza to Ascalon was an easy march. Ascalon and Ekron, like Gaza, became famous in later history, and have preserved their names from those remote ages to the present day. They are all remarkable for the extreme beauty and profusion of the gardens which surround them. The scarlet blossoms of the pomegranates, the enormous oranges which gild the green foliage of their famous groves, lent attractiveness and fascination to the vices by which they were defiled; and doves "still fill with their cooings the luxuriant gardens which grow in the sandy hollow within the ruined walls." * *"Askelon with the coast thereof, and Ekron with the coast thereof,"*—Ekron being the most northern, as Gaza is the most southern city of Philistia,—were successively taken; thus apparently completing the conquest of that region; for "*the Lord was with Judah.*" †

Thus far the career of the two tribes had been successful. The mantle of Joshua had fallen upon the captains of Simeon and of Judah, and his parting words were being verified: "One man of you shall chase a thousand; for the Lord your God, He it is that fighteth for you." ‡ They had asked and had

---

* Stanley, p. 257. "In Ascalon was entrenched the hero of the last gleam of history which has thrown light over the plains of Philistia. Within the walls and towers still standing, Richard *Cœur de Lion* held his court; and the white-faced hill which, seen from their heights, forms so conspicuous an object in the western part of the plain, is the 'Blanche-Garde' of the crusading chroniclers, which witnessed his chief adventures."

† Jud. i. 17.   ‡ Josh. xxiii. 10.

received direction from on high. Deprived of their visible head, they had relied upon the power and promise of God ; nor had they relied in vain. Like the apostles after the ascension, though deprived of the visible presence of their Lord, these elders of Israel were clothed with power, and advanced from strength to strength. Had they maintained this faith—had they resisted the deceitfulness of unbelief —nothing could have prevented them from effecting the entire subjugation of the country, and realizing all the blessing of that good land which the Lord' had promised to their fathers. But they were not thus faithful. After this brief and brilliant career of victory, their annals record a series of failures, all traceable more or less directly to their unbelief. These failures laid a foundation for the miseries and misfortunes of succeeding generations ; while indirectly they led to the raising up of those mighty men of faith, the judges of Israel.

2

THE CANAANITES NOT EXPELLED

A SUCCESSION of brilliant victories, worthy of
the name and fame of Israel, had crowned the
arms of the two tribes who had first gone up at the
command of the Lord to fight against the Canaanites.
The promise which had encouraged Judah at the
outset, "Behold, I have delivered the land into his
hand," * had been fulfilled, as his triumphant army,
reducing one great fortress of the enemy after another,
went on "from strength to strength." Soon, however, the history assumes a different complexion.
The evil heart of unbelief, the "mystery of iniquity,"
which wrought so early and so fatally in the New
Testament Churches,—which, operating in divers
forms and under manifold disguises, bewitched the
Galatians, seduced the Ephesians from their first love,
taught the Churches at Pergamos and Thyatira the
doctrines of Balaam and Jezebel, led the Laodiceans
into lukewarmness, and raised before the eyes of St.
John the spectre of Antichrist already come,—this
mystery of iniquity and unbelief operated so early
and so powerfully in the Hebrew Church after their

* Jud. i. 2.

settlement in Canaan, that its history, even in the first chapter of the record, ceases to be a history of triumph, and becomes a chronicle of failures.

The first failure recorded is that of the victorious tribe of Judah itself. " *The Lord was with Judah; and he drave out the inhabitants of the mountain; but could not drive out the inhabitants of the valley, because they had chariots of iron.*" *

The rugged and mountainous parts of Palestine were for the most part conquered and occupied by the men of Israel, while the plains and level tracts * were left to a great extent in possession of the enemy.   Looking at the matter otherwise than with the eye of faith, this was easy enough to be understood.   The Israelites were a nation of infantry; and they could not deal with an enemy who could bring horses and chariots into action.   It is true that some of their first victories after Joshua's death were, as we have seen, achieved in a level country, when Judah and Simeon seized three out of the five great cities of the Philistian plain.   But although they took these cities they could neither hold them, nor drive out the inhabitants; for we shortly afterwards find the " five lords of the Philistines " included in an enumeration of the enemies who were left unsubdued. †

---

* Jud. i. 19 : the Hebrew word *emek*, "valley," is "not applied to ravines, but to the long broad sweeps sometimes found between parallel ranges of hills."—*Stanley's Heb. Vocabulary* ' *Syr. and Pal.*," p. 481.

† Jud. iii. 3.

This inability, though so readily explained, was a direct consequence of their unbelief. The sphere of faith lies, not in that which is visible, and calculable according to that lower reason which can only grasp "the things that are seen," but in that which is invisible, and to be calculated according to that higher reason which grasps "the things that are not seen." *
Therefore in Judah's inability to drive out the chariots of iron we may trace the first stage of unbelief, and of the consequent powerlessness and degradation of the Church.

Their unbelief was the more inexcusable, inasmuch as a promise had been given expressly to meet this very difficulty : " When thou goest out to battle against thine enemies, and seest horses, and chariots, and a people more than thou, be not afraid of them : for the Lord thy God is with thee, which brought thee up out of the land of Egypt." † Under ordinary circumstances, an army of foot soldiers might reasonably hesitate to engage with horses and chariots. But the warfare of the Israelitish people, like the spiritual warfare of the Christian, was not to be thus calculated. They had a promise from the Unseen God ; and that almighty Arm which had divided the Red Sea would be their strength, whatever forces might be arrayed against them, if they would only believe Him. Joshua had thus believed. To him therefore, although he possessed no cavalry, the "horses and chariots very

---

* Heb. xi. 1.   † Deut. xx. 1.

many" of the combined armies of Palestine, though accompanied by soldiers "even as the sand that is upon the sea shore in multitude," seemed no invincible force. "To-morrow about this time," said the Lord to him, "thou shalt hough their horses, and burn their chariots with fire;" and "Joshua did unto them as the Lord bade him." *

Occasionally, in the subsequent history of this people, the war chariots of their enemies were routed, when some captain, full of faith in God, was raised up to deliver Israel, as in the time of Deborah and Barak. But as a general rule horses and chariots proved too formidable for them, and their enemies invariably gathered courage whenever they could bring these into action. Five hundred years after the times of which we are now speaking, the Syrians encouraged each other to a renewed attack upon the Israelites by this argument: "Their gods are gods of the hills, therefore they were stronger than we; but let us fight against them in the plain, and surely we shall be stronger than they." † So chronic was that condition of unbelief which first developed itself among the hitherto faithful and victorious men of Judah, who "could not drive out the inhabitants of the valley, because they had chariots of iron."

The next failure related is that of the tribe of Benjamin. They "*did not drive out the Jebusites that inhabited Jerusalem ; but the Jebusites dwell*

---

* Josh. xi. 4–9.   † 1 Kings xx. 23.

with the children of Benjamin in Jerusalem unto this day ;*—that is, to the time of the prophet Samuel, by whom probably the book of Judges was compiled.

Although the Israelites made themselves masters, for the most part, of the hilly districts, there were some exceptions to this, of which the failure of Benjamin to take Jerusalem is the most remarkable. Soon after the tribes had crossed the Jordan, the then king of Jerusalem joined in a confederacy with other neighbouring kings, all of whom Joshua put to the sword. It does not appear that Joshua attacked the city itself ; but the statement that he " smote all the country of the hills " † would seem to imply that Jerusalem, one of the most important strongholds of that region, was subdued. The men of Judah, we read, had "taken Jerusalem, and set the city on fire ;" but the Jebusites re-entered it, and dwelt with the children of Judah ‡ and Benjamin, the city lying upon the border line of the two tribes. It is spoken of in the book of Judges as a " city of the Jebusites," and a " city of a stranger ;" § nor was it recovered until the time of David, who, having offered rewards to any of his men who would scale the precipitous sides of the ravine, " took the stronghold of Zion," and, seeing no doubt at a glance the matchless strength of its situation, at once took up his residence " in the fort," and " built round about " it.‖ The

---

* Jud. i. 21.   † Josh. x. 40.   ‡ Josh. xv. 63.
§ Jud. xix. 11, 12.   ‖ 2 Sam. v. 7-9.

men of Benjamin, however, "could not drive out the
Jebusites :" they could not retain what their predecessors had gained, but were content with a divided
supremacy. We have here a key to the subsequent
moral state of Jerusalem. The city was not in the
beginning purged from idolaters ; the tares and the
wheat grew together from the beginning—"representing," as a commentator justly remarks, "a lax
state of the Church of God, due to men's sin ;"* nor
can we wonder at its subsequent history and fall.

Passing from the tribe of Benjamin to that of
Manasseh, the sacred record enumerates the places
which the men of that tribe were unable to subdue.
"*Neither did Manasseh drive out the inhabitants of
Beth-shean and her towns*"—her *daughters*, if we
translate the text literally ; that is, the smaller places
situated near the principal city—"*nor Taanach and
her towns, nor the inhabitants of Dor . . . nor
of Ibleam . . . nor of Megiddo and her towns ;
but the Canaanites would dwell in that land.*"†

The situation of these places, with the exception of
Ibleam, is well ascertained. From their positions, as
well as from the way in which they are mentioned,
both in earlier and in later records,‡ it is evident that
they must have been among the most important places
in Manasseh's territory. They are all situated in that
great plain of Jezreel or of Esdraelon, § which extends

---

* Bishop Wordsworth.   † Jud. i. 27.

‡ Josh. xvii. 11 ; 1 Chron. vii. 29.

§ *Esdraelon* is merely the Greek form of the Heb. word *Jezreel*.

quite across the centre of Palestine, from the Mediterranean on the west to the Jordan on the east, cutting the country in two, and dividing the mountain ranges of Samaria from those of Galilee.

Beginning at the Jordan end of the plain, the writer first names *Beth-shean*, the "house of rest," called in later times Scythopolis and now *Beisân*, a place situated two or three miles west of that river, just on the brow of the descent where the plain begins to drop towards the Jordan level. Four streams run through or near the town. The abundance of water, the exuberance of the soil, and the facility afforded by the level country for the use of "chariots," may explain why the Canaanites struggled to keep, while the Manassites were unable to conquer, the fruitful Beth-shean. *Taanach* and *Megiddo* are situated at the western or seaward end of the plain. Taanach still retains its ancient name; and Megiddo, beside whose waters Sisera's host was routed, and whose name is associated with memories of Solomon and Josiah, and with the prophetic battle of Armageddon, or "mount Megiddo," * is visible from it; where some columns and rubbish heaps and building stones along the banks of a little stream are the only vestiges left of the royal city of the Canaanites. *Dor* was upon the sea coast, not far from the base of mount Carmel. It was an ancient royal city of the Canaanites; it became afterwards a residence of one of Solomon's twelve

* 1 Kings ix. 15 ; 2 Kings xxiii. 29 ; Rev. xvi. 16.

purveyors ; it went through various fortunes in the times of the Maccabees and Romans;* it is now a heap of low ruins, the district being almost wholly deserted, in consequence of the periodical raids of the wild Bedouin, who pasture their flocks on the plain of Sharon.

" The Canaanites would dwell in that land," says the historian, repeating the words used in reference to the same tribe and the same places in the book of Joshua.† The Hebrew word which our version renders " *would* ‡ dwell," intimates that the Canaanites wished to arrange the matter agreeably ; that they made friendly overtures to the men of Manasseh to be permitted to remain—a permission which was granted them on condition of their paying tribute.   Such is the attitude which, in these latter days, the world frequently assumes toward the Church of Christ in Christian countries.   It is willing enough to pay tribute, both in gold and outward forms of deference, if only the Church will allow it a peaceable lodging, and refrain from using against it the sword of the Spirit.   Too often has the Church, like the men of Manasseh, consented to accept tribute money, whether of the state or of private individuals, as the price of permitting the world to remain unmolested within its borders ; and how often has she found, in her bitter

---

* Josh. xii. 21, 23 ; 1 Kings iv. 11 ; 1 Macc. xv. 11.

† Josh. xvii. 12.

‡ Compare Gen. xviii. 27, Exod. ii. 21, 1 Sam. xii. 22, Josh. vii. 7 ; where the Hebrew *Yaal* (Hiphil) is variously rendered in our Authorized Version.

experience, the degrading and enslaving effect of such compromises—verifying to the letter the prediction of Joshua in regard to such unhallowed connections : " they shall be snares and traps unto you, and scourges in your sides, and thorns in your eyes !" *

We come, next, to the powerful tribe of Ephraim, which is recorded to have failed in only one instance —that of Gezer†—to drive out the heathen who dwelt within its boundaries. This failure is mentioned in the book of Joshua, where it is added, "the Canaanites dwell among the Ephraimites unto this day, and serve under tribute."‡ Gezer was probably a place of great commercial importance, well able to pay a heavy tax. It was situated, it is believed, on the maritime plain which lies between the hills of Ephraim and the Mediterranean coast, along which passed the traffic between Phœnicia and Egypt. Tempted by worldly interest, the Ephraimites disobeyed God's command. " He is a merchant," said the prophet Hosea concerning Ephraim ; "the balances of deceit are in his hand." § So well content was this money-grasping tribe with the bargain which they had made, that no subsequent attempt appears to have been attempted to disturb the traffickers of Gezer. As late as the time of Solomon the place was still in possession of the Canaanites, and apparently independent. ‖ Instead of serving God with

---

* Josh. xxiii. 13.　　† Jud. i. 29.　　‡ Josh. xvi. 10.
§ Hos. xii. 7.　　‖ 1 Kings ix. 16, 17.

all their heart, the Ephraimites preferred that the Canaanites should enrich them. The gold of Canaan made way for the idols of Canaan; until at length the spiritual death knell of the tribe was sounded—" Ephraim is joined to his idols; let him alone." *

Concerning the tribe of Zebulun, along whose fair and fertile allotment lay "the way of the sea,"†— the great road from Damascus and the East to the Mediterranean, and whose people from the time of their first settlement must have had constant intercourse with merchants of Syria and Phœnicia and Egypt, travelling to and from the "haven of ships"‡ which formed their western border—the history states that they did not *drive out the inhabitants of Kitron, nor the inhabitants of Nahalol; but the Canaanites dwelt among them, and became tributaries.*" § The situation of these places has not been ascertained. They may have been situated in the great plain of the Buttauf, which is almost equal in extent and fertility to the plain of Jezreel, with the immense advantage of not being, as that was, the high road of the Bedouin.

The territory of Asher, the "happy," contained some of the richest land in Palestine; verifying the prediction of Jacob that "his bread should be fat," and that he should "yield royal dainties;" ‖ while its mineral wealth illustrated the prediction of Moses that his "shoes" should be "iron and brass."¶   Yet,

---

* Hos. iv. 17.   † Isa. ix. 1.   ‡ Gen. xlix. 13.   § Jud. i. 30.
‖ Gen. xlix. 20.   ¶ Deut. xxxiii. 25.

although shod with the iron which lay in abundance beneath his feet, Asher was from the beginning disposed, as Moses had foretold, to "dip his foot in oil," and to "wash his steps" with the "butter"* of a self-pleasing and luxurious course. The Asherites effected less than any other tribe toward removing the heathen from their borders. Of the tribes already mentioned, it is said that the Canaanites were allowed as tributaries to dwell among the Israelites; but in the case of Asher a lower depth of degeneracy was reached, for it is said that "*the Asherites dwelt among the Canaanites*," literally, in the bowels of the Canaanites, —"*the inhabitants of the land, for they did not drive them out.*"†

The enemy was permitted to hold all the places of chief importance in the land of Asher,—" Accho," the modern St. Jean d'Acre;—"Zidon," literally "fishery," a great port, celebrated in many a chapter of later history;—"Ahlab," the situation of which is uncertain;—" Achzib," the *Casale Huberti* of the Crusaders, and the modern *es-Zib*, a few miles north of Acre;— " Helbuh," probably in the plain near Zidon;— "Aphek," and " Rehob," whose situations have not been identified. The daintiest feeder and the most opulent trader among his brethren, Asher represents that sordid commercial instinct, far from unknown in our own day, which prefers moral slavery and political degradation, together with fulness of bread, to liberty

---

* Job xxix. 6.   † Jud. i. 31, 32.

and honour, with fighting and hard fare. How dangerous are abundance and luxury !

> " Is Heaven tremendous in its frowns ?   Most sure ;
> And in its favours formidable too.
> Its favours here are trials, not rewards ;
> A call to duty, not discharge from care ;
> And should alarm us full as much as woes." *

Of Naphtali, dwelling in the land of forest-clad mountains, it is stated that he failed to expel the heathen from two of their strongholds ;—" *Beth-shemesh*," the " house of the sun," the Phœnician deity, " in which," says Jerome, " the primitive worshippers remained ; " and " *Beth-anath*," a place not elsewhere mentioned in Scripture, but spoken of by early Christian writers as having been famous for its medicinal springs.   Naphtali, so far from destroying the pagan altars, went and " *dwelt among the Canaanites*," in a city avowedly devoted to idolatry.

Lastly, we read of the " children of Dan," that the Amorites " *forced* " them " *into the mountain ; for they would not suffer them to come down to the valley*." †   They forced them up from the cornfields of the Philistian plain, to the villages whose ruins still crown the adjacent hills ;—hills which at this day. are dotted here and there with squalid villages of the miserable Moslems, whose cornfields and gardens are in the plains below, but whose homes are in the rugged mountain-sides, for safety from the ravages of

---

* Young's " Night Thoughts," Night I.
† Jud. i. 34, 35.

the Bedouin,* built frequently on the ruins of the ancient towns and villages of Dan. It was a signal mark of their unfaithfulness, and a singular aggrava- tion of their shame, that " *the Amorites would dwell in mount Heres, in Aijalon.*" On the scene of Joshua's victory, where he had commanded the sun and moon to stand still, on that very spot the hand of the Canaanite now prevailed. But is not the Christian Church equally put to shame by the domination of the Moslem throughout Syria and North Africa, where in bygone ages mighty signs attended the preaching of the word, and hundreds of flourishing Churches were gathered ?   " When the Church of God declines from her first faith and love, even the battle-fields of her noblest victories will become the witnesses of her defeat and ignominy." †

Such is the account which the first chapter of the book of Judges supplies of the failure of the tribes to eject the heathen from their respective territories. The tribes of Reuben and Gad being on the other side Jordan, and having more completely dispossessed the heathen during the lifetime of Moses, are not in- cluded in the enumeration ; Simeon is viewed as incorporated with Judah ; and the fortunes of Issachar appear to have followed those of Naphtali. Like the ruined abbeys of England, the forts and settlements of the Canaanites were to be found wherever there

---

* Porter's " Giant Cities," p. 202.
† Bishop Wordsworth.

were fertile plains, fruitful vales, and pleasant streams in the land of Israel. The more pleasant and luxuriant their allotment, the more reluctant were the tribes of Israel to undertake the fatigue and self-denial of fulfilling the duty which God had assigned to them, and the more readily they were drawn into the snare of the enemy.

3

THE ANGEL AT BOCHIM

THE second chapter of the book of Judges opens with an account of a second great assembly of the Israelitish people. On the former occasion the tribes had met, in anxiety and fear, to inquire of the Lord which of them should be the first to march against the Canaanites. An answer had been given, and victory had crowned the arms of Judah. On this occasion they met, lamenting their unfaithfulness, being stung by the sharp reproofs of a messenger of the Lord for not having continued to drive out the inhabitants of the land. It is probable that they were assembled at one of the periodical festivals, which at that time were held before the ark at Shiloh, that central yet secluded spot in the land of Ephraim, which continued for ages to be the great sanctuary of the house of Joseph. The name *Bochim*, or *Weepers*, by which the place is designated, appears to have been given in commemoration of their out-cries of grief; but as it does not occur again in the sacred history we may infer that the name did not permanently attach to the locality.

While the tribes were assembled, an unknown messenger presented himself. He is described as "*an angel of the Lord*," who "*came up from Gilgal to Bochim*." As to the real nature of this extraordinary messenger, opinions have been various. It has been conjectured that he was the high-priest for the year, or that he was a prophet commissioned for this particular message, and standing forward, like Elijah, no man knowing his antecedents. Our belief is, that he was neither a mortal prophet or priest, nor a created angel, but the Second Person in the Blessed Trinity. For the Son of God was pleased, on many occasions previous to that manifestation of Himself when He pitched His tent here on earth for more than thirty years, to appear to His servants under the old covenant in a visible form, and to converse with them in an audible voice. This was the Angel whom Jehovah had promised to send before Israel, to bring them into the place which He had prepared ;* who revealed Himself to Joshua as Captain of the Lord's host ;† who bare and carried His people all the days of old ;‡ and whom we shall find, in the course of this history, appearing again to Gideon at Ophrah, and to the parents of Samson in the field of Zorah.§

He "*came up*," we are significantly told, "*from Gilgal to Bochim*." Gilgal was the place of the manifestation of Jehovah's power, and of His people's triumph. Gilgal was the first place in Canaan at

---

* Exod. xxiii. 20.   † Josh. v. 14.   ‡ Isa. lxiii. 9.
§ Jud. vi. 11, xiii. 9–11.

which they had halted, after the miraculous passage of the Jordan ; it was at Gilgal that the reproach of Egypt had been rolled away from Israel by the circumcision with the knives of stone ; Gilgal was the first place in Canaan where they had kept the pass-over ; and from Gilgal the mercies of God and the conquests of Joshua in Canaan dated their origin.* The prophetic phrase, "from Shittim unto Gilgal," represents the progress of the Church of Israel from sin, shame, and misery, to a glorious resurrection and recovery;† and now the phrase "from Gilgal to Bochim," or the *Weepers*, bespeaks her decline from primitive holiness and honour, to a state of abasement and woe.

The words of this Divine Messenger were few, but they were powerful; so that "*the people lifted up their voice and wept.*" He declared that it was He Him-self who had brought them out of Egypt and made a perpetual covenant with them ; but that because they had forsaken Him, and had been in league with the inhabitants of the land, He had subsequently said that He would no more exert His power in their behalf, but would leave them to be chastised by the heathen and deluded by their gods.‡

The charge thus laid against the Israelites is amply sustained by the facts detailed in the latter part of the first chapter of the book.‖ We are told that

---

* Josh. iv. 19, v. 2–10.
† Mic. vi. 5 ; Num. xxv. 1 ; Josh. iii. 1.   ‡ Jud. ii.
‖ Jud. i. 19–21, 27–39.

even victorious Judah "could not drive out the inhabitants of the valley, because they had chariots of iron;" so feeble was his faith, and so readily, like sinking Peter, were his fears aroused. Joshua had not been afraid of these iron chariots; but timorous Judah, of little faith, dared not face them. "The children of Benjamin" too, hardy and fierce though they were reputed to be, were lax in the performance of the task assigned to them; they "did not drive out the Jebusites that inhabited Jerusalem," but permitted them to reside there with themselves. Manasseh and Ephraim, instead of driving the Canaanites out of their border, listened to their overtures, accepted their tribute money, and permitted them to dwell beside them as neighbours and friends, and afterwards became enslaved under their yoke. In the same way Zebulun became degenerate, and instead of using his strength to glorify God, he used it to enrich himself with the tribute money of the heathen whom he ought to have destroyed. Asher was more degenerate still; for he was content to incorporate himself and dwell with "the Canaanites, the inhabitants of the land." The same is said of Naphtali, who was content, instead of extirpating the enemy, to dwell quietly among them "in Beth-shemesh," the "city of the sun," the high place of their idolatry. Worst of all, the children of Dan, in Aijalon, the place where Joshua had commanded the sun to stand still, so far from being animated by the memory of their leader's faith, were actually driven back by the heathen, and forced to take shelter in the mountains; thus turning the noblest battle-field of the Church of God into a scene of defeat and shame.

Such were the facts on which the Angel at Bochim founded His reproof and threatening. "*I said, . . . Ye shall make no league with the inhabitants of this land; ye shall throw down their altars: but ye have not obeyed My voice? why have ye done this?*" Rebellious man turns aside from God's path to find indulgence and ease, but in the end he is bitterly disappointed. The Lord now threatened Israel with misery and suffering through those very Canaanites whom, for their own selfish ends, they had permitted to live: "*I will not drive them out from before you; but they shall be as thorns in your sides, and their gods shall be a snare unto you.*" *

The narrative of the Angel's appearance at Bochim is followed by an anticipatory sketch, in which the sacred writer reviews the entire history of the period of the Judges; showing the unfaithfulness of the generations that followed Joshua, their constant back-slidings from God in pursuit of the idolatry which they had sinfully permitted to live amongst them, the anger of God against them, their frequent repentances when severely chastised, God's mercy in raising up from time to time judges to deliver them, and the obstinate persistency of the people, notwithstanding, in "their own doings" and "their stubborn way." †

---

* Jud. ii. 2, 3.   † Jud. ii. 6–23.

We are thus presented with a general view of the entire period of the Judges, in which three points stand prominently before us. The first is, the command which God had laid upon the Israelitish people, to drive out and destroy the Canaanites ; the second is, their disobedience in permitting the Canaanites to remain ; and the third, the punishment they had to suffer for this disobedience, the Canaanites becoming as thorns in their sides, and their gods being a snare unto them. The whole of this is also a Divine parable or mystery, the hidden meaning of which, like that of Christ's spoken parables, is not perceived by " them that are without," but is full of instruction and blessedness to those unto whom " it is given to know the mystery of the kingdom of God."*

I. The commands laid upon the Hebrew people with reference to the destruction of the Canaanite idolaters were so explicit and so frequently repeated, that it was impossible to plead ignorance, or to mistake their meaning. God, who is the sole Lord and Giver of life, had devoted these nations to destruction, and appointed the Israelites executioners of His will. The Israelites were solemnly charged to enter into no league, to form no connections with them. They were to show no mercy toward the gods of the land, or its idolatrous abominations. They were to destroy and drive out all the old inhabitants, and to take possession of the country by Divine gift. And although,

---

* Mark iv. 11.

as a general rule in war, they were expressly directed to spare the enemy's women and children, a special exception to this rule was made in regard to the cities of Canaan, of whose inhabitants they were to "save alive nothing that breatheth," but utterly to destroy the whole.*

This terrible severity was no act of mere private vengeance. It was expressly declared to be a judgment of God upon some of the vilest nations that had ever existed. So execrably wicked were they, that the land is represented as nauseating and vomiting them forth with intolerable loathing. After a catalogue of abominable offences, we find it enjoined upon the Israelites, "Defile not ye yourselves in any of these things; for in all these the nations are defiled which I cast out before you: and the land is defiled; therefore I do visit the iniquity thereof upon it, and the land itself vomiteth out her inhabitants." †

This command to extirpate the Canaanites is regarded by many as one of the chief difficulties in the Old Testament. The difficulty lies not so much in the thing itself, as in our defective views of God, or of man's relation to Him, or of the supernatural character of the revelation made to Moses. As it has ever been a favourite ground of attack with the enemies of revelation, and is felt as a difficulty by

---

* Deut. vi. 2–6, xii. 2, 3 ; Num. xxxiii. 51–53 ; Deut. xx. 16–18.
† Lev. xviii. 24, 25.

many sincere believers in the Divine authority of the Bible, we will turn aside from the regular course of the narrative, to consider briefly the supposed injustice of this command to extirpate the Canaanites.

The objection, it will be observed, is grounded (or it has no force) upon the supposed inconsistency of this command with the Divine righteousness and equity. Yet there are other acts of God, equally terrible and equally indiscriminate in their effects, which we never presume to call in question. When, for example, the Almighty sends an earthquake or a pestilence, there is no complaint of injustice; and yet earthquake and pestilence spare neither age nor sex nor rank, but involve all in the same ruin. The fire and brimstone which consumed the cities of the plain—the earthquake in which Korah and his company were swallowed up—the plague which smote the people in the time of David—did these spare the young or the aged, the mother or the infant at her breast? Do fire, or famine, or cholera, discriminate between the sexes, or spare the aged or the young? If the sword of Israel was commissioned to destroy all that breathed of the Canaanites, it certainly was not more indiscriminate than these other judgments of God. If we dare not assert or even insinuate injustice in the case of the one, neither can we rationally do so in the case of the other; nor can we deny to the Almighty the right to choose this or that method of chastising a guilty people, whether earthquake or famine, pestilence or war.

We may further remember that the annihilation of a people is so far from being a new, or an unexampled occurrence, that similar events in the overruling wisdom of God have been continually taking place ever since the dawn of history. For an example of it we need not travel beyond our own shores. Where are the original inhabitants of England ? The Briton was subdued by the Saxon, the Saxon was driven out by the Norman and the Dane, each race leaving however some trace of itself in the stock and blood of the country. Yet the original race has been more completely extirpated than ever the Canaanitish races were during the Hebrew occupancy of Palestine.

Still more complete has been the disappearance of the North American Indians. The red man has been driven farther and farther towards the setting sun, till the race seems threatened with absolute extermination, and is actually extinct over an area twenty times as great as that of Palestine. It appears to be an unvarying law, that the savage recedes before the civilized man. We cannot justify all the means by which this result is accomplished, or palliate the dark and monstrous crimes which have been perpetrated in the name of civilization ; yet it is an evident fact that the Ruler of nations is pleased to ordain, or to permit, that nations should be driven from their ancestral inheritance, and their places filled by others. Thus we see that what happened to the Canaanites is happening continually in the history of nations. In this view the phenomenon of the destruction of the Canaanite nations does not stand alone.   It can be referred to a class.   And there is no more ground for disputing the Divine justice in regard to the destruction of these people than in regard to the disappearance of scores and perhaps hundreds of other ancient races from the face of the earth ; for it cannot be contended that there is any difference, as it regards justice and equity, whether a nation be extirpated by war, destroyed by famine or pestilence, or left to perish, like the aborigines of Australia, by hopeless and helpless exhaustion.

There is therefore no ground for questioning the justice of the sentence against the Canaanites, which will not equally apply to a thousand other works of Him who " rendereth not unto man an account of His ways."   We recur to the point, that their extirpation was the Israelites' duty.   They were not to judge for themselves in the matter.   They were not even to gratify a natural feeling of compassion ; but to regard themselves as the ministers of God's righteous vengeance, the executioners of His awful will.   The same Voice which had spoken to them the words of the Ten Commandments bade them dispossess the Canaanites and take possession of the land promised to Abraham ; it forbade them to hold " any fellowship with the unfruitful works of darkness," or even so much as to make inquiry how the heathen served their gods ; and, their duty being performed, it promised them a plentiful and lasting and peaceful inheritance.

II. "*But*," said the Angel at Bochim, "*ye have not obeyed My voice.*"

This disobedience is so far from being charged against the men who, under the leadership of Joshua, first entered and took possession of the land of promise, that the Holy Spirit accords to those men the illustrious distinction of having "served the Lord all their days." * It was when a fresh generation had arisen, who had not with their own eyes "seen all the great works of the Lord, that He did for Israel," that the spirit of unbelief and the law of selfishness so far prevailed, that at length a supernatural Messenger was sent to reprove and threaten them for their disobedience. Of the generation contemporary with Joshua, it may be said that, like Thomas after the Lord's resurrection, because they had seen they believed. The generations that followed failed to attain to the blessing promised to those who "have not seen, and yet have believed."†

The accusation against them at Bochim was negative rather than positive. They were not charged with any specific act of avowed rebellion, but with having failed to obey the voice of God. There are degrees of guilt in the rebellions of the Church against her Head ; and as yet the Israelites were not charged, like Ahab afterwards, with doing "very abominably in following idols : " ‡ still less had they reached the villany of Manasseh at a yet later period, who even

---

* Jud. ii. 7.   † John xx. 29.   ‡ 1 Kings xxi. 26.

" overpassed the deeds of the heathen," for he " did wickedly above all that the Amorites did, which were before him," and " shed innocent blood till he had filled Jerusalem from one end to another." * It is true that their downward course, after they had once placed themselves on the smooth deceitful gradient, soon became rapid and headlong ; but as yet they are expostulated with chiefly for sins of omission : " *Ye have not obeyed My voice; why have ye done this?*"

But when the Church has begun to habitually neglect any one of her Lord's known commands—still more when she begins to " break one of these least commandments, and teach men so "—the day is not far distant when, unless arrested in her career by the mercy or the judgments of God, she will be found openly consorting with the mammon-worshippers by whom she is surrounded. Even so it was in the history before us. We have seen how Judah quailed before the chariots of iron, and Benjamin allowed the Jebusites to hold Jerusalem ; how Ephraim and Manasseh, instead of driving the Canaanites out of their heritage, compromised matters with them, and consented to take tribute money at their hands ; how Asher and Naphtali, and Zebulun and Dan, were even content with a bare toleration, with being permitted to dwell among the people whom they ought to have expelled in the name of the Lord. From sparing the lives of the enemies of the Church, it was an easy

---

* Jer. v. 28 ; 2 Kings xxi. 11, 16.

step to make comfortable agreements with them. Such agreements once entered into, the mortal enmity, the irreconcilable antagonism, between the Church and the heathen was at an end; and it was a natural step to enter into various associations with them of a more or less friendly nature. Then, as the lascivious and ungodly practices of the heathen were more in accordance with "the desires of the flesh and of the mind" than the pure and self-denying precepts of the law of God, it was natural that familiarity should weaken repugnance and lead to imitation; and so—it is the old story, yet how few take warning !—we are prepared to hear without the slightest surprise the next statement of the inspired historian, to the effect that "*they forsook the Lord God of their fathers, which brought them out of the land of Egypt, and followed other gods, of the gods of the people that were round about them;*" and still further, that they even left off the form of worshipping God, and joined in the public celebrations of the pagan worship: "*they bowed themselves unto them, and provoked the Lord to anger; and they forsook the Lord, and served Baal and Ashtaroth.*" *

"Which things," says St. Paul—for surely we must not limit the principle to the one incident of Sarah and Agar there mentioned by him—"which things are an allegory." † Not only the narrative of the wanderings of the Hebrews in the wilderness, but surely,

---

* Jud. ii. 12, 13.   † Gal. iv. 24.

also the history of their victories and their sins after they had entered the land of promise, is to be reckoned among those "things written aforetime," concerning which the same apostle declares that they were "written for our learning." * Whoever reads the book of Judges without this key reads it with the veil on his eyes and on his heart, for the whole history here recorded is, if I might so express it, an acted parable—a scene in the vast drama of this world's history, specially recorded by the Holy Spirit, because of its occult sense, its typical or allegorical character. And those are "able ministers of the New Testament" who are ministers "not of the letter, but of the spirit" †—not of the outward historical sense only, but of the inward and spiritual meaning.   The lessons furnished by this part of the history are manifold and instructive.

I. The Canaanites in this history represent the enemies of the Church of God, and also the inward besetting sins of individual members of that Church.   We view them at present more especially as representing the inward sins of Christian believers.   Need we specify them ?   Need we name pride, and lust, and covetousness, and self-conceit, and envy, and worldliness, and impatience, and fretfulness, and revengefulness—a band of brothers, tall sons of Anak, diverse in feature, yet all showing the ancestry and lineaments of the serpent ? Need we mention others of the same kindred—jealousy,

---

* Rom. xv. 4.   † 2 Cor. iii. 6.

and sloth, and worldliness, and levity, and procrastination, and presumption, and unbelief? In every age the Church of God has to drive out her spiritual Amorites—Unbelief, Ungodliness, Heresy, Idolatry, the setting up of man's inventions and forms in place of the pure truth of God ; and unless she is diligent and bold these enemies will beleaguer and infest her, and will at length drive her out of her inheritance.

These are the enemies who will dispute with the heirs of promise every foot of their expected heritage. With these it is no child's play at arms, but a veritable struggle for life ; for as the spies reported of "the sons of Anak, which come of the giants, we were in our own sight as grasshoppers, and so we were in their sight"*—so these bold gigantic foes are not afraid of the utmost efforts the believer can put forth by the mere force of his own will. Still less are they to be overcome by any of those ecclesiastical forms in which we are apt to place a mistaken confidence. They will not retreat at the sound of an intoned prayer or at the swell of an organ ; they fear neither the robes and mitre of a bishop nor the broadbrim of a Quaker ; they defy alike the laver of Baptism and the outward elements of the Supper : either we must, through our Joshua's help, turn them out of our hearts, or they will keep us out of the kingdom of heaven : for without holiness no man shall see the Lord.

---

* Num. xiii. 33.

2. It follows, then, that the believer's warfare is not completed when he has been made a partaker of peace through believing in Christ; for "we are made partakers of Christ" only "if we hold the beginning of our confidence steadfast unto the end." * When the Lord brings us up out of the legal wilderness, filling our hearts with the first joys of faith and adoption, it is not to be imagined that our salvation is fully wrought out. This is not the end of the warfare, though it may appear so to the soul contemplating it from afar off.

The Israelites in the desert, as they looked towards the hills of Canaan, may have imagined that if they could only cross yonder Jordan, and march triumphant up those promised hills, their warfare would be accomplished ; but they found in reality that there must be a lifelong struggle for possession and for conquest. So, although we may have spiritually entered, as believers in Christ, into the good land, and have therefore, in a sense, "entered into the rest,"† we shall find that the Canaanites are still lurking around us, and that it will be our work to subdue and to expel them. "Put off," says the Scripture, "the old man, which is corrupt according to the deceitful lusts." Mighty task !—for this "old man" is not easily ousted from his ancient habitation. He fights hard for possession ; and except we "give diligence," even after we have obtained our "calling and election," to

---

* Heb. iii. 14.   † Heb. iv. 3 (Greek).

"make it sure," * we shall fall into the same snare as that into which the generation that succeeded Joshua fell, and shall incur the reproofs of some angel of wrath, making the place a *Bochim* as he thunders in our alarmed ears the words of the Lord, " Ye have not obeyed My voice."

3. We are reminded that many of the spiritual Israel stop short of a full salvation , for it is to be remembered that these men had partially obeyed. They had begun well. Judah, by the Lord's help, had routed "the inhabitants of the mountain ;" other tribes had so far reduced the heathen as to compel them to pay a tribute ; Israel was not driven back into the wilderness, but effected his settlement in the land. Still, like multitudes in the Church in every age, they only half did their work. Unlike Caleb and Joshua, who followed the Lord fully, they stopped short of the faith and labour necessary to ensure a full salvation. Worst of all—and how true the resemblance holds !—they were content in this inglorious state. They just managed to avoid being driven back toward Egypt ; content, though heirs of conquest, to drag on a dishonourable existence, be-grudging the self-denial which would have been requisite in order to put them fully in possession of the privileges of their covenant.

4. The history illustrates the causes of the weakness of the Church and people of God.

---

* 2 Pet. i. 10.

(1.) One of these causes was indolence. "They neglected to destroy the nations, not because of want of inclination, but because they were deficient in strength in consequence of their guilt ; not from feelings of compassion, but from want of holy zeal and from slothfulness."* If a few wishes, or an occasional effort in a revival, were all that is required, multitudes who now fall short of salvation would be saved. Multitudes there are who pray now and then, and even display a brilliant zeal on particular occasions, whose idle souls recoil from the precept to pray without ceasing, and to whom "patient continuance in well-doing" is the most irksome of injunctions. The laziest of savages will arouse themselves at times to wonderful activity ; it is only the trained and civilized man who can endure consecutive labour. And patient labour there must be, if we would win the prize of our high calling. The athlete cannot retain his strength without daily exercise ; the vocalist cannot retain his power and command of voice without incessant practice ; and the child of God cannot go on to perfection without a daily spiritual gymnastic, "exercising himself with a view to godliness,"† as an athlete with a view to the games. Faith and love, correcting the indolence of our nature, will make this holy toil delightful. In the second century it passed into a proverb, when men would express the impossibilty of a thing, to say "You may as soon

---

* Hengstenberg on Psalm cvi.   † 1 Tim. iv. 7 (Greek).

take off a Christian from Christ;" and our blessed Master, whose example is the most perfect rebuke of slothfulness, declared that it was His meat and drink, not merely to begin, not merely to carry on, but to *finish* His Father's work.*

(2.) Another cause of spiritual weakness is a secret love of sin. The Israelites found in the habits of the men of Canaan much that was congenial to their own corrupt inclinations. In our own day there are degraded Englishmen who have settled among the savages of New Hebrides or Fiji, on purpose to be free from all moral restraint, and who outdo the worst of the heathen in every kind of abomination. In religious families there are sons and daughters who, although outwardly restrained by the circumstances of their position, cherish a bitter hatred of religion, and a secret love for a dissipated life. And even in the hearts of the faithful what strange occasional lingerings towards evil! What treacherous trifling with things forbidden! What hovering about the devil's ground! What secret inclinations to taste the poisoned cup! What strange revival, at times, of the power of old habits which we had imagined subdued for ever! What infatuated dancing on the brink of hell, like the moth fluttering round the candle to its destruction! Who can explain the depth of that hidden treason? who can disclose the inner sources of that secret alienation from the adora-

---

* John iv. 34.

ble God, that lusting of the flesh against the spirit, which so many of the faithful mourn ? Had Israel hated the sins of Canaan, they would not have failed to subdue the men of Canaan ; nor would they have entered into league with their armies, if they had not been secretly inclined to their ways. " Never," says Calvin, " does the love of piety sufficiently flourish in our hearts unless it begets in us a hatred of sin." To the same effect writes the psalmist : " Do not I hate them, O God, that hate Thee ? and am not I grieved with them that rise up against Thee ? I hate them with a perfect hatred, I count them mine enemies." *
No wonder we languish in spiritual weakness, when the world or the flesh has a secret share in our affections.

(3.) Another cause of spiritual weakness is unbelief, if indeed this one cause does not sum up and exhaust the whole subject. Unbelief is vitally connected with that alienation of heart and affections from God, in which the deepest ruin of man consists. For example : it was partly because of the secret distaste which the Israelites in the wilderness felt for the professed blessings of the land of Canaan that they were so slow to believe God's promise of possessing it. Souls that craved the leeks and onions and fleshpots of Egypt, rather than the good land flowing with milk and honey, were not predisposed to put much faith in promises of possession. Here is the great secret of unbe-

---

* Ps. cxxxix. 21–23.

lief—it is "the evil heart, departing from the living God." *   And is it for this cause, O ye Israel of God, that ye are so slow to believe even in the possibility of being sanctified wholly, and of being preserved blameless unto the coming of the Lord ?   Is this the reason why ye so stoutly contend that although the inbred foe, the spiritual Canaanite, may be humbled and put to tribute, it is impossible he should be utterly destroyed on this side the grave ?   The men who believed not of old time were the same men who hankered after the gods of Egypt, and turned aside to serve the gods of Canaan.   Is there any merit in such unbelief ?   Have Caleb and Joshua, the men who believed that the Church of their day was " well able " to go up and possess the land, ceased to be patterns of following the Lord fully?   When the heart pants after the living God, is it pleasant to think that, in this life at least, He will never take full and complete possession, but that some damnable lust will always be there to dispute with Him for the supremacy? When the Bride weeps after her Bridegroom, and mourns His long delay, surely it is hard to think that in this world at least He will never, never come !   Oh let us not encourage unbelief by theoretical doubts of the possibility of a full salvation, but let us rather rejoice in the glorious hope of perfect love.

It was this heart of unbelief which actuated the men of Israel in the times we are now studying.   Its

* Heb. iv. 12.

blinding influence prevented them from seeing what was their high calling as the chosen people of God, and as heirs of the promises; its enervating influence disabled them from putting forth the necessary exertions; its stupefying and sensualizing influence quenched all desire for the kingdom of God. In the deep gloom which settled on the nation we learn to appreciate the greatness and the mighty virtue of those MEN OF FAITH, whose deeds will presently come under review, and whose light shines with the more splendid lustre because of the darkness encompassing it on every side.

III. A terrible series of penalties were the consequences of Israel's unfaithfulness. The Angel at Bochim drew tears of anguish from the assembled multitudes as He followed His reproof with the sentence of punishment: *"I will not drive them out from before you; but they shall be as thorns in your sides, and their gods shall be a snare unto you."* *

How soon this sentence begun to take effect is evident from the narrative which immediately follows; how long and how fully the sentence was fulfilled will appear in the sequel of this history. The tears shed at Bochim were scarcely tears of genuine repentance. The feelings of the people were moved, but their hearts were not turned; they wept at the prospect of coming misery, but such tears avail nothing unless the heart turns away from its cherished sin—indeed,

---

* Jud. ii. 3.

they leave the heart harder than it was before. We find accordingly that soon after their short-lived repentance they relapsed into worse disobedience. The evening twilight soon fades into total darkness ; so their negative evil soon degenerated into positive revolt : "they did evil in the sight of the Lord, and served Baalim," * or idols. For a time, perhaps, the worship of God and the worship of idols were observed together ; but a further step in the downward course—their abandonment of Jehovah and open adoration of the Canaanitish idols—was not long in being taken : "they forsook the Lord, and served Baal and Ashtaroth." †

The whole of the subsequent history is an unfolding of the fulfilment of the Angel's threat. Never was there a more warning instance of the progressive tendency of sin in the Church of God, and of the certainty that chastisement will follow sin, than is afforded in the book of Judges ; of which we shall see more in the sequel. This second chapter is an epitome of the period, a general view of those ages of sorrow and confusion. " *The anger of the Lord*," says the historian, "*was hot against Israel, and He delivered them into the hands of spoilers that spoiled them, and He sold them into the hands of their enemies round about, so that they could not any longer stand before their enemies.*" ‡ In this feeble and degraded condition one trace after another of

---

* Jud. ii. 12.   † Jud. ii. 13.   ‡ Jud. ii. 14.

their former glory and greatness disappeared : the might of faith was exchanged for the disgrace of subjugation ; and the descendants of the conquerors who followed the standards of Joshua, unable to face the enemy in battle, withdrew to the fastnesses of the hills and the gloomy shelter of mountain caves.   For it was not merely that they had lost their strength ; the Lord had become their adversary : "*whithersoever they went out, the hand of the Lord was against them for evil, as the Lord had said, and as the Lord had sworn unto them; and they were greatly distressed.*" *

If we contrast this miserable condition with those glorious days of a bygone age, when the sight of Israel's banners struck terror into the idolater ;— when "all the kings which were on this side Jordan, in the hills, and in the valleys, and in all the coasts of the Great Sea, gathered themselves together to fight against Joshua, and with Israel, with one accord ;" † when "they went out, they and all their hosts with them, much people, even as the sand that is on the seashore in multitude, with horses and chariots very many ; " ‡—when over all those embattled myriads the sword of Israel was victorious ;—the contrast between the might of faith and the weakness of unbelief becomes manifest.

" Mercy shown to our lusts is cruelty to ourselves," says Bishop Horne ; and how many periods of such cruelty, ending in misery and shame, there have been

---

* Jud. ii. 15 ; Lev. xxvi. 17 ; Deut. xxviii. 25.
　† Josh. ix. 1.　　　‡ Josh. xi. 4.

in the Churches of God and in the souls of believers, is known only to Him who searches all hearts. Too often do Christians pass weeks, or months, or even years, in spiritual sloth, in self-indulgence, in indifference and unbelief, making terms with God's enemies, whom they ought to have driven out of His heritage.

All such unfaithfulness brings its sure punishment. If we wilfully spare a single Canaanite, or enter into a tacit agreement with the enemy, though we may perhaps not fail of heaven at last, we shall have stripes of sorrow on our journey thither : " they shall be as thorns in your sides, and their gods shall be a snare unto you." Our prospects will be dim, our usefulness will be impaired, our light will be turned into darkness, and our songs into dirges of lamentation; while the remorseless, tyrannous lust humbles us again and again, sinks us lower than the dust, and reduces us to exquisite and abject misery : the just penalty of refusing to take up the cross and deny self, that we might follow Christ.

Merciful Lord ! deliver me and Thy whole Church from the humiliation and bitterness of being subject to the Canaanite !

4

MISSION AND SUCCESS
OF THE JUDGES

IF unbelief and rebellion had been permitted to run
an unobstructed course, the glory would soon have
departed from Israel, and their name would have
perished. It was not their own salvation only, but
the whole future of mankind, which was involved in
the maintenance amongst them of the worship of God
and the expectation of a Redeemer. It was not solely
on their own account, but also because "unto them
were committed the oracles of God," and because God
in His sovereign grace had chosen the seed of Abraham, and would perform His covenant,* 'that so
wonderful a series of providential interpositions mark
their national history. Of these interpositions the
raising up of judges during the four centuries following the death of Joshua is not the least remarkable.
The sacred historian prefaces his narrative of these
centuries with a general view of the office of the
judges, and of the effect of their administration upon
the people.† It may not be a useless preparation for
the sketches which follow, to devote this chapter to a

---

* Deut. ix. 4–6.   † Jud. ii. 16–19.

consideration of the nature of their calling and commission—the functions they were called to discharge
—the effects upon the people of their labours and
administration,—and their figurative character as
types or shadows of things to come.

I. The office of the judges must not be confounded
with that of the subordinate functionaries whom Moses
appointed to administer justice while the tribes encamped in the wilderness.   The great legislator found
his work to overwhelm him; and acting on the
suggestion of Hobab, his father-in-law, he appointed
officers whose duty it was to "judge the people at all
seasons,"* reserving only cases of peculiar difficulty
for his personal decision.   These "judges" Moses
solemnly charged at the time of their appointment to
"judge righteously," and "not to be afraid of the face
of man, for the judgment is God's;"† and the arrangement, temporary at first, was afterwards confirmed
and made permanent by express revelation: "judges
and officers shalt thou make thee in all thy gates."‡

There can be no doubt that a magistracy of this
description continued to exist after the settlement in
Canaan, but the method of election cannot be now
stated with certainty.   The probability is that it soon
reverted to the ancient form of patriarchal government, according to which each of the twelve tribes
had its own chief, under whom were the heads of the
great families or clans of which the tribe was composed,

---

* Exod. xviii. 13–26.   † Deut. i. 16.   ‡ Deut. xvi. 18.

and under these again the heads of houses *—a mode of government to which an exact parallel still subsists among the Arab and Tartar tribes.

Whatever may have been the mode in which these local judges received their appointment, their office was totally different from that of those extraordinary messengers of the Divine will, called judges, some of whose deeds this book of Scripture records. These were raised up from time to time, irrespective of tribal or family claims, by the special appointment of God. Like the prophets in succeeding ages, the judges were men set up in Israel, filled with the Holy Spirit, commissioned for special work, and endued with marvellous powers, not in a defined order of succession, like the priesthood, but at irregular intervals, according as the Most High willed them to appear. This Divine and extraordinary character of their mission is directly asserted, not only in the twice repeated declaration in the chapter before us that it was "the Lord" who "raised them up judges,"† but also afterwards by Samuel‡ and by Nehemiah,§ and in the New Testament by the apostle Paul.‖

These men, in some of whom the miraculous operations of the Holy Spirit were singularly manifested, did not enter upon their office by popular election, or by hereditary succession, or by military despotism, or through personal or family influence. The common-

---

* Josh. vii. 16–18.   † Jud. ii. 16, 18.   ‡ 1 Sam. xii. 11.
§ Neh. ix. 27.   ‖ Acts xiii. 17, 20.

wealth of Israel was neither an oligarchy, nor a monarchy (except as God was their king), nor a republic. The judges of Israel were not chosen, like the suffetes of Carthage, with regal powers for a year; nor like the archons of Athens, with divided and carefully defined responsibilities; nor like the dictators of Rome, chosen to exercise uncontrolled power during extraordinary emergencies. They were not chosen by the people at all. They were sent forth by the Divine King of Israel—impelled by an inward inspiration, which was in several instances confirmed by outward miraculous signs, to act in His great name. Nor did they appear in an uninterruped succession. There were intervals during which there was no judge in Israel. They were raised up as the exigencies of the times required ; and their presence and their absence were alike calculated to keep alive in the nation a sense of dependence upon its invisible King.

The judges were, in a certain sense, the successors of Moses and of Joshua. Though in a humbler sphere, yet they were as truly extraordinary messengers of God's will and purpose as either of those illustrious men. Moses was raised up to bring the Israelites out of Egypt, to conduct them forty years through the wilderness to the borders of Canaan, and to unfold the law of the Old Covenant. Joshua was raised up to lead them into the promised land, to defeat and drive out the heathen, and to establish the chosen people in their inheritance. And when afterwards the Canaanite or the Amorite endeavoured to reassert his old supremacy, like the unclean spirit, saying, " I will return unto my house from whence I came out,"* a judge or "saviour" was raised up to "overcome him, and to take from him all his armour wherein he trusted, and to divide his spoils:"† thus helping to conserve the work which Joshua had begun.

The twelve ‡ judges whose names are recorded in this book were as truly called of God, and inspired by His Spirit, to maintain the honour of His name, in danger of being lost, in the Jewish Church, as the twelve apostles afterwards were to preach Christ and the resurrection, and to lay the foundations of the Christian Church. And the narrative of their deeds, in times when the priesthood and the people were alike disposed to forget their God, is full of encouragement to the Christian Church in every age ; showing that when ordinary means fail, and the recognised defenders of the truth are either asleep or perverting the people, the Lord can raise up occasional and extraordinary instruments of His will, to retrieve the honour of His name, and to check the spread of corruption or the advance of Antichrist.

II. The functions which the judges were called upon to discharge may be partly understood by referring to the position in which Moses and Joshua stood in relation to the twelve tribes. The judges were God's

---

* Matt. xii. 44.   † Luke xi. 22.

‡ Othniel, Ehud, Shamgar, Deborah, Gideon, Tola, Jair, Jephthah, Ibzan, Elon, Abdon, Samson. The acts of Eli and of Samuel are not narrated in the book of Judges.

vicegerents. Although their recorded exploits are chiefly of a warlike nature, yet, when we read of Othniel and of Gideon, "that the land had rest forty years"* between their victories and their death—of Tola, who judged Israel twenty-three years; and of Jair, who judged Israel twenty-two years † ; of Ibzan, and Abdon, and Elon, who held the office for shorter periods,‡ without any reference being made to deeds of war—we cannot but suppose that their unrecorded acts consisted chiefly in the exercise of civil government. There being "no king in Israel," and "every man doing that which was right in his own eyes,"§ the want of a supreme central authority would frequently be felt in times of peace scarcely less than in times of war. It is not certain, however, that every judge ruled the entire land of Canaan. Some of them, probably, were judges of certain tribes only, and their period of office may have run parallel to that of other judges in other parts of the country.

The parallel between the office of the judges and that of Moses or Joshua was not, however, complete. In so far as they were specially raised up to be God's vicegerents in Israel, it holds good ; yet it was a separate and distinct form of government, and is recognised as such by St. Paul.‖ Moses and Joshua were called, each of them, to introduce a new order of things. But during the period of the judges,

---

* Jud. iii. 11 ; viii. 23. † Jud. x. 1–3. ‡ Jud. xii. 8–14.
§ Jud. xvii. 6. ‖ Acts xiii. 20.

nothing, in respect of God's covenant, was put upon a new footing. The history of the people is a succession of various fortunes, afflictions, and deliverances, alternating according to their public sin or their repentance ; but no change occurred, permanently or deeply affecting their public condition.

As often as the sins of the people brought down God's chastisements, and chastisement produced repentance, judges were raised up to repel the invader, and to restore peace and tranquillity. Hence they are frequently called, in the sacred history, "deliverers and saviours."* Usually, however, they are denominated judges ;† nor is the meaning and usage of the Hebrew word restricted, as our English term might seem to imply, to matters of judicature or of litigation. It signifies not merely administrators of justice, but avengers—rulers, in the wide

---

* Othniel is called (Jud. iii. 9) "a deliverer," in the Hebrew *moshia*, from the same root (the prefix being changed) as *Joshua* and *Jesus*. To Ehud the same term is applied (iii. 15). The same word is applied (Jud. x. 1) to Tola, our version rendering it "to *defend* Israel." Nehemiah speaks of the judges as a class, as *moshiaim*, "saviours." See Pearson on the Creed, art. 2, p. 72.

† *Shophetim*, from *shaphat*, to "judge" (Exod. xviii. 22); to "avenge" (2 Sam. xviii. 31; Isa. i. 23) ; to "punish" (2 Chron. xx. 12 ; Ezek. vii. 3) ; to "rule :" king Amaziah being a leper, his son, Jotham, "*judged* the people of the land" (2 Kings xv. 5)— that is, he exercised the functions of king instead of his father. The Israelites asked, "Make us a king to *judge* us like all the nations" (1 Sam. viii. 5). In this sense of *ruling*, the word is to be understood generally throughout the Book of Judges.

sense of that term. It expresses not merely the functions of a judge, as we now understand that word, but rather those of a king, though without the regal state and title. The judges were the chief magistrates of the Hebrew commonwealth.

As such, they had to deal with religious, no less than with civil, affairs ; for the sharp line of separation between these which modern ingenuity has invented did not then exist. It was the duty of the Levites to attend to the religious instruction of the nation, and of the priests to attend to the worship and sacrifices ; but the apathy and ungodliness of those consecrated sinners may be inferred from the continual defections of the nation from the worship of God. It became the duty of the judges to stir up the people to return to the Lord ; and hence they needed to be themselves men of faith. The Israelites were perpetually forgetting that covenant of God, to which they owed their national existence. Notwithstanding the splendour of the miracles wrought in behalf of their fathers, and the wonderful fulfilment of the promise which had been made to Abraham that his seed should possess the land of Canaan, they would not believe in the Unseen ; they were, as Moses had described them, " children in whom is no faith." * Stupefied by earthliness and sensuality, they preferred imitating the degraded heathen around them to following God's commandments ; and they would have been utterly

---

* Deut. xxxii. 20.

lost, had not men been raised up to whom, whatever may have been their errors, the THINGS UNSEEN were present realities ; men who possessed a living FAITH in that covenant which the priest and the Levite taught merely as a matter of form :—" Gedeon, and Barak, and Samson, and Jephthae, . . . who through faith subdued kingdoms, wrought righteousness, obtained promises, stopped the mouths of lions, quenched the violence of fire, escaped the edge of the sword, out of weakness were made strong, turned to flight the armies of the aliens." *

III.   With regard to the effect of their administration upon the nation of the Jews, I am inclined to think that the period of the judges was, upon the whole, a period of national advancement.   The prevailing idea is, no doubt, opposed to this view.   It contemplates the period of the judges as an unbroken series of idolatries and crimes and miseries, relieved only by the occasional appearance of a Barak or a Gideon, like a momentary gleam of sunshine on a dark, tempestuous day.   But a deeper study of the times tends to modify and correct this idea.

For, in the first place, the rule of the judges secured long periods of public tranquillity.   Of history in general, it may be justly said that it brings into bold relief a nation's wars and discontents, while epochs of peace and prosperity are either thrown into the background, or left unnoticed.   The exceptions, rather

---

* Heb. xi. 32–34.

than the rule, are recorded ; just as a voyager, nar-
rating the story of his crossing the ocean, dwells
chiefly on a storm or two which befel him, and passes
lightly over many a week of smooth and pleasant
sailing,—or as a physician, who in summing up the
history of his patient's life, remembers the attacks of
sickness, and scarcely mentions the long intervals of
health in which nine-tenths of that life was passed.

It is thus with the Book of Judges.   The period of
which it treats was not a period of incessant warfare ;
but it was marked by long and frequent intervals of
repose.   War and disgrace were, after all, the exception ; peace and tranquillity were the rule.   Thus,
after the victory achieved by the first judge, Othniel,
" the land had rest forty years ; " after Ehud's victories, " the land had rest fourscore years ; " after the
rout of Sisera, " the land had rest forty years ; " a little
later, " the country was in quietness forty years in the
days of Gideon ; " the twenty-three years of Tola, the
twenty-two years of Jair, the twenty-five years following the death of Jephthah, all passed without any
recorded national struggle ; and the forty years of
Eli's official life were free from war till its melancholy
close.*   And although the people's lapses into idolatry were frequent, they were so far checked and
restrained, that of 450 years, according to the computation of a learned writer, † there were not less than

---

* Jud. iii. 11, 30 ; v. 31 ; viii. 28 ; x. 2-4 ; xii. 8-14 ;
1 Sam. iv. 18.

† Graves on the Pentateuch, p. 182.

377 years during which the worship of God was generally maintained.   Gloomy and fearful as are some of
the details furnished in the Book of Judges, the Hebrew nation was nevertheless in a better state during
that period, morally, politically, and spiritually, than
it became afterwards during the reigns of the later
kings.

For these long intervals of tranquillity and of rest
from the enemy—during which many a family, no
doubt, followed the Lord in quietness and faith, according to that lovely picture of domestic piety given
us in the Book of Ruth—the Church of those days
was indebted, under God, to the judges, who, through
faith, "wrought righteousness, and obtained promises."

Not only the intervals of repose, but also the
periods of warfare, must be taken into account in
estimating the benefits of their rule.   In general, they
exerted themselves to prevent idolatry, dissuading the
people from their besetting sin ; but there were times
when the people "would not hearken unto their
judges ; " and further, "when the judge was dead,"
they took advantage of the interregnum which sometimes occurred, and "returned and corrupted themselves more than their fathers." *   These apostasies
were followed by chastisements.   The Lord forsook
them ; He permitted their enemies to oppress and
torment them ; "the east wind from the wilderness "†
dried up the fountain of their strength ; until, at the

---

* Jud. ii. 17, 19.   † Hos. xiii. 15.

point to die, they bethought themselves of His holy name. Miserable and forsaken, their name might have been blotted out for ever, but for the "saviours"*—figures of a greater Saviour—whom their God raised up to deliver them.

Nor was success denied to these men in that which they undertook. Unlike Elijah, whose work appeared to himself so ineffectual that he longed to die ; unlike Isaiah, who said, I "have laboured in vain and spent my strength for nought ; " † unlike the later prophets, who were persecuted and slain,—the judges, with the strange exception of Samson, hereafter to be considered, were visibly victorious. "The Lord was with the judge, and delivered them out of the hand of their enemies all the days of the judge." ‡ The kings of Mesopotamia, of Moab, and of Canaan ; the fierce mountaineers of Ammon ; the innumerable hordes of the Bedouin ; the lordly and persistent Philistines, were in turn humbled and subdued by these men, who through faith "quenched the violence of fire, escaped the edge of the sword, waxed valiant in fight, turned to flight the armies of the aliens."

On the whole, during this period, the Hebrew nation increased in importance and strength. After Joshua's death there had been a rapid decline ; but if we take as the commencement of the period the state of things in the time of Othniel, the first judge, and compare it with the state of things in the time of

---

* Neh. ix. 27.   † Isa. xlix. 4.   ‡ Jud. ii. 18.

Samuel, who was the last, the advancement is too manifest to be disputed. The Jewish state went on from that time increasing in glory till it reached its culminating point a century later in the reign of Solomon : after which commenced its long and unretrieved decline. In the period of the Judges, notwithstanding the defections from God, the rebellions, the outrages, the confusion, the bloody civil strifes, which the historian records, so that at the close of the book we seem to behold, as a learned writer observes, "an overclouded sunset, almost a dark eclipse, of the glory of Israel," * yet idolatry was neither so frequent, so open, so obstinately continued, nor so shamelessly immoral, as it became in the later period of the monarchy. The rulers of the people, instead of being hereditary tyrants, and sensualists who taught their people to sin, were special messengers of God, men of faith and power, capable of checking public disorder, and of restoring religion and faith. Notwithstanding frightful interruptions, like the deep rents and yawning chasms which meet the traveller ascending their own Lebanon, the general tendency and direction of the period of the judges was not downward, but upward toward the heights beyond.

IV. It only remains to add a few words respecting the spiritual or typical interpretation of these narratives of the judges.

In modern times it has become the fashion to ignore

---

* Wordsworth, preface to Ruth, p. 158.

almost completely this kind of interpretation.   Commentators and writers on Jewish history have treated the book as if it were nothing more than a secular narrative ; — allowing, indeed, its canonicity and inspiration, but seeing in it nothing beyond the letter. Fathers in the Church of Christ have warned young ministers against allegorizing and spiritualizing, and the advice has become so popular that books on Jewish history have become favourites, whose authors appear as unconscious of any deeper meaning in these ancient records as the Jew, Josephus, himself. Without undervaluing the immensely important labours of modern criticism, and of recent explorations, travels, and researches, I cannot but think that some of the Greek and Latin fathers,—as Chrysostom and Theodoret, Augustine, Jerome, and Ambrose—notwithstanding their ignorance of many illustrative matters with which we in this day are familiar, had a juster and a fuller understanding of the contents of this book than many expositors of modern times.

Unless we read the inspired story with veiled eyes, like the Jews when Moses is read, * in those Canaanites and others who opposed, seduced, and tyrannized over the elect people of God, we shall perceive an emblem of those powers of darkness, those invisible foes of the Church in every age, those seducing spirits and those secret sins which rule in the hearts of the disobedient, and perplex the faithful.   In the men

---

* 2 Cor. iii. 15.

who were raised up and filled with mighty power to defeat these hosts of the enemy and to deliver Israel, we shall perceive a foreshadowing of that greater Deliverer, who will finally, after the long struggles of His Church, overcome all the powers of Antichrist, and secure for His people what the judges could not secure, an unbroken enjoyment of the promised inheritance. The selfsame foes and the selfsame Deliverer exist now as in the days of Barak and of Gideon ; and the conflicts of ancient Israel are being reproduced to-day in another sphere, further removed, it is true, from the sensible and the external, yet none the less real.

Why should the follower of Christ, who truly believes that He is the Alpha and the Omega in His own revealed Word, refuse, or be loth to recognise in these ancient narratives, types or foreshadowings of Him ? Do we not lose the best part of this book, if we shut Christ out of it ? Are these views fit only for the illiterate, and are they not rather worthy the deepest attention of the Christian student ? Ought we to suppose that He, " of whom Moses in the law, and the prophets did write," is wholly excluded, in His covenant character, from this record ?

Let us not therefore be ashamed to see in " Jael, the wife of Heber the Kenite," an emblem of that Seed of the woman who bruised the head of the mighty destroyer, the spiritual Sisera, with the wood of His cross ;—in Gideon's fleece, an image of the Hebrew Church and of the Church universal ;—in "the day of Midian," a foreshadowing of the final rout of the innumerable hosts of error, by the trumpets of His word and the lamps of His truth breaking in upon the spiritual darkness;—in the self-devotion and meek beauty of Jephthah's daughter, a wonderful and mysterious adumbration of another meek and holy One, sacrificed for our sakes;—in the marvellous feats of Samson, images of Him who bore away a burden heavier than the gates of Gaza, and whose death is the death-knell of all the enemies of His Church, and the salvation of His Israel from the hands of the enemy!

At the same time, we must beware of the notion that every resemblance which an acute student may be able to discover, is a true and real type. Without pushing such analogies to a fanciful length, the chief spiritual lesson to be learned from this book seems to be, as an ingenious author succinctly states it, "the failure of the elect in heavenly places,—failure arising from making leagues with Canaanites instead of overcoming them." * This lesson will become more and more obvious as we proceed with the subject.

---

* Jukes's " Types of Genesis," p. ix.

5

ISRAEL TESTED AND TRAINED

THE atmosphere with which our earth is encompassed furnishes one of the most wonderful instances of the skill of the Creator. Let us imagine the problem to have been proposed, to construct a substance enveloping the entire globe, which should be at once the food of all vegetable organisms, the life of all animated creatures, and a shield to prevent their destruction by the earth's rapid motion through space ;—which should at the same time be the vehicle of light, the medium of colour, and the generator of sound in all its endless variety of tones and gradations ;—which should also be a reservoir of heat and of electricity, a home for the clouds and rain, and a force at once so gentle as not to break the leaf of the snowdrop, and yet so powerful as to lash the ocean into fury, and waft ponderous ships across its surface ; —which should accomplish each one of these and many other purposes as perfectly as if its sole function lay in that one object :—how hopeless must such a problem have appeared, until it was solved by the wisdom of the Creator !

Instances of a similar skill in the combination of

results may be discovered in the phenomena of the moral world. It is true that in many instances these phenomena defy our analysis and elude our research. God's "judgments are far above, out of our sight." Yet we often find occasion to observe how one and the same event or series of events in the arrangements of the Divine government, is made to serve the most varied and apparently opposite purposes. Indeed, scarcely an event can happen to us, from the new experiences of infancy to the hour when we sink into the grave, which is not calculated to answer more than one moral end.

It is thus that the imperfect subjugation of the nations which had inhabited Canaan was made to serve a variety of moral ends. It was a punitive visitation upon races steeped in wickedness. It furnished an exercise to the chosen people in the art of war, teaching them by the most imperious necessity to confront their enemies. It supplied an evidence of God's faithfulness to His promise uttered five centuries before, and of His mercy in providing a home for His people. It was a type for the instruction of all following ages, of His Church's conflict with sin and an evil world.

The special interpositions of Providence ceased when the people became idle and unbelieving. "Because that this people hath transgressed my covenant which I commanded their fathers, and have not hearkened unto my voice, I also will not henceforth drive out any from before them of the nations which

Joshua left when he died." *   No more commanding
the sun and moon to stand still! No more great
stones from heaven thundering down as upon the
fugitive host in the way to Beth-horon! †   No more of
the "terror of the Lord" falling upon all the heathen
round about, constraining them to exclaim in pallid
fear, "Now shall this company lick up all that are
round about us, as the ox licketh up the grass of the
field." ‡   Through their sloth and unbelief the covenant people had lost the shield of the Divine protection, and Jehovah would no more interpose to drive
out their enemies.

Thus, in the style familiar to us in the Hebrew
scriptures, the Lord is said to have "left" the various
tribes of the heathen in the land of Israel. "*These
are the nations*," the historian writes, "*which the Lord
left, to prove Israel by them.*" That is represented as
a direct act of God which was a consequence of His
having withdrawn His special aid and presence, as is
always the case when, in His terrible judgments, He
leaves backsliders in heart to be filled with their own
ways.

In this chapter we shall review the list furnished by
the author of the Book of Judges of those heathen
"nations which the Lord left," and also the moral
purposes or reasons why they were so left, "*to prove
Israel by them; even as many of Israel as had not
known all the wars of Canaan; only that the genera-*

---

* Jud. ii. 20, 21.   † Josh. x. 11.   ‡ Num. xxii. 4.

tions of the children of Israel might know to teach them war, at the least such as before knew nothing thereof;" and *"to know whether they would hearken unto the commandments of the Lord, which He commanded their fathers by the hand of Moses."* *

I. In the preceding chapter it has been shown that the judges were to a great extent successful in accomplishing the purpose for which they were raised up. Their duty was, as "saviours" to deliver and defend, and as "judges" to rule, the chosen people. They were not called to extend the territory of Israel beyond the limits of the conquests of Joshua, but only to repress and keep down the heathen within those limits. In general they were successful; yet some important exceptions are noted in the sacred narrative.

The third chapter of the Book of Judges opens with a brief enumeration, altogether different from that which we have already examined, † of the nations which were left unsubdued. If some expositors have explained this second catalogue as being a short summary of the first, it has been through their not having compared the two with sufficient care. The former catalogue enumerates the various places, within the allotments of the several tribes, where the Canaanites were still suffered to remain, most of them under tribute; whereas the passage now before us speaks of "nations" which were left unconquered,—

---

* Jud. iii. 1–4.   † In section II.

"these are the nations which the Lord left, to prove
Israel by them." *   The enemies here referred to
resided not among the Israelites, but for the most
part in their own territories, not acknowledging the
supremacy of Israel.

It cannot be too distinctly pointed out, that the
limits of the "land of promise," as they had been
described by Moses, were far wider than the limits of
the land of possession, as actually subdued and in-
herited by the Hebrew people.   The actual conquests
of Joshua extended northwards " even unto Baal-gad
in the valley of Lebanon under Mount Hermon ;"†
but the promised border of Israel extended much
farther.   In the word of the Lord, spoken by Moses,
it had been laid down with singular exactness : " This
shall be your north border ; from the Great Sea ye
shall point out for you Mount Hor ; from Mount Hor
ye shall point out unto the entrance of Hamath ; and
the goings forth of the border shall be to Zedad ; and
the border shall go on to Ziphron, and the goings out
of it shall be at Hazar-enan."‡

Without going into minute topographical details§
it may be sufficient here to state that Baal-gad, the
utmost limit in this direction of Joshua's conquests,
is about a hundred miles south of " the entrance of
Hamath," to which the promised boundary of the

---

* Jud. iii. 1.   † Josh. xi. 17 ; xii. 7.   ‡ Num. xxxiv. 7–9.
§ See Stanley's " Sinai and Palestine," p. 407 ;   Van de
Velde, i. 113 ; Porter's " Giant Cities," p. 303.

land extended.   The intervening region embraces
the ranges of Lebanon and Anti-Lebanon, the valley
of Cœlo-Syria, and the plain of Hamath ; a magnificent country, which the successors of Joshua ought
to have subdued, in order to complete their covenanted inheritance, but which, until the time of David,
they never entered.   In this noble country resided
" *The Hivites that dwelt in mount Lebanon from
mount Baal-hermon*," — which was most probably
identical with Baal-gad just mentioned—"*unto the
entering in of Hamath.*"*   This country, though distinctly within the boundaries of the land of promise,
was not so much as allotted to any of the tribes.
Joshua divided the land so far as he had conquered
it ; but before his death the Lord reminded him that
" there remaineth yet very much land to be possessed,"
particularly specifying " all Lebanon toward the sun-
rising, from Baal-gad under mount Hermon unto the
entering into Hamath."†   This country, then, remained unsubdued.   The Israelites did not so much
as enter it.   The Hivites remained unmolested in the
hills and valleys of Lebanon.   Unlike the Canaanites
of southern and central Palestine, who were at least
partially subdued, and whose land was divided among
the Israelitish tribes, these " nations " of the north
were not brought under the yoke, nor was their land
occupied as an inheritance.   The faith of Israel waxed
feeble ; they could not go on to new conquests ; and

---

a great part of the land of promise never came, at least during the period now under review, into their possession, but was left entirely to the heathen.

" These," then, (to adopt the words of the sacred narrative) "are the *nations* which the Lord left, to prove Israel by them, even as many of Israel as had not known all the wars of Canaan." Besides the nation of the Hivites, who occupied the region of Lebanon, there were "the Sidonians,"—a remarkable and powerful people, whose history is famous alike in sacred and in classic story ; whose territory lay within the bounds of the land of promise, as they had been defined by Moses, yet was never actually possessed by the Jewish people. These " Sidonians," who are called also " Canaanites," were the far-famed Phœnicians of antiquity, and "the Lord left them " in possession of their land, "to prove Israel by them, to know whether they would hearken unto the commandments of the Lord."*

One of the most remarkable of the physical features of Palestine is the strip of lowland, varying from twenty miles to two miles in breadth, which extends from south to north along its entire seaboard. In the southern part of the coast this strip widens into a spacious plain of twenty miles across, having the Mediterranean on the west, and on the east the mountains of Judah ; this plain is Philistia. In the central section of the coast the plain becomes narrower, and is shut

---

* Jud. iii. 4.

in by the mountains of Manasseh and Ephraim ; this is the plain of Sharon. In the northern part of the coast, extending for a hundred miles beyond the " White Cape " and the " Tyrian Ladder," the plain becomes a mere strip of two or three miles in width, having the sea on one side and the mountain-range of Lebanon on the other ; this strip is Phœnicia. Contracted as is the territory, its commerce, like that of our own little island in modern times, became celebrated throughout the known world. Part of this strip was included in the allotment of the tribe of Asher ; and Zidon itself, the early metropolis of the region, has been already mentioned as one of the cities of the heathen which Asher failed to subdue. But Zidon was the most northerly point to which his allotment extended ; whereas beyond this, for a distance almost equal to the entire length of Palestine from Dan to Beersheba, the Phœnician plain extended, all of which, as well as the mountain region of Lebanon which runs parallel to it, had been included within the divinely appointed limits of the land of promise.

The subsequent fame of Phœnicia, of Tyre its capital city, and of the ingenious and enterprising Sidonian race, the English of antiquity—their connection with the fortunes of the Israelitish people, with the Greeks and Romans, and with the ancient inhabitants of Britain—their extraordinary opulence, and the marvel of their predicted fall, and of the utter desolation of their country according to the word of the Lord by His prophets *—these are subjects which do not lie within the scope of this volume.   Our purpose here is simply to explain that important section in the Book of Judges which points out that, in addition to the towns and villages scattered throughout the land of Israel where the heathen were still permitted to reside, there were whole "nations" which "the Lord left, to prove Israel by them."   The Sidonians were one of these nations of idolaters, and they became "snares and traps" to Israel.   In the times preceding Jepththah, they are spoken of as having oppressed Israel † by violence ; while their luxurious mode of life, "dwelling careless and secure," ‡ was perhaps more fatal than even their political tyranny to the faith and morals of God's people.   Women of Zidon persuaded Solomon, in the infatuation of his luxurious old age, to worship the lewd "Ashtoreth the goddess of the Zidonians." §   Of king Ahab, the inspired historian relates, as a crowning mark of his wickedness, that " as if it had been a light thing for him to walk in the sins of Jeroboam the son of Nebat, he took to wife Jezebel, the daughter of Ethbaal king of the Zidonians, and went and served Baal, and worshipped him."|| In the time of our Lord, Phœnicia was considered as altogether Gentile ground.   Once only, during His public ministry, is He recorded to have passed the bounds of what was recognised as Jewish territory.

---

* Isa. xxiii. 24 ; Ezek. xxvi. 28.   † Jud. x. 12.
‡ Jud. xviii. 7.   § 1 Kings xi. 5, 33. || 1 Kings xvi. 31.

It was when He "went into the borders of Tyre and Sidon," and spoke to the woman who was "a Gentile, a Syrophenician by nation,"* in language which attested in the most decisive manner the Gentile character of the land and of the people.

Besides the Hivites of mount Lebanon, and the Sidonians of the Phœnician plain, there was yet another "nation," at that time more powerful than either, which "the Lord left" within the bounds of the land of promise. These were the Philistines,† whose five great cities, with towns and villages intervening, stood upon the broad and noble plain which lies between the mountains of Judah and the sea. Although three at least of these cities had been taken, as we have seen, by the tribes of Judah and Simeon, it is evident that the power of the Philistines was far from broken. They regained possession, and throughout the whole period of the judges continued to be formidable troublers of Israel.

II. The continuance of these nations in their original possessions, and the consequent contraction of the limits of the land of promise, as compared with the boundaries which had been promised to Abraham and to Moses, was a direct consequence, and in a certain sense a punishment, of the unbelief of God's people. Other ends, however, were answered by it. Israel was tested, and was trained for war. These nations were left "*only that the generations of Israel might know,*

---

* Mark vii. 26, margin.   † Jud. iii. 3.

to teach them war, at least such as before knew nothing thereof." And further, they were left, *" to prove Israel by them, to know whether they would hearken unto the commandments of the Lord, which He commanded their fathers by the hand of Moses." ∗*

It was God's will, then,—it was a necessity for the Israelites—that they should "learn war." But in what way were they to learn it ? Were they to learn it by keeping up a standing army, by maintaining an effective military discipline, by any of the usual pro-cesses of the soldier's art ? Nothing of the kind. In their case, "learning war" meant learning that God alone could fight for them. Their instructions, re-peated again and again in the writings of Moses, amounted to this—that they were to keep all the commandments and ordinances of God's law, and that if they did this the Lord would help them to fight, and would render them victorious over whatever ene-mies might rise up against them ; whereas, if they disobeyed God, no power on earth would be able to save them from defeat and misery.† It was in this spirit that all the wars of Joshua had been conducted. That great conqueror's science of war might have been summed up in one word—FAITH. And the psalmist, celebrating his victories, declares, " They got not the land in possession by their own sword, neither did their own arm save them : but Thy right hand, and

---

∗ Jud. iii. 2, 4.   † Deut. xxviii. 1, 7, 47, 48.

Thine arm, and the light of Thy countenance, because Thou hadst a favour unto them." *

The miraculous aid rendered to Joshua had taught the Israelites that their power to conquer did not consist in their numbers or in their skill, but solely in the omnipotent might of their covenant God, which they could only possess so long as they continued faithful to Him. This lesson the generations that followed Joshua had forgotten, and consequently they did not understand how to make war. To impress this truth upon them—this great truth, upon which the very existence of Israel depended—the Lord left the nations on the north and on the south of their borders, as well as the Canaanites scattered through the land. " Necessity teaches a man to pray. The distress into which the Israelites were brought by the remaining Canaanites was a chastisement from God, through which the Lord desired to bring back the rebellious to Himself, to keep them obedient to His commands, and to train them to the fulfilment of their covenant duties. In this respect learning war— *i. e.*, learning how the congregation of the Lord was to fight against the enemies of God and of His kingdom —was one of the means appointed by God to tempt Israel, or to prove whether it would listen to the commandments of God, or would walk in the ways of the Lord. If Israel should so learn to war, it would at the same time learn to keep the commandments of God." †

---

* Ps. xliv. 3.   † Keil, p. 274.

It is thus that the All-wise Father, in His infinite mercy, overrules evil for good. Israel had disobeyed His command; but in His infinite longsuffering, His next purpose was that their disobedience might still be overruled for good; that the faith, patience, and steadfastness of Israel might be tried and exercised, and so might receive a reward; that where sin had abounded, grace might much more abound.

Are not the same principles of government apparent in the treatment by our Divine Lord of His Church in these latter days? Do not the Canaanites of Unbelief, Heresy, and Worldliness still remain? And is not the evil of their remaining presence overruled for a twofold good—that of teaching His Church how to make war, and of proving their faithfulness toward Himself? When unbelief abounds, is it not that faith may be awakened in the Lord's elect, teaching them " earnestly to contend for the faith once delivered to the saints?" Were not the ancient creeds produced through the spread of heresies, and is not the revival of sacerdotal superstition amongst us at the present day, teaching the lovers of the simple gospel to furbish their weapons anew, and to prepare for a war in defence of the truth, which is infinitely better than sluggish stagnation?

Let us not be dismayed, therefore, if we see the conquests of the Church yet incomplete. That they remain so is doubtless her sin and her punishment. If throughout the ages she had "hearkened to God's commandments," halcyon days might have dawned

before this, and her enemies having been all subdued
and her days of warfare accomplished, her "peace
might have flown as a river." But it is not unmixed
calamity to the faithful. The unsubdued enemies,
whether around or within them, shall be the means of
training them to a higher obedience; and "the trial
of their faith, which is much more precious than of
gold that perisheth, though it be tried with fire, shall
be found unto praise and honour and glory at the
appearing of Jesus Christ." *

---

* 1 Pet. i. 9.

Part 2
BARAK

BARAK

MORE than a hundred years have passed away since the death of Joshua. During that period the chosen nation has not been permitted to remain altogether at peace. True to their hereditary character, the Israelitish people have again and again provoked their God to anger—not merely, as all sinners of mankind do, by individual or secret sins, but by open abandonment of His worship and national revolt against His authority. They intermarried with the families of the Canaanites, who had been permitted to remain in the country ; and being thus "unequally yoked with unbelievers," the natural consequences followed. They "served the gods" of the heathen with whom these prohibited alliances had been formed. They deserted the sanctuary of Jehovah, and "served Baalim and the groves." *

Again and again have these defections occurred in the century and more which has elapsed since Joshua's death. Again and again has punishment been inflicted on them, with the effect of producing a temporary, but only a temporary, repentance ;—a history

* Jud. iii. 7.

strangely similar to the secret history of the Christian's heart. Without commenting at length upon every verse of the Book of Judges, it may be sufficient merely to allude to the histories contained in the third and fourth chapters ; how the Israelites were delivered for eight years into the hands of the king of Mesopotamia, Chushan-rishathaim, and were rescued by the judge Othniel, who secured for them forty years of rest ; how at the expiration of that time they again "did evil," and were brought under the yoke of Eglon, king of Moab, who worsted their army in battle, and reduced them to a state of servitude for eighteen years, until he was put to death by Ehud, the judge, "a man fierce and undaunted," as Lord Bacon describes him, "and one that in a sort neglected his life for the good of his people," the terror of whose name secured to his country afterwards eighty years of tranquillity ; how "in the days of Shamgar," the next judge, through incursions of the Philistines, public security again became endangered ; "the highways were unoccupied, and the travellers walked through byways" * for fear of the invader, until, by feats of unparalleled personal prowess, slaying "six hundred men with an ox goad," Shamgar "also delivered Israel." These punishments and mercies have alike failed to produce more than a transient effect, and the history now brings into view a new condition of disaster and degradation,

---

* Jud. v. 6.

from which the people were delivered through the instrumentality of one whose name is enshrined in the epistle to the Hebrews as a MAN OF FAITH—a man who through faith "waxed valiant in fight," and "turned to flight the armies of the aliens." *

---

* Heb. xi. 34.

6

THE ENEMY

THE offences of which the Israelites in the time of Barak and Deborah were guilty, and which brought upon them the calamities about to be described, were probably a repetition of those for which previous generations had suffered. They "did evil again in the sight of the Lord when Ehud was dead."* They repeated their former crimes, and especially their inveterate sin of idolatry, which, while it included in its abominable accompaniments every other sin, furnished a visible index of the utterly depraved condition of their hearts.† Unhappy Israel, to forget so soon and so often the glory and covenant of their fathers' God!

The consequence was that, in the startling language of the historian, "*the Lord sold them into the hand*" of a hereditary enemy. This was no more than Moses had predicted in the inspired song which he left as a permanent warning to his people.‡ "Have the wicked," exclaims a venerable commentator, § "never done with the consequences of their sin? Do the waves in succession break against them, and are

---

* Jud. iv. 1.   † Mark vii. 21.   ‡ Deut. xxxii. 30.   § Sutcliffe.

they never to expect repose?" As we proceed with
these sketches, we shall discover yet more fully the
inconceivable folly, ingratitude, and depravity of that
"evil heart of unbelief in departing from the living
God,"* of which the Hebrew nation afford so monitory
an example, through a series of generations; and which
in its dismal monotony of disobedience realized only
too exactly the melancholy foreboding of their great
lawgiver, "Behold, while I am yet alive with you
this day, ye have been rebellious against the Lord;
and how much more after my death?"†

The enemy into whose hand the Lord sold them,
in the period now under review, was one of those
kings of northern Canaan who bore the name of
Jabin. Like the Abimelechs and subsequently the
Pharaohs of Egypt, or, in a later age, the Cæsars of
Rome, the successive rulers of this region appear to
have adopted the same hereditary title—Jabin, "the
discerning." Their capital city, and the head, in the
earliest times, of all the kingdoms of northern Palestine, was Hazor; a name which still lingers on the
rugged slopes above the site of the ancient Cæsarea,
where a few rude stone blocks on a rocky eminence,
and a deep circular grove of ilexes close beside them,
mark the probable site of the capital of the Jabins, ‡
and of the grove so long identified with that worship
of Astarte, the Canaanite Venus, by which the Israelites polluted themselves.

---

* Heb. iv. 12. † Deut. xxxi. 27. ‡ Stanley, p. 397.

In the time of Joshua, a hundred and fifty years previously, one of this race of Jabins appeared as the convener of the most formidable confederation against which Joshua ever had to contend.* He seems to have been the recognised head of all the chieftains of northern Palestine, from Esdraelon to Hermon ; and it was he who first brought "horses and chariots very many" into the field against the Israelites. One of the greatest of Joshua's battles ensued. On the eve of the battle, he was within a day's march of the lake of Merom, where Jabin and the confederate armies lay encamped, " even as the sand that is upon the sea shore for multitude." On the morrow, by a sudden descent, Joshua with his host fell like a thunderbolt upon them before they had time to rally. They were utterly routed ; the horses which had seemed so formidable were hamstrung and the chariots were burned with fire ; and Hazor, the capital city, suffered a similar fate. After making " war a long time with all those kings," "Joshua took all that land ;" and the Hebrews appear to have held the supremacy for a century or more after their great commander's death.

Now, however, the case is reversed. Another king appears, bearing the same name, inhabiting the same capital rebuilt from its ashes, and formidable from the same cause as his conquered predecessor; "*for he had nine hundred chariots of iron, and twenty years he mightily oppressed the children of Israel.*" †

---

* Josh. xi. 1–13.   † Jud. iv. 3.

These were probably two-wheeled chariots armed with iron scythes fixed to the axles, and braced together with iron clamps. They may have been similar in design to the chariots which, as early as the times of Joseph, had been in use in Egypt, or to those of which we read as being common afterwards in Assyria and Persia ; or they may have resembled the *currus falcati*, or hooked chariots, which, as appear from the commentaries of Cæsar, were possessed by the ancient Britons. The city where Jabin's general, Sisera, dwelt, " Harosheth of the Gentiles," a city whose exact situation has not been identified, may also have been the place where these chariots were fabricated, if we may judge from the name. It was at Harosheth, at least, that Jabin's nine hundred chariots were collected together by Sisera for the attack upon the little army of Barak.

For twenty long years the oppressions and exactions of Jabin continued. Their servitude under Jabin was in one respect more humiliating to the Israelites than any of the previous oppressions which they had suffered. For eight years they had served Chusan-rishathaim, king of Mesopotamia, and for eighteen years they had served Eglon, king of Moab. But then both of these were foreign potentates ; whereas Jabin rose and reigned in the region which had been won by the arms of Joshua, and assigned to the tribe of Naphtali. Foreign armies, indeed, had invaded the country and laid the tribes under tribute ; but never until now had a king risen up in revolt within the bounds of the land, and shaken off the dominion of Israel in his newly-acquired inheritance. Like the demoniac described by our Lord, into whom the unclean spirits returned after having been cast out, the "last state" of the Israelitish people, humbled and subdued by the idolater, whose ancestors they had crushed beneath their feet, would have been "worse than the first,"—worse than their slavery in Egypt, unless their covenant God had interposed and raised up for them a deliverer.

Such was the tyranny under which faithless Israel succumbed for twenty years. Their ancient foe, whom they had conquered, rose gradually from his prostration. He rebuilt his castle; he repossessed the lands; he multiplied his armies. At length he defied and "*mightily oppressed*" the chosen people. The wanton cruelties inflicted in our own time by Theodore, king of Abysinnia, upon his subjects, may aid us in forming a conception of the miseries which backsliding Israel suffered at the hands of the heathen tyrant. The Lord's elect had sown to the flesh, and now of the flesh they reaped corruption. Enticed by the fair and wanton forms of the idolatresses, the men of Naphtali had forgotten the covenant of their God; lust had conceived and brought forth sin, and sin completed was now bringing forth national and spiritual death.

Is there no modern parallel to this? Are there not multitudes even now who "fall after the same example of unbelief"? How has this history been re-enacted a thousand times in the experience both of individual believers and of Christian Churches! How many there are who answer to the description given by St. Peter: "After they have escaped the pollutions of the world through the knowledge of our Lord and Saviour Jesus Christ, they are again entangled therein, and overcome"!* The Canaanite was slain, but he reappears and resumes his ancient tyranny. Exploded errors revive. Slain heresies live again and triumph on the very spot where they received what was deemed their death-blow. The Romish foundry furnace roars, while new artillery are being forged after the pattern of the old which were shattered in the wars of long ago. The subjugation and prostration of the Church may not be as complete as was the twenty years' slavery of Israel under the second Jabin, yet is not the fortress of Hazor being rebuilt in this land? Are not the furnaces of Harosheth being rekindled? And are not the papal workmen busy fabricating chariots of iron wherewith anew to scour the plains which valiant Protestants of old won in the name of the Lord and of His truth?

---

* 2 Pet. ii. 20.

7

THE PROPHETESS

THE tyranny of Jabin was not exercised over the whole of the land of promise. It did not, for example, prevent the law from being administered in southern Palestine. At this time the judicial functions were discharged by a woman—the earliest instance on record of female government. "*Deborah, a prophetess, the wife of Lapidoth, she judged Israel at that time. And she dwelt under the palm-tree of Deborah, between Ramah and Bethel, in mount Ephraim; and the children of Israel came up to her for judgment.*" * It is incorrect to suppose, as several learned and pious writers have done, that Deborah was raised up in answer to the prayers of the Israelites when they "cried to the Lord" for deliverance from Jabin and Sisera. She was already not only a judge, but, to use her own expressive words, a "mother in Israel." Her position was not as in the case of other judges, acquired by any warlike exploit; nor do we read that it was conferred upon her through any direct or sudden revelation. It seems to have grown out of the respect and honour which were paid

---

* Jud. iv. 4, 5.

to her as one taught of God, and eminent for wisdom, sagacity, and the power of prophetic utterance. This led to her being much consulted and referred to, and eventually to a universally acknowledged influence and status. She thus became, through a Divine appointment, none the less genuine because it was developed gradually, the recognised judge of the Israelitish nation.

The name Deborah, which signifies a bee, has been variously commented upon. Jerome has magnified it into an emblem of "industry, wisdom, chastity, and eloquence;" while an English puritan quaintly remarks that, like the bee, Deborah had "honey for the friends, and a sting for the enemies of Israel." To her the people came, not compelled by legal enactment, but voluntarily, from all parts of the land. All men knew that she was to be found "under the palm-tree of Deborah, between Ramah and Bethel," the chosen spot where, following the custom of the patriarchs, this "mother in Israel" sat in judgment. As Abraham pitched his tent under the oak at Mamre, so Deborah pitched her tent under the palm-tree at Ramah. It is probable that then, as now, trees in that part of Palestine were so scarce as to form the most noticeable feature of the landscape; in that region, at the present day, it is not unusual to find a village better known by some remarkable tree than by its proper name. A namesake of Deborah had been buried four hundred years before under a terebinth oak not far from the spot, and which for ages was distinguished as "*Allon-bachuth*,"—the oak of weeping.*

To the chaste dignity of a mother in Israel, and to the function of a judge, there was added, in the case of Deborah, the gift of prophecy. The term is used in Scripture with considerable latitude of meaning; nor does the fact of her being spoken of as a "prophetess," in itself render it absolutely certain that her sublime ode, which, under the inspiration of the Holy Spirit, has been incorporated in the Book of Judges, is to be received as itself directly inspired from heaven. The ode itself contains no assertion of this; it is not prefaced with the authoritative formula "Thus saith the Lord;" and it may be regarded as an outburst of the feelings of gratitude and triumph which moved the Hebrew Church, uttered by the most gifted minister of that Church, after the rout and downfall of its enemy. Aaron is called in Scripture a "prophet," in respect of his gift of eloquence, and because he was interpreter for Moses; and Miriam, their sister, is called a "prophetess," apparently in respect of her kindred gift of music and song.† The title of prophets is repeatedly given to the musicians who sung the praises of God, or who accompanied the song with musical instruments. ‡ It is also given to the theological students, or the students of sacred music, in the colleges first founded by Samuel, and continued afterwards

---

* Gen. xxxv. 8.   † Exod. vii. 1 ; xv. 20-21.
‡ 1 Chron. xxv. 1 ; 1 Sam. x. 5.

probably to the captivity.*   It is thus, that in respect of her gift of poetry alone, Deborah might be called a prophetess.   At the same time, it is to be remembered that she displayed the higher gift of foretelling the future, and that her message to Barak was prophetic in the highest sense.

The condition of affairs in Deborah's time was such as to afford little hope of a successful resistance being offered to the Canaanite tyrant.   Since the triumphant times of Joshua, there had been a gradual decline of faith ; and although the judges preceding Deborah had effected temporary deliverances for their countrymen, they had not been able permanently to turn the ebbing tide of the national life, or to restore the flow of piety and prosperity.   The miserable aspect of the country is described by Deborah, in the second strophe of her ode, in language which brings it vividly before the eye.

> " In the days of Shamgar, the son of Anath,
>   In the days of Jael, the highways were unoccupied,
>   And the travellers walked through by-ways.
>   The villages ceased, they ceased in Israel,
>   Until that I, Deborah, arose,
>   That I arose, a mother in Israel.
>   They chose new gods :
>   There was war in the gates :
>   Was there a shield or a spear seen
>   Among forty thousand in Israel ? " †

Throughout the lifetime of preceding judges, as

---

* I Sam. x. 11 ; I Kings xviii. 4 ; xx. 35, etc.
† Judg. v. 6–8.

Shamgar and Jael, new forms of idolatry had arisen among the chosen people. They chose new gods until Deborah arose. But when she arose, her influence as a judge, as a prophetess, and as a mother in Israel, checked the further development of idolatry ; nor is it unlikely that it was owing to her influence that the northern tribes, when oppressed by Jabin, bethought themselves at length of the covenant of Jehovah, which they had forsaken.

In the stanzas just quoted, there are four illustrations of the miserable condition of the country.

First, " *the highways were unoccupied, and the travellers walked through by-ways.*" There was no security for property or life in passing from place to place. Travelling ceased ; people only left their homes on occasions of the utmost urgency ; and when obliged to take a journey, to lessen the risk of being plundered or murdered, they abandoned the high-roads, and stole from place to place by obscure and unfrequented routes. "We have ourselves known in the East," says a well-known traveller, "in unsettled times, persons afraid to stir for months together beyond their towns and villages, and for still longer periods travelling wholly abandoned, or undertaken in large and well-armed bodies."*

In the days before Deborah, lawlessness and terror prevailed, and the intercourse of commerce was unknown. The sons, afraid to traverse the plains their

---

* Kitto's Bible Illustrations, vol. ii., p. 343.

fathers had conquered, stayed shivering at home. The picture drawn by the poetic hand of Isaiah in a later age was realized in this: "The highways lie waste, the wayfaring man ceaseth." Or that by Zechariah, of the time of the captivity; "The land was desolate after them, that no man passed through nor returned." *

Secondly, "*the villages ceased in Israel.*" Villages are the characteristics of a settled country. The villages of England, dotted here and there on every landscape, and without the slightest protection, furnish the strongest possible evidence of the security and peace our nation enjoys. In unsettled countries, the people dare not live thus unprotected, but are collected in walled towns. In Israel it had not always been thus; but from the time the people began to choose new gods, public security began to diminish, and "the villages ceased."

But not even in the walled towns were they secure; for our poet notes, thirdly, that there was "*war in the gates.*" The enemy approached their fortified cities, even though, like the cities of the dispossessed Anakim, they were "walled up to heaven," † and inclosed with "gates of brass and bars of iron;" ‡ nor could all their precautions prevent their being surprised and plundered. Hostile bands attacked the very gates where Israel's magistrates sat in judgment;

---

and the threatening of Moses was being accomplished " He shall besiege thee in all thy gates, until thy high and fenced walls shall come down, wherein thou trustedst, throughout all thy land." *

Fourthly, Israel had no means of resistance left, having been completely disarmed.   While Jabin the Canaanite possessed his nine hundred chariots of iron, and his foundry at Harosheth, every weapon of defence which the Israelites had possessed had been taken from them, so as effectually to prevent their offering resistance in defence of their liberties; and Israel had been so stripped and impoverished that, although money would doubtless have procured them a supply of arms from the smiths among their neigh- bours the Philistines, " *not a shield or a spear* " was to be seen " *among forty thousand in Israel.*"

Such was the condition of the people who had " chosen new gods ;"—an emblem of the condition of all, in every Church and in every age, who forsake "the fountain of living waters," and " hew out to themselves cisterns, broken cisterns, that can hold no water." †   And is it merely for historical purposes that we possess this narrative ?   Does not a spiritual truth lie underneath, or rather upon, its very surface ? In this picture of the Israelitish people, disarmed, dejected, and degraded, may we not perceive the in- evitable doom of all who, faithless to their baptism, their Church, and their Saviour, cease to worship God

---

* Deut. xxviii. 52.   † Jer. ii. 13.

in spirit and in truth, and permit themselves to be ensnared by the corruptions of the world?

In this sombre picture there is, however, one relieving picture. The people, after twenty long years of servitude, "*cried unto the Lord*." Yet from what quarter was deliverance to arise? How could a weaponless and impoverished people resist the man who had nine hundred chariots of iron? But Israel need not despair. For as their fathers "gat not the land in possession by their own sword, neither did their own bow save them," * so the sons shall find that a new deliverance can be effected without sword or spear. Although no human weapons are at hand, a pardoning God can summon "the stars in their courses"† to fight against the enemies of His repentant people.

---

* Ps. xliv. 3.   † Jud. v. 20.

8

THE DELIVERER

IN the apportionment of the land of Canaan among the twelve tribes, the lot of the great tribe of Naphtali was not drawn till the last but one. Yet although ten of the tribes had already selected their respective portions, the allotment obtained by Naphtali, though remote, was perhaps the noblest region of Palestine. The physical features of the country are different from those which prevail in Southern Palestine—a difference readily perceived by the traveller viewing the vast panorama from the top of mount Tabor or from the heights of Hermon. The hills, which are higher than those of Ephraim or Judah, "contain or sustain green basins of table land just below their topmost ridges." * These green peaceful basins are linked to the mountains above them by rocky spurs or ridges. On these ridges the chief cities of Naphtali were built, and they are to the present day dotted with their ruins. A ruined village, called Kades, standing on one of these rocky eminences, just on the western edge of the basin of the *Ard-el-Huleh*, the great depressed basin or tract through which the Jordan makes its way to the sea of Merom, has been

---

* Stanley, pp. 365, 390.

identified by Dr. Robinson as the ancient Kedesh-naphtali,—"the holy place of Naphtali," which was appointed by Joshua as one of the six cities of refuge. *
It was here that Joshua routed the combined hosts under the command of the first Jabin; and it was here that another Joshua was residing, in the sorrow-ful times now under review, who was destined to overwhelm the hosts of the second Jabin with a defeat no less signal.

It was by direct revelation that Deborah *"sent and called Barak out of Kedesh-naphtali."* The Lord had chosen him. His name, Barak or "lightning," might symbolise the suddenness and force of his movement, as well as the superhuman character of his victory. To him the prophetess despatched a summons in poetic form, and in the name of the Lord:

> " Hath not Jehovah God of Israel commanded,—
> Go and draw toward mount Tabor,
> And take with thee ten thousand men
> Of the children of Naphtali and of the children of Zebulun ?
> And I will draw unto thee to the river Kishon
> Sisera, the captain of Jabin's army,
> With his chariots and his multitude ;
> And I will deliver him into thine hand."†

In this summons, with its definite orders, and its promise equally definite and plain, we have a remark-

---

* Robinson, iii. pp. 366–368. Mr. Macgregor, who viewed these ruins from the heights above, describes them as being "in a valley."—*Rob Roy on the Jordan*, p. 284 : but the two ac-counts contradict each other only in appearance.

† Jud. iv. 6, 7.

able instance of answer to prayer.   Not more eagerly does a mother fly to the rescue of her babe, screaming with its clothes ablaze, then does the Merciful One interpose to provide help for His chosen in the hour when they call upon Him.

The command to Barak, to collect ten thousand men of Naphtali and Zebulun, and to advance with them to mount Tabor, was too precise to be misunderstood.   These were the tribes best known to him ; the tribes which had suffered most from the enemy ; the tribes from which soldiers could be most quickly obtained.   The terms of Deborah's order sufficiently prove that she was recognised as possessing, through a Divine commission, supreme political power.   It was, perhaps, by inspiration that she knew that, even in those evil times, ten thousand men were to be found in those two tribes, who, if not equally pure as the seven thousand in Elijah's days who had never bowed the knee to Baal, had at least faith and courage enough to rally round an untried captain, and to risk at fearful odds an encounter with their mighty oppressor.   How much more hopeful, after all, was this state of things than that which prevailed in the time of the later monarchy, when not a man was to be found in the streets of Jerusalem who sought the truth !*   Like the difference between a young prodigal, who, although he has wandered far and foully, has not yet lost all tenderness of heart ; and an old

---

* Jer. v. i.

transgressor, grown grey in wickedness, and whose heart is past feeling, having become "hardened through the deceitfulness of sin."

The promise was as clear as the command. It declared, first, that Sisera, with his chariots and his army would be drawn to the river Kishon. To an unbelieving mind, indeed, this part of the promise might occasion alarm rather than assurance, inasmuch as the plains through which this river flows was peculiarly favourable for the operation of Sisera's chariots—the very spot where the footmen of Israel would be placed at the greatest disadvantage. But the promise was addressed to a man of faith, who looked not at human possibilities, but at the word of the Supreme God, Who had expressly declared that He would "draw" Sisera's forces to that very spot, unlikely as it might appear, that they might be delivered into the hand of Israel. As the fishes in the sea of Tiberias were drawn from all around so as to be inclosed in Peter's net when lowered at Christ's command: so the Canaanites would be drawn, by an invisible hand, to the spot where, in answer to His people's cry, God had decreed their destruction. How slow are we to remember that the Lord God is King over all! "Assemble your men on mount Tabor," said the Lord in effect to Barak. "That is all you have to do. Leave the rest with Me. I will draw the enemy into My snare, from which he shall not escape,* and I will

---

* Compare Isa. xxxvii. 29.

show to you, at the needed moment, but not before, the path of victory."

The man of faith was obedient to the summons. We cannot agree with those who impugn the faith of Barak because of his stipulation with Deborah, "*If thou wilt go with me, then will I go* ; *but if thou wilt not go with me, then I will not go.*" To these words some ancient versions add the following : "for I know not the day when the Lord will send His angel with me." * Barak may have felt that, not being himself Divinely inspired, he needed, both for his own direction and for the encouragement of his followers, the presence of the prophetess. He feared lest he might, through his own infirmity, and in the absence of that guidance which her inspiration could afford, mistake the precise moment for action. He wished to show that he considered himself throughout as merely an instrument in God's hands, and that he desired all his followers to understand this. Therefore, when Deborah, foreseeing the issue, told them that the journey would not be for his honour, that Sisera would fall into the hands of a woman, she said nothing for which this dutiful and self-forgetting soldier was not perfectly prepared. Barak must gather his army to Tabor, as the warriors must go round Jericho, in proof of faith and obedience to God.

---

* So two editions of the Septuagint, and the old Vulgate, as quoted and commented on by Augustine in his " Quæstiones," and by Ambrose in his treatise " De Viduis."

The alacrity with which the people of the two tribes responded to Barak's summons, may be inferred from the opening strains of Deborah's ode of victory:

> " Praise ye the Lord for the avenging of Israel,
> When the people willingly offered themselves."*

In the fifth strophe of the ode, the theme is resumed:

> " Speak, ye that ride on white asses,
> Ye that sit on carpets,
> Ye that walk in the way:
> Saved from the archer's noise in the places of drawing water,
> There will they rehearse the righteous acts of the Lord,
> The righteous acts, His villages in Israel;
> Then did the people of the Lord return to the gates.
> Awake, awake, Deborah,
> Awake, awake, utter a song,
> And lead thy captivity captive, thou son of Abinoam."†

The prophetess calls on different classes of her countrymen to unite with her in blessing God for the willingness with which the people offered themselves. The nobles and the wealthy who rode out upon white asses,‡ the people who sat quietly at home upon carpets of tapestry or needlework, and the wayfaring poor who travelled on foot, are invited to rehearse in their villages the Lord's mercies toward His people, when they returned to those " gates " of the great city of Naphtali from which they had before been forced to fly, for fear of the enemy, assembling by

---

* Jud. v. 2.

† Jud. v. 9–12. I have given the above with some variations from our Authorized Version.

‡ Compare Jud. x. 3, 4 ; xii. 13, 14.

thousands for the march to mount Tabor. In this view the song corresponds exactly with the narrative, which states that, Deborah having arrived in accordance with his request, " *Barak called Zebulun and Naphtali to Kedesh ;* " and that the response was so immediate and general, that he " *went up* " from Kedesh to Tabor " *with ten thousand men at his feet.*"*

Besides Zebulun and Naphtali, other tribes also appear to have been summoned. In the ode of the prophetess, we have a judicial record of the conduct of the several tribes, designed, like the song of Moses, to be a witness against the people in days to come.† First, those are mentioned who were obedient to the call. Out of Ephraim came a root or remnant of those who had of old distinguished themselves against Amalek. The tribe of Benjamin, though small and distant from the fight, supplied a contingent. Manasseh, here called " Machir," from the name of his only son,‡ sent his "governors" or chief men, and Zebulun sent those that "handle the pen of the writer," enrolling the names of all who mustered for the combat. Issachar also, sent his "princes," to be numbered with those who should descend from the summit of Tabor into the valley of Kishon, to meet the chariots of Sisera. So we may understand the following strain :—

"Out of Ephraim was there a root of them against Amalek :
After thee, Benjamin, among thy people :

---

* Jud. iv. 10.   † Deut. xxxi. 19–21.   ‡ Num. xxvi. 29.

Out of Machir came down governors,
And out of Zebulun they that handle the pen of the writer :
And the princes of Issachar were with Deborah,
Even Issachar, and also with Barak ;
He was sent on foot into the valley." *

Such commendation, however, could not be bestowed upon all the tribes. The pastoral tribe of
Reuben preferred to abide among the sheepfolds.
They deliberated, indeed ; there were "great searchings of heart ;" but they did not act. They were not
firmly of one mind ; as their father Jacob foretold of
Reuben, " Unstable as water, thou shalt not excel ;" †
and at length, after all their consultations, as is usual
with those who require long deliberation when there
is a plain and stirring call of duty, they preferred the
bleating of their flocks to the martial sound of the
trumpet in the battle of the Lord. " Gilead," that
is the tribe of Gad, and the eastern part of Manasseh
beyond Jordan, did not come up to the help of the
Lord, but " remained beyond Jordan." Dan preferred
his commerce and his fisheries ; and Asher, in his fat
land, full of "royal dainties," ‡ remained lazily in his
" breaches" or indented bays on the sea shore, while
his brethren were "jeoparding their lives unto the
death." As we read this poem, how can we fail to
perceive its lesson for our own times ? Is it not just
so now when the Lord's battle is to be fought ? Some,
like Reuben, remain at home absorbed in rural life,
and care not for the conflict, the din of which is out of

---

* Jud. v. 14, 15. † Gen. xlix. 4. ‡ Gen. xlix. 20.

their hearing ; others, like Dan, are too full of their
commerce, their imports and exports, their bargain-
ings abroad and at home, to regard it ; while others,
like Asher, born to competence and comfort, prefer a
life of ease, indolence, and luxury, to the toil and
self-denial involved in a hearty consecration of themselves to Christ and His Church, such as that which
was displayed so heroically by the men of Zebulun
and Naphtali.

> " For the divisions of Reuben
>   There were great thoughts of heart.
>   Why abodest thou among the sheepfolds,
>   To hear the bleatings of the flocks ?
>   Gilead abode beyond Jordan ;
>   And why did Dan remain in ships ?
>   Asher continued on the sea-shore,
>   And abode in his breaches.
>   Zebulun and Naphtali were a people
>   That hazarded their lives unto the death
>   In the high places of the field." *

The muster-roll is now complete.   The ten thousand
of the prophetic summons have assembled.   Men
mightily oppressed for twenty years, impoverished,
disarmed ; but men who have cried to the Lord, and
are ready to lay down their lives for His sake.   Not
a chariot is among them ; scarcely a weapon of war.
But there is a prophet amongst them ; the appointed
representative of Him who has " chosen the foolish
things of the world to confound the wise, and the weak
things of the world to confound the things that are

---

* Jud. v. 15–18.

mighty." *   And at their head there is a MAN OF
FAITH, believing in the covenant, and therefore
undismayed by the nine hundred chariots of iron ;
knowing that " with God all things are possible." †
In this faith the ten thousand move from the sanctuary
of Naphtali toward the summit of Tabor.

---

* 1 Cor. i. 27.   † Matt. xix. 26.

9

THE VICTORY

THE movements of Barak and his ten thousand were not unobserved by the wandering Bedouin. Encamped in their black tents, in the marshy ground to the north of lake Huleh, in the neighbourhood of Kadesh ;* or perhaps in a green plain, studded with terebinths, which lay to the southward of that sanctuary,† was a party of Kenites, under Heber their chief, and Jael his wife. They had severed themselves from the main body of their tribe, whose tents were pitched in the dry region in the extreme south of Judah,‡ and had found pleasanter camping ground in the upland plains of Naphtali. Between the Israelites and the main body of the Kenites a friendly alliance had always existed. Descended from Abraham by

---

* Smith's " Dictionary," art. *Zaanaim*.

† Stanley's " Jewish Church," p. 324 ; localities 197. The " plain of Zaanaim," mentioned as the camping place of Heber, has not been satisfactorily identified : but the word " plain," here, as elsewhere (Gen. xii. 6 ; xiii. 18 ; xiv. 13 ; Jud. ix. 6, 37, etc.), is a mistranslation. It should rather be " oak." See Smith's " Dictionary," art. *Plain*, sec. 7 ; the modern Hebrew lexicons ; and Stanley's " Syria and Palestine," p. 519.

‡ Jud. i. 16.

his wife Keturah,* the Kenites had been intimately associated with the Israelites in the time of Moses,† had followed them in their wanderings in the desert,‡ had pitched their tents in the land of promise, and remained not only to the days of Saul and David,§ but to the Babylonish captivity.‖ One of their sheikhs, however, Heber by name, had wandered northward in the days of Deborah, and finding the Israelites in adversity, had allied himself with their enemy. It was this company of faithless Kenites who communicated to the Canaanite commander information of the movements of Barak and his men, and *"showed Sisera that Barak the son of Abinoam was gone up to mount Tabor."* ¶ Little may Heber have imagined, while betraying the ancient allies of his fathers, that his treason would be the means of entrapping their mighty enemy to his destruction.

It was in this way, however, that the word of the Lord to Barak was literally fulfilled : *"I will draw unto thee,"* as a wild animal into a snare, *"unto the river Kishon, Sisera, the captain of Jabin's army, with his chariots and his multitude."* The heathen general having received information from the Kenites, summoned all his forces for a contest which he expected,

---

* Compare Gen. xxv. 2, with Exod. ii. 15 ; iii. 1 ; and Jud. i. 16.

† Num. x. 29.

‡ Their tents were seen by Balaam when he viewed the encampments of the twelve tribes from the mountains of Moab (Num. xxiv. 21, 22).

§ 1 Sam. xxvii. 10 ; xxx. 29.   ‖ Jer. xxxv.   ¶ Jud. iv. 12

no doubt, would result in the annihilation of the Israelitish band.   Nine hundred chariots of iron, and all the people that were with him—all the forces which king Jabin could bring together—were summoned at Harosheth, and marched from thence "unto the river of Kishon," * where the chariots would be in the best possible position for action, on the flat alluvial plain.

Let us pause to contemplate the two armies, each now in position, and awaiting the battle.   There, on the summit of Tabor, "a level, oval-shaped area, about a mile in circuit," † stand Barak's ten thousand, waiting till the eagle-eyed prophetess, watching Sisera in the plain below, gives the signal of attack.   Around them lay that wonderful panorama, which, once seen, can never be obliterated from the memory, and every point of which, notwithstanding their apparently hopeless inferiority, might serve to enkindle their faith, and to animate their hope.   On the north, the brown peaks of their own Naphtali running in a serried ridge across the glowing sky, a corner of the sea of Galilee in its deep bed, and the glittering top of Hermon towering over it like a guardian angel.   On the east, the long purple ridge of Gilead, rising like a colossal wall from the Jordan valley.   On the south, the battle-field of the enemy, the plain sweeping round the base of the mount upon whose top the men

---

* Jud. iv. 13.
† Porter's " Giant Cities of Bashan," p. 243.

of Israel stood, and extending like a sea of verdure across to the hills of Samaria. On the west, the wooded heights of Galilee, extending to the dark ridge of Carmel and the distant Mediterranean. The steep sides of mount Tabor, probably less entangled at that time with brambles and brushwood than they are at the present day, afford a ready path for a rapid descent upon the enemy occupying the plain. But, once descended from the summit, how fearful the venture! How could a small company of wretchedly equipped footmen withstand, even for an instant, the onward rush of the enemy's swift chariots, supported by column after column of his well-armed and impetuous legions. To descend the mountain-side was like rushing into the jaws of destruction. With so great a disparity of force, nothing could prompt the movement, but either faith, or the wild and reckless courage of despair.

But despair finds no place in the heart of Barak so long as he has the Lord's prophetess at his side. A true man of faith, he is as humble and docile as he is swift and courageous. When commanded, he moves as the lightning, or as the "angels that excel in strength," those "ministers" of Jehovah, who "do His pleasure;" * but until commanded, teachable and quiet, his "soul is even as a weaned child:" † a wonderful example, for the Church in all ages, of that phase or manifestation of faith which unites the most

---

* Ps. ciii. 20, 21.　　　† Ps. cxxxi. 2.

impetuous ardour with perfect self-abnegation and humility.   Peter was perhaps as ardent, when he drew his sword to defend his Master against the four hundred who came to apprehend Him; but he was not as docile.

At length the prophetess gives the word of command.   Sharp, clear, and full of mysterious encouragement, it was characteristic of her whose summons had first drawn Barak from his retirement in Kedesh-naphtali.   "*Up! for this is the day in which Jehovah hath delivered Sisera into thine hand! Is not Jehovah gone out before thee?*"* It may be asked, Was there any outward sign by which Deborah knew the precise moment for the attack? Did she hear, like David in the valley of Rephaim, "the sound of a going" in the tree-tops, † or like Nahum before the destruction of Nineveh, "the noise of the rattling of the wheels, and of the prancing horses, and of the jumping chariots?"‡ Or did she, like Elijah's servant, distinguish from the mountain-top "a little cloud," § which she prophetically saw to be the precursor of that tremendous tempest which was to overwhelm the enemy's army with destruction? Whatever she saw or heard, it was given her to know that "the Lord was gone out" from His holy place. Her challenge to Barak, "Is not the Lord gone out before thee?" was a direct and singularly encouraging reference,

---

* Jud. iv. 14.　　† 2 Sam. v. 24.　　‡ Nah. iii. 2.
§ 1 Kings xviii. 44.

which he would be quick to understand, to the words of Moses encouraging Israel to go up against the sons of Anak: "The Lord thy God is He which goeth over before thee; as a consuming fire He shall destroy them, and He shall bring them down before thy face; so shalt thou drive them out, and destroy them quickly."[*] Thus, at the critical moment, Barak was fortified by the threefold encouragement of a promise from the law of the Lord, an instance of His past faithfulness, and an inspired assurance of present success.

No sooner had the prophetess spoken than the ten thousand obeyed, and descended to meet the enemy. The narrative gives no particulars of the engagement ; it only records the completeness of the victory : "*The Lord discomfited Sisera, and all his chariots, and all his host, with the edge of the sword before Barak. And Barak pursued after the chariots, and after the host, unto Harosheth of the Gentiles: and all the host of Sisera fell upon the edge of the sword ; and there was not a man left.*"[†]

In the text, as thus rendered in our version, no intimation is conveyed of extraordinary phenomena, such as is suggested by the Hebrew word *yaham*, which is there translated *discomfited*. The word occurs comparatively seldom, and chiefly in connection with direct interpositions of God ; as in the account of the discomfiture of the Egyptians at the Exodus, when " the Lord looked through the pillar of fire and of the

---

[*] Deut. ix. 3.   [†] Jud. iv. 15, 16.

cloud, and *troubled* the host of the Egyptians;"* or as
when the Lord *discomfited* the army of the five kings
in the time of Joshua, by " casting down great stones
from heaven upon them ; "† or as the psalmist prays,
" Cast forth lightnings and scatter them ; shoot out
thine arrows and *destroy* them."‡   " The expression
places the defeat of Sisera and his army in the same
category as the miraculous destruction of Pharaoh,
and of the Canaanites at Gibeon.   Jehovah threw
Sisera and his army into confusion, and like a terrible
champion fighting in front of Israel, smote him without quarter."§

The song of Deborah supplies some further particulars which confirm this view.

> " The kings came and fought,
>   Then fought the kings of Canaan
>   In Taanach by the waters of Megiddo ;
>   They took no gain of money.
>   They fought from heaven ;
>   The stars in their courses fought against Sisera.
>   The river of Kishon swept them away,
>   That ancient river, the river Kishon.
>   Then were the horsehoofs broken by the plungings,
>   By the plungings of the mighty ones." ‖

From the top of Tabor to Taanach, where the army
of Sisera was assembled, is about twelve miles. Sisera
had marshalled them apparently on the south bank

---

* Exod. xiv. 24.   † Josh. x. 10.
‡ Ps. cxliv. 6 ; compare 2 Sam. xxii. 15 ; Ps. xviii. 15.
§ Keil, p. 304.   ‖ Jud. v. 19–22.

of the Kishon, between Megiddo and Taanach—the latter name is still preserved in an isolated *tell* covered with ruins. News arrived that Barak was descending from Tabor. Sisera turned to meet him. While the distance was being traversed, and the armies were rapidly approaching each other, a tempest of unparalleled force and grandeur was arising. "A little cloud," it may be, " arose out of the sea ;" not the harbinger, on this occasion, of an " abundance of rain" to refresh the parched earth, but of a terrific storm, "the stars in their courses " fighting against the Canaanite. The waters pouring down the mountain-sides presently swelled the river Kishon, till its torrent rose into a flood which turned the alluvial banks of the river into a quagmire, overflowed the plain, stopped the movement of the chariots, carrying them away in its eddies, or rendering their progress impracticable in the soft morass; the " *horsehoofs being broken by the pransings of the mighty ones*,"—the drivers urging the animals to escape at a pace beyond their strength, till in their desperate plunging they broke their limbs or became otherwise disabled.

"In the spring of 1858, " says a veteran traveller, " I saw the low parts of Esdraelon, previously hard and dry, turned into a dangerous morass by a few hours' heavy rain ; and the Kishon was swollen to such an extent as to render it altogether impassable at the ordinary fords."*

---

* Porter's " Giant Cities," p. 255.

In the beginning of 1869, a renowned British oarsman visited the river, and he thus describes it :—" The treacherous nature of the Kishon exceeds that of any river I have seen.   Even after a long spell of fair weather, a few hours' rain may render a passage impossible.   Descending the steep bank, my horse entered the river, which is there about fifty feet broad, but we had not advanced two yards into the channel before the water came up to my knees in the saddle, and all endeavours to cross were futile.   It is readily understood, then, how Sisera's army might have easily crossed the Kishon before a storm, and yet be 'swept away' in the very same place after rain had flooded the river."

The same traveller describes "another peculiarity of the plain," which illustrates the narrative.   " On certain tracts of its surface there is strong adhesive mud.   Now when horses and mules pass over such places, they are often unable to pull out their feet.   If a horse's foot is buried in the mud long enough to allow the clay to close over it from above, he finds it extremely difficult to draw his leg out again, and he instantly changes his gait to a series of plunges, with rapid, short, and jerky steps, snorting and groaning the while with terror, and panting and steaming in the wildest excitement.   Therefore it was that the steeds of Sisera were discomfited, flying before Israel, 'so that Sisera lighted down off his chariot,' and Deborah could sing in her hymn of triumph, ' Then were the horsehoofs broken by the means of the pransings, the pransings of the mighty ones.'"*

It was however in no ordinary tempest, but in a storm of rain, hail, and thunder, of unprecedented violence, that the armies of Sisera and of Barak met ; the storm, according to Josephus, being from the east and in the face of the Canaanites. Panic and confusion seized the hosts of Jabin. The battle became a rout. Sisera, confounded by the tempest, and unable to control his panic-stricken army, left caring for the battle, which he saw to be lost, and sought only to preserve his own life. He "*lighted down off his chariot*," which could no longer be forced through the soft morass, "*and fled away on his feet;*" while the victorious men of Israel, picking up the swords dropped by the enemy, slew the flying fugitives with their own weapons as they pursued them through the driving storm to the very gates of Harosheth, until "there was not a man left" in regular array of battle.

Can it be necessary to dwell upon the moral of this wonderful story? Of the lessons which it suggests, two or three may in the briefest manner be indicated.

1. That which was the chief boast of the heathen oppressor and the chief terror of the trembling Israelites, proved to be one of the principal causes of the enemy's overthrow, and of Israel's salvation. It was

---

* " Rob Roy on the Jordan," pp. 439-441.

not the multitude of Sisera's soldiers that so greatly terrified the Israelites; it was his nine hundred chariots of iron, the symbols of his protracted tyranny and of Israel's subjugation. Yet it was these very chariots which hindered the flight of his legions, and hastened their destruction in the day of Jehovah's vengeance. Footmen might have escaped more swiftly, but "the horsehoofs were broken," the flight of the chariots was impeded, and "the river of Kishon swept them away." It is thus that the earthly might of the infidel and the oppressor, which alarms a feeble and persecuted Church, may become a weapon swift and sure for his own destruction. It is thus that Churches possessing wealth and temporal grandeur, and treating poorer and less favoured Churches, though equally sound in the faith, with neglect and disdain, may expect to find the wealth and position in which they have deemed themselves secure, turned against them to hasten their downfall. How little, if we had true faith, should we fear mere human pomp and greatness! The chariots of the enemy shall but accelerate his ruin.

2. Closely connected with this is the thought which will receive more abundant illustration as we proceed with these sketches, that faith is the highest reason. Reason and faith are commonly spoken of as if they were antagonistic principles. And, indeed, faith is antagonistic to low, carnal, self-sufficient reason : to reason which shuts out of view the living God, and trusts to no better guide than its own imperfect and ever

changing conclusions. But to that higher reason which recognises an omniscient God, and submits implicity to His declared will, faith is not merely not opposed, for in fact the two are one. Which is the higher exercise of reason on the part of a young child : to adhere obstinately to its own notion or way, or to submit its little intellect and will to its father ? And what is the disparity between an infant and a man, when compared with the infinite disparity between the wisest of men and the Eternal God ? When He speaks, the highest exercise of reason and will of which we are capable is, to listen, to believe, and to obey : and this is also faith. Was Barak a man of faith ? Did he not also put in exercise the highest intelligence ? Earthly, short-sighted reason—the wisdom which is merely human, would have pronounced his movements extravagant and absurd. But his soul dwelt in a higher sphere. He heard a voice which no gross ear can hear. He caught a ray from the Throne of Light, which it would have been madness and sin to neglect, but the perfection of intelligence and wisdom to follow. The purer, higher reason, then, is not abnegated when faith is called into exercise. Faith, on the contrary, is the highest reason. And as the wisdom of Barak's proceedings was vindicated when the shattered hosts of the enemy were flying in disorder before him : so in a higher sphere, the wisdom of the humble disciple, who for the sake of our Lord Christ has willingly been accounted a fool by scoffing professors of a mere human philosophy, shall be manifested when, victorious at last, he enters into rest.

3. In the overthrow of Sisera's host may be discerned a type of the final overthrow of Satan. Long indeed has the enemy triumphed :—Sisera for twenty years over the children of Israel ; Satan for thrice twenty centuries over the race of redeemed . men. The place of the heathen tyrant's overthrow, " by the waters of Megiddo," seems to have suggested the locality of that mystic battle of Armageddon,* where there were voices, and thunders, and lightnings, and a great earthquake ;" and when " great Babylon came in remembrance before God, to give unto her the cup of the wine of the fierceness of His wrath." In that great and terrible day, "there came a great voice out of the temple of heaven, from the throne, saying, It is done."

We may also profitably regard this great victory as an emblem of encouragement to ourselves in the daily struggle with evil. Weaker in ourselves than was Barak's little band in comparison with the great armament of Sisera, we need not fear when He who makes the clouds His chariots, and rides upon the whirlwind and the storm, is near to our help. We may conclude this section with the words of two great teachers of the ancient Church. " In that victory," says Ambrose, " we may see a figure of our own conquests over our own spiritual enemies, by faith and

---

* Rev. xvi. 16.

prayer." *   " Let us," says Origen, "crucify our own lusts, and destroy the Siseras within us ; then shall we go and sit down with Deborah under her palm-tree, her tree of victory, and sing a song of victory with her for evermore."

---

* Amb. de Viduis, chap. viii.

10

JAEL

"SO let Thine enemies perish, O Lord," was the
exclamation with which, in allusion to the destruction of Jabin's host, and more especially to the
ignominious end of Sisera, its commander, Deborah
closed her song of victory.* The faithful will say
Amen to her prayer, so far as relates to the interposition of the Almighty, who "cast forth lightnings and
scattered"† His enemies by directing against them
the tempest and the storm. But can the Amen be so
readily uttered in regard to the circumstances of
Sisera's death?

The act of Jael does not fall exactly within the
boundary of our subject. It can scarcely be regarded
as an example of faith. From early times her conduct has been viewed with opposite feelings, and the
diversity of opinion continues to this day. On the
one hand, her act has been stigmatized as an unpro-
voked murder, committed under circumstances of the
highest aggravation. On the other hand, it has been
contended that when she killed Sisera she was acting

---

* Iud. v. 31.   † Ps. cxliv. 6.

under a direct Divine impulse, and she has been exalted into a type of the Gentile Church. Midway between these views are such sentiments as those of Dr. Chalmers:—" One cannot help a recoil from the deed of Jael, in which there were both treachery and cruelty, sorely aggravated to our natural feeling by the circumstance of her being a woman. Yet God does employ the instrumentality of what in itself is evil for the furtherance of His own purposes. Nor are we to know in how far there might not have been a Divine commission for the particular act which would completely legalize it; even as the commission given to the Israelites did to exterminate the Canaanites." *

Sisera, having lost all control over his battalions, and his horses being helpless to drag his chariot through the adhesive clay, while the victorious Israelites were in full pursuit behind him, "lighted down off his chariot and fled away on his feet." Hastening up one of the ravines in the wooded hills to the north of the plain of battle, he presented himself at the tent of Jael, whose husband was sheikh of a Bedouin tribe of Kenites, friendly with Jabin. Here he would feel more secure than in any other place to which he could betake himself; † and having been served by Jael

---

* Chalmers' Posthumous Works, vol. ii., p. 8.

† Pococke relates how, in one of his journeys, he was taken to an Arab's tent, the wife having a separate harem or apartment. " I was kept," he continues, " in the harem for greater security, the wife being always with me; no stranger ever daring

with refreshments, and having directed her to deny his presence if any question should be asked, exhausted with excitement and worn out by fatigue, he lay down to sleep.

When Jael received him, she did so no doubt in good faith, nor had she heard of his overwhelming disaster. She would be only too ready to afford shelter to the proudest warrior of those regions. It is not unlikely that while he was sleeping she began to reflect upon the strangeness of his being in a condition to need such succour; and that from fugitives and others passing by, she learned the story of that eventful day. She found that it was no longer a victor, but a baffled and helpless fugitive who lay in her tent. If she were discovered giving shelter to him, what vengeance might she not expect at the hands of Barak? Anyhow she must be quit of such a visitor. Her memory would recall countless instances of the cruelty of this torturer of the Hebrew people during twenty years. She probably had a dim idea also of his character, as an enemy of the God of heaven whom the Israelites worshipped.

A sudden impulse seized her; she would despatch him as he lay. Was he not the worst of oppressors? Did he deserve to live? Besides, the cries of the pursuers already echo through the mountains, and their weapons flash amid the foliage. The wretched

---

to come into the woman's apartment, unless they are introduced."—Harmer's Observations, i., p. 295.

Sisera is too exhausted to offer a dangerous resistance. She enters the apartment and strikes him. He staggers up; then in a swoon he falls at her feet.* An iron tent-pin, to which the cords of the tent were fastened, is in her hand, and a mallet. She drives the iron pin through his temples into the earth, with a blow given in the superhuman strength of frenzied excitement. Then voices are heard in the forest. The pursuers have come up; it is Barak himself. *" And behold, as Barak pursued Sisera, Jael came out to meet him, and said unto him, Come, and I will show thee the man whom thou seekest. And when he came into her tent, behold, Sisera lay dead, and the nail was in his temples."*

"Beneath the shade of a terebinth," says a living traveller, "by the ruins of Kedesh, I read this tragic tale. Before me, in a forest glade, were the black tents of some Turkmans, modern representatives of the Kenites. I saw the large iron tent-pins; I saw the mallets with which the women drive them into the ground when encamping, for this is their work. I saw the women themselves; strong, active, fierce-looking women, just as fancy would picture a Jael. There was little wanting to complete the scene. That little imagination easily supplied; and there again was realized before me one of the most graphic of Bible stories."†

---

* Compare Jud. v. 26, 27, with iv. 21.
† Porter's "Giant Cities," p. 268.

The whole story appears perfectly natural; nor is there any need for the supposition of Jael acting under a Divine impulse, or a special Divine commission. Her act was dictated as much by self-interest as by any other motive. It was a moment of wild excitement, and cannot be judged by the rules of our peaceable and decorous time. If in the great Indian mutiny, we had heard of Nana Sahib having been entrapped and killed by some wild woman of a wandering tribe, the public opinion of England would not have scrutinized too closely the morality of the action, in its joy at being rid of the most infamous of murderers.

It is, in fact, the eulogy pronounced by Deborah which has constituted the difficulty. And a difficulty it must always remain to those who believe that every word uttered by those who of old had the name and rank of prophets, is a direct utterance of the Divine will. According to this view, this heathen woman, Jael, who is twice declared to be "*blessed above women*,"* must be ranked among the chief servants of God. The difficulty, however, disappears if we view the splendid ode of Deborah as being included by the guidance of the Spirit of God among the records of His ancient Church, and as expressing the feelings of an Israelite patriot of that day. The holiest and most devout of the Church of that age would respond to Deborah's language. Any of them would have re-

---

* Jud. v. 24.

joiced to have acted Jael's part, who, in the impulse
of a moment, turned upon the merciless torturer of
twenty years, and laid him dead at her feet; and
would have united in the antiphon, "*So perish all
Thine enemies, O Lord.*" Whether such sentiments
would be appropriate in our own day is not in question: we believe in the doctrine and in the fact of
progressive light.

Part 3
GIDEON

11

THE MIDIANITE SPOILERS

IN studying any account of military operations, nothing is more necessary than a correct knowledge of the country. As this general remark is peculiarly applicable in regard to the exploits of Gideon, we cannot perhaps more fitly commence the study of his history than by recalling the features of that portion of Palestine where he lived and fought and conquered:—the plain of Esdraelon, the heights of Manasseh, and the cornfields of Issachar.

Between the elevated lands of Southern Palestine on the one hand, which extend in bare rolling hills of greyish limestone from Hebron to Samaria, and the bolder mountains of Northern Palestine on the other, there is a rent, or a depression of the surface, averaging about twelve miles in width. It cannot be described as a chasm, nor as a defile between two mountain ranges: it is much too wide, and not sufficiently deep, to answer to either of these descriptions. It is a low tract, an uneven plain, lying between more elevated regions which bound it like a lofty wall of irregular height on either side; and in its length it stretches across the entire width of Palestine proper, from the shore of the Mediterranean on the west to the valley of the Jordan on the east. Towards the coast, or western end, the mountains on either side approach each other more and more closely, till at length the plain narrows into a mere gorge, through which, for two or three miles, flows the river Kishon; the plain then opens out again upon the sea shore. In its central or widest portion it is level without interruption from the southern hills of Samaria to the northern hills of Galilee. Towards the east it rises to a slight elevation, and then slopes irregularly down till it meets the right bank of the Jordan; on the other side of which river there is a free and unobstructed course eastward and southward, away to the deserts of Arabia. In the spring, the aspect of this plain is that of a vast waving cornfield, interspersed with olive-trees; the green and fertile tract, so wide, so long, and so rich, presenting a charming contrast to the huge bare masses of hill—bare at least in their upper regions—which bound it on either side.

At the present day, this plain, and also the lower tracts of the mountain-sides, are dotted with villages. These almost all retain their ancient names, and they are usually situated either on the lower slopes of the mountains which bound the plain, or else on slight eminences rising out of it. Such was the pleasant and fruitful land which on more than one occasion tempted the cupidity of the enemies of Israel. Looking down upon it from the lofty heights of Carmel on the west, or from the dome-like summit of Tabor on the east, the prospect is one of such pleasant fertility, that men could scarcely refrain from envying the tribe of Issachar, whose lot it was to possess this productive tract. But the men of Issachar, in other days, as well as in those of Gideon, were under the power of spoilers who invaded their country. Less hardy and less resolute than their brethren of the mountain districts, they had the character of too often preferring a dishonourable peace to an honourable though difficult resistance. Their father Jacob, on his dying bed, had foretold this of them :—" Issachar is a strong ass, crouching down between two burdens : and he saw that rest was good, and the land was pleasant ; and bowed his shoulder to bear, and became a servant unto tribute."*

Such is the plain of Esdraelon, and such was the character of its inhabitants in the days of Gideon's youth. Some fifty years had passed since the victory of Deborah and Barak, and the defeat of Sisera, upon this very plain. But forgetful Israel, after that memorable deliverance, soon turned again from the Lord, and now a more formidable enemy than Jabin or Sisera ravaged the country.

The plains of Palestine are the most defenceless portion of the country. The narrow passes of the

---

* Gen. xlix. 14, 15.

mountain regions afford strong positions of defence against an invader, and the caves and fastnesses afford ready shelter ; but over the open plains the wandering tribes of the desert can range more freely. In our own times, every summer, numerous hordes of Bedouin come up from the Arabian desert, cross the Jordan, and pitch their tents all over the plain of Esdraelon, and in the creek-like narrow valleys which run far up between the adjacent hills, plundering whatever they can lay their hands on, and rendering the district all but uninhabitable. But of all the recorded migrations of Bedouin into Palestine, the most gigantic was that with which the Israelitish people were scourged in the days of Gideon. The invaders are described as "the Midianites, and the Amalekites, and the children of the east." It was a general migration of the combined hordes of the desert ; the same phenomenon, a thousand times magnified, as occurs summer after summer at the present day, when the roving Arabs of the Hauran and of Gilead come far up the plain of Esdraelon, plundering all they meet with.

Among these desert tribes the principal aggressors were the " Midianites "—wild, wandering corsairs of the desert : the same people who ages before had bought Joseph for a slave, and sold him in Egypt ; against whose beguiling arts and wiles Moses cautioned the Israelites. Moses was himself expressly commanded to " vex the Midianites, and smite them ;" and again, to " avenge the children of Israel of the Midianites," before he should be gathered to his fathers; which he did with such effect, that they cried to each other in consternation, " Now shall this company lick up all that is round about us, as the ox licketh up the grass of the field."*

The times were now changed. Israel was no longer triumphant. Now, instead of being a victorious people, whose very name struck terror into the hearts of the nations round about, they were fain to hide in " *the dens which are in the mountains, and in caves, and strong holds,*" because " *the hand of Midian prevailed against them.*" † The number of these wandering robbers was incalculable; "*they came up with their cattle and their tents, and they came as grasshoppers for multitude; for both they and their camels were without number.*" The ravages which they committed were fully in proportion. " No one in present days," says a recent traveller, " has passed this plain without seeing or hearing of the assaults of the Bedouin Arabs, as they stream in from the adjacent desert. Here and there, by the well-side, or amongst the bushes of the mountains, their tents or their wild figures may always be seen, the terror alike of the peaceful villager and of the defenceless traveller. What we now see on a small scale constantly, is but a miniature representation of the one great visitation which lived for ages afterwards in the memory of the Jewish people."‡

---

* Num. xxi. 17; xxxi. 2 ; xxii. 4.   † Jud. vi. 2–5.
‡ Stanley, p. 340.

The narrative of the sacred historian, though brief, gives a vivid picture of the ravages of the Midianites, and of the pitiable distress to which Israel was reduced. They chose the spring, when the seed had been sown, and came up with all the accompaniments of Bedouin life, "with their cattle, their tents, and their camels." They ranged over the entire plain, beginning at the bank of the Jordan, and proceeding farther and farther westward, "*until thou come to Gaza*," on the low-lying sandy shore of the Mediterranean. They carried their plundering incursions far up into the hills of Manasseh, of Zebulun, and of Naphtali. They arranged no regular campaign, but pitched their tents wherever they pleased ; roaming in armed parties over the whole country, and spreading terror in every direction. The farmers, instead of combining in self-defence, fled to the hills, or sheltered themselves in caves ; leaving their produce to the robbers, who "*destroyed the increase of the earth*," carried off the cattle, and "*left neither sheep, nor ox, nor ass*," nor any kind of sustenance for Israel. After they had plundered all, they withdrew till the following season, when they again came up from the desert, after the seed had been sown, to renew their depredations. For seven successive years were these ravages committed—ravages more terrible than those of war, until the Israelitish people had become not only "*greatly impoverished*," but utterly disheartened. At length their miseries led them to remember Him whose worship they had neglected, and whose name they had dishonoured.   In hunger and wretchedness they bethought themselves of Him whom they had wickedly forsaken in the days of their prosperity. The altars of Baal were, in some instances at least, forsaken for the invisible Throne of the All-merciful— *" the children of Israel cried unto the Lord."*

"Ah, sinful nation, a people laden with iniquity, a seed of evil-doers, children that are corrupters! They have forsaken the Lord, they have provoked the Holy One of Israel to anger, they have gone away backward." *   The famished, terror-stricken fugitives, are they indeed the sons of the men of old before whom the elders of Moab and of Midian trembled, and against whom the prince of sorcerers confessed that no enchantments could prevail? These crouching slaves that timidly peep from behind projecting rocks, or shiver in the damp darkness of caverns, are they indeed the sons of the men who vanquished Sihon, king of the Amorites, and Og, king of Bashan, in whose sight the sun and moon stood still, and great hailstones from heaven scattered their discomfited enemies? Where are the old traditions of victory? Where is now "the shout of a king," which was of old in their camp? Where is the national character—the energy of the race?

National character, ancestral traditions, energy of race! Yes, I am not denying that such things exist. They do exist; they have potency and value. But

---

* Isa. i. 5.

there is one law, higher, wider, deeper, than all these, and which modifies and controls them all. It is the everlasting law of right and wrong; the law of conscience; the law of retribution. Discourse as you will about organization and race and character and climate: a greater difference than can arise from any of these causes is the difference in the same man when he is doing consciously wrong, and when he is doing consciously right. " The wicked flee when no man pursueth, but the righteous are bold as a lion." If these Israelites had never yielded to the seductions of the heathen—if they had retained that brave and dauntless heart which faith and a good conscience can inspire—would they thus have cowered before marauders from the desert? Would Midian have feasted on the plunder, if Israel had not sinned against the Lord? It is thus that the sacred narrative states the case: *"The children of Israel did evil in the sight of the Lord, and the Lord delivered them into the hand of Midian seven years."* It was the Lord, then, who delivered them into the hand of Midian. He withdrew the protection of His omnipotent arm. He no longer placed a restraint upon the Bedouin of the desert. They crossed the Jordan, and among the cornfields of Issachar they found a people who were cowards at heart—a people whose strength was gone because of their guilty conscience. Israel had forsaken Jehovah, and had fallen into the licentious practices of the heathen; therefore they became an easy prey to the spoiler, whose audacity increased, while Israel's strength diminished, year by year of that calamitous seven.

The same laws are still in force, for the whole world is a theocracy. Men talk in a shallow way about the Jewish dispensation, as if God's manner of ruling the world then was radically different from what it is now. It is not so. The "mint, anise, and cummin" of symbols and sacrifices may have been superseded; but "the weightier matters of the law, judgment, mercy, and faith," remain unalterably the same. Those who sin may expect to suffer, and to suffer in proportion to the light and knowledge against which they have sinned. If we act as the Israelites acted we shall suffer as they suffered. Spoilers will come upon us,—spoilers in the form of tumultuous passions; spoilers in the form of mighty lusts; spoilers in the form of wretched, remorseful thoughts, which will devour our happiness, and make us ready to skulk away into the farthest corner of the darkest cave, to avoid the light of the sun. This irruption of the Midianites into the fruitful vales of Palestine was no accident. The world is not governed by chance. Israel had bowed to the gods of the heathen, therefore they must bow to the tyranny of the heathen.

In a subsequent part of Gideon's history we find an illustration of the idolatry then prevalent. The Lord said to him, "Throw down the altar of Baal that thy father hath, and cut down the grove that is by it." * In Gideon's own family, then, there was an

---

* Jud. vii. 25.

altar, and a grove (or shrine) of Baal.   That idol and
that altar had been set up in defiance of the first and
of the second commandments of the decalogue, and
in defiance of the express injunction laid upon the
people by Moses: "Take heed to thyself, lest thou
make a covenant with the inhabitants of the land
whither thou goest, lest it be for a snare in the midst
of thee : but ye shall destroy their altars, break their
images, and cut down their groves." *   Yet here is an
altar and a shrine among the hills of Manasseh, upon
land which belongs to one of the " chiefs of thousands "
of her people ; and doubtless the practice was
general.

This practice of setting up an image of Baal to
worship, became in after-ages a fatal snare to the
Jewish people, and was the occasion at length of their
national overthrow.   It is necessary to recollect not
only what the idol was in itself, but what it represented and symbolised.   The Israelites had first of all
hankered after the vices of the heathen ; they had
fallen into those vices ; the consequence was that
"they did not like to retain God in their knowledge."
They lost, in the first instance, the spirit and the
habit of obedience ; their heart departed from the
living God; afterwards they abandoned the very forms
of a worship which was a continual reproof to their
wickedness, and adopted another form which opposed
no resistance to their licentious passions.   Thus the

* Exod. xxxiv. 12, 13.

shrines and images of Baal represented, not a harm-
less illusion, but the utter demoralization of the
people, "inflaming themselves with idols on every
high hill, and under every green tree." * Hence their
abject weakness. Their conscience had become defiled, their understanding had become besotted, their
energies were paralysed by a secret sense of guilt,
they became too weak and pusillanimous to offer
resistance to an invader. "How should one chase a
thousand, and two put ten thousand to flight, except
the Lord had sold them, and their Rock had shut
them up?" † It was because they had committed sin,
and loved to continue in it, that their ancient strength,
the offspring of faith, had left them, and they were
become the helpless prey of a contemptible enemy,
who stripped their fields and devastated their country
with impunity.

A thousand times has this history been re-enacted
since the days of Gideon. Why is it that so many
of the spiritual Israel are strangers to a real, hearty
cheerfulness? What mean those reproaches and fears
which, like an insect swarm, settle upon the heart and
devour all its verdure? How is it that the soul is
invaded with detestable thoughts over which we have
no power? How is it that we cannot drive out these
Midianites, but are become their easy prey, and are
greatly impoverished—nay, have become, perhaps, so
feeble and craven in spirit as to acquiesce in their do-

---

* Isa. lvii. 5. † Deut. xxxii. 30.

minion over us ?   Alas, notwithstanding our baptism and our high calling, we have given our hearts to the world and sin. There is an idol's shrine in the heart, set apart for wanton revellings of a defiled imagination. There is an image of Baal in the heart, sitting, like the idol in the grounds of Joash, enthroned upon the top of a rock. There is an altar in the heart, on which we minister to our cherished idol, and do him service. Therefore it is that our years are wasted and our joys are few. The Eternal Father seeks for worshippers who worship Him in spirit and in truth ; but, though the Church may not have been forsaken, our hearts have turned aside from that true inner worship to the worship of a Baal of our own choice.   Therefore it is that we are delivered into the hands of the Midianites ; and sad forebodings, or shivering fear, or gloomy discontent, or restless self-reproach, or devouring remorse, march up like swarming Arabs from the desert, and turn into a dreary and desolate wilderness those fields which might have smiled with plenty, and echoed with songs of happiness and praise.

12

THE PRAYER AND THE PROPHET

depth of despair

" AND *the children of Israel cried unto the Lord.*"*
     We may well cling to these few words, and
dwell upon them with ever-increasing gratitude. They
admonish us never to despair. While the prodigal
son was rioting in the far country, it might appear
that he was utterly reckless, and that the last link
which had bound him to his father's house was broken.
Yet such was not the case. Amidst all his riots, the
father's house had never been totally forgotten ; and
although it cost a sharp pang to return in rags, yet
when roysterers and harlots had stripped him of his
all, whither could he turn with such hope as to the
house of his father ? Thus at length the disobedient
profligates of Israel, after seven years of untold misery,
" cried unto the Lord."

     To whom else could they cry ? Could Baal hear
them in the day of their distress ? Or was there any
compassion in Baal ? Had they not heard how God
had descended to Moses in the cloud, and proclaimed
His own blessed name : " The Lord, the Lord God,
merciful and gracious, longsuffering, and abundant

---

* Jud. vi. 6.

in goodness and truth, keeping mercy for thousands, forgiving iniquity and transgression and sin"? It has been a prevalent fashion to represent the God of the Hebrews as a narrow, malignant Being, implacable in vengeance and incapable of mercy ; but such a notion is utterly repugnant to the whole tenor of the Jewish history, which is one long record of God's marvellous forbearance. The contemporaries of Gideon did not entertain this view of Jehovah. If they had conceived Him to be a dark, relentless avenger, would they have ventured, after openly neglecting His worship, and embracing idolatry, the sin which He had branded with His especial displeasure, to return to Him and implore His mercy in the day of their trouble? They would rather have dreaded even to mention His name, lest instant vengeance should come upon them. But so far from this, it was to Jehovah that they turned when their distress had become intolerable. Wretched and sinful, they did not give way to despair, but turned in sorrow and penitence to the All-merciful One.

Their prayer was heard and answered. But it was not answered at first in a way calculated to bring either immediate relief to the country, or immediate consolation to the people. Rather it would add poignancy to their sorrows. A Divinely commissioned messenger appeared amongst them ; but for what purpose? Not to chase the Midianites, not to rally round him the soldiers of Manasseh and Naphtali, not to promise them a speedy deliverance, not even to speak comfortable words to soothe their anguish, " *The Lord sent them a prophet ;*" but the prophet brought no message of mercy, no healing balm— nothing but reproof and conviction of sin.   " *Thus saith the Lord God of Israel, I brought you up from Egypt, and brought you forth from the house of bondage ; and I delivered you out of the hand of the Egyptians, and out of the hand of all that oppressed you, and drave them out from before you, and gave you their land ; and I said unto you, I am the Lord your God ; fear (or worship) ye not the gods of the Amorites, in whose land ye dwell : but ye have not obeyed my voice.*"*

The name of this prophet is not preserved to us. Without adopting either the tradition current among the Jews, that it was Phinehas, Aaron's grandson, or the supposition of Augustine and others, that he was an angelic messenger, we are content to believe that this prophet was a man of God, of veritable flesh and blood, but whose name, like those of the messenger at Bochim, of the man of God who bore the fatal message to Eli, and of the prophet who foretold to Ahab victory over the Syrians, the sacred historian has not recorded.   Neither are we informed whether he addressed the people in some vast assembly— whether he confined his message to the chiefs of the tribes—whether he roused the nation, like John the Baptist, by assuming an austere appearance, and by preaching in unfrequented places—or whether he

---

* Jud. vi. 8–10.

travelled from village to village, and from one hiding-place of the scattered people to another, delivering his message as he might happen to find them. In whatever form or manner the message was delivered, the burthen of it was these few and awful words :—" *Thus saith the Lord : Ye have not obeyed my voice.*"

Awful words, but not unmixed with mercy. If the wounds of a friend are faithful—if it be a kindness when the righteous smites us—how much more when our heavenly Father is pleased to reprove ! Severe and unsympathising as the utterances of this prophet might sound in the ears of a crushed and dejected people, they were a necessary preparation for the coming deliverance. Before the Lord sent them a deliverer, He sent to them a prophet to preach repentance ; to remind them that their own disobedience had been the real cause of all their miseries ; to prepare them for salvation by piercing them with a sense of sin. It is a mercy if the silence of the skies is broken, even though it be by the voice of correction. If that word which is like a two-edged sword be humbly and dutifully received, the word which heals and restores will presently follow. Thus it was in Gideon's time ; a messenger of reproof prepared the way for a messenger of victory.

13

THE WINEPRESS AT OPHRAH

WE now leave the plain of Esdraelon, where the tents of the Bedouin are seen in every direction, and ascend the hills of Manasseh. In a secluded spot of this rugged, broken country—a spot shut in, we may suppose, by rocks on every side—a young man of noble countenance,* and in the prime of early manhood, is occupied in threshing out a bundle of wheat. The young man is one of the sons of the owner of the estate; his father has many servants in his employ, and holds a position of authority in the district. In ordinary times the wheat-threshing would be performed upon the broad levelled threshing-floor by a machine drawn round and round upon heavy rollers, by oxen. But the enemy is abroad; the threshing-floor is in an open situation, where the wind can play freely over it, to blow away the chaff; the hum-drumming of the machine, and the occasional lowing of the oxen, might attract the attention of the enemy. So the wheat is threshed by hand, in unaccustomed places, and in small quantities for daily use. In Palestine, the vintage is not gathered till four months

---

* Jud. viii. 18.

after the wheat harvest, so that at the season when threshing is most rife, the winepress lies idle ; and this farmer's son, Gideon the son of Joash, has chosen the winepress—a hollow basin, hewn out of the rock, probably in a secluded corner of the farm—as a place of secrecy, where he can thresh out his bundle of sheaves, so as "*to hide it from the Midianites.*"

Raising his eyes for a moment from his work, the young man perceives a stranger, whose approach he had not noticed—a Man with a staff in his hand, quietly seated under the spreading canopy of the solitary oak which grows there. In such fearful times the sight of any stranger was calculated to excite apprehension : but the Man with a staff in his hand, fixes his gaze steadily on Gideon, and accosts him in a manner altogether unexpected :—

"*Jehovah is with thee, mighty man of valour !*"

There is something in the speech and in the mien of the stranger which excites involuntary awe. The flail is still, and Gideon's thoughts are instantly transferred from the straw and the corn-ears which lie at his feet, to the miserable condition of his forsaken country. The stranger's salutation puzzles him. "Mighty man of valour !"—what can he mean? A man of valour indeed, slinking behind these rocks to thresh out a handful of corn! "Jehovah with us" indeed, when we are obliged to hide ourselves in caves for fear of these thieves from the desert! Still, there is something in the stranger's appearance which, while it inspires profound respect, inspires confidence too : and in the fulness of a heart all but despairing of his country, Gideon replies :—

" O my Lord, if Jehovah be with us, why then is all this evil befallen us? and where be all His miracles which our fathers told us of, saying, Did not Jehovah bring us out of Egypt? But now Jehovah hath forsaken us, and delivered us into the hand of the Midianites."

Is this the speech of a mighty man of valour? Can despondency such as this exist in the breast of a hero? Is it possible for a man possessing true and genuine faith, to say of the chosen people, " The Lord hath forsaken us, and delivered us into the hand of the enemy"? Before adopting any view unfavourable to Gideon thus replying, it may be well to consider his words more fully.

Here is a man who forgets himself through concern for his country. He is accosted with words referring exclusively to himself, words calculated to arouse any dormant vanity which might be in him : *" The Lord is with thee, thou mighty man of valour !"* A vain man or a selfish man thus accosted, would have found all his thoughts at once turned toward himself ; undefined, brilliant images of future celebrity and glory would have floated before his fancy ; and his first anxiety would have been to ascertain in what way he was to attain to fame. But in the heart of this faithful young Israelite there dwells no such low ambition. Gideon forgets himself, and remembers only Israel. The cause of his suffering brethren is his cause ; their humiliation is his humiliation; nor can any prospect of personal promotion or honour be acceptable, unless in connection with the deliverance of his country.

Here is a man who is striving hard, under the sorest discouragements, to retain his faith: " *Where be all the miracles which our fathers told us of?* " This man, then, is not one of the sottish multitude who have forgotten the wonders of the old time. He has heard of the mighty works of Jehovah two hundred years before. In his boyhood those glorious tales had fired his imagination and filled his soul. He had probably never read, perhaps never seen, the written records of those events ; but he had "heard with his ears, and his fathers had told " him of them, and he had received the word, like Timothy in his youth, with unfeigned faith. But now he muses upon these histories with a settled melancholy. The events of the last seven years had led him to fear that the warning of Moses had come to pass ; and that on account of the sins of his countrymen, the Lord had in anger forsaken them, and brought cursing upon them instead of the good things which He had promised.

It is only a great and noble heart which could be thus dejected. It is from among spirits of such depth and tenderness—spirits capable of a sorrow which dull men and selfish men and covetous men and trivial men are utterly unable to fathom—that God has usually chosen His messengers of liberty and regeneration. Gideon, being accosted as a hero, has not an instant to spare for self-gratulation, but bursts out into eloquent grief for the vanished glory of Israel. He displays neither unbelief nor feebleness nor unreasoning dejection. There is a time to weep ; and the heart which has known unselfish mourning is alone qualified to make other hearts rejoice.

The next feature of the scene, as recorded by the sacred writer, is the investiture of Gideon with a Divine commission as judge and saviour of the Israelitish people. At this point also we learn who the Man was that sat under the oak with the staff in his hand : " *And Jehovah looked upon him, and said, Go in this thy might, and thou shalt save Israel from the hand of the Midianites : have not I sent thee ?*"

The Man was therefore the Jehovah-angel—the Divine and eternal Son of God, manifesting Himself, as He had already in past ages manifested Himself, in human form. The Jews maintain that the visible presence was not Jehovah, but a created messenger ; and that the words which Gideon heard were uttered from an invisible uncreated Presence behind the messenger. But Christians, who believe that " God was manifest in the flesh " in the person of Jesus, are not under the same necessity of tampering with the obvious meaning of the sacred text. Those momentary appearances of Jehovah in human form were preparatory to, and in a certain sense prefigurative of, His incarnation in a subsequent age, when He more fully assumed that human nature, which henceforth is indissolubly united with the Divine.

At the commencement of the narrative we read that "the angel of the Lord appeared to" Gideon. In the next scene, we are not only informed that this messenger was himself Jehovah, but also that "Jehovah looked upon him." That look, directed in anger, had troubled the embattled hosts of Pharaoh. That look, directed in pity, had been the salvation of the Hebrews from their bondage in Egypt. That look, directed in remonstrance, in an after-age, "broke unfaithful Peter's heart." And now, beneath the shade of the oak in Ophrah, beside the winepress of his father Joash, that look transformed the rustic son of the Abi-ezrite into the commissioned deliverer of Israel.

At this solemn moment Gideon received his commission. The terms in which it was conveyed, though brief, were precise and unequivocal: "Go in this thy might, and thou shalt save Israel from the hand of the Midianites: have not I sent thee?" Here is the word of command, "Go," and no option was left him but to obey;—the unchallengeable Divine commission and authority, "Have not I sent thee?"—the strength for the execution of his duty, "in this thy might," for whom the Lord sends He will strengthen for their duty;—and the assurance of success, "Thou shalt save Israel from the hand of the Midianites." In the might of the wonderful look with which these words were accompanied, he was to begin to summon his countrymen to enlist under his banner. In all his subsequent labours and dangers, he was never to forget—

how could he ever forget?—the penetrating power, the matchless majesty, the animating energy of that glance of the God-man under the oak at Ophrah. In anxieties, in desertion, faced by innumerable enemies, he was to invigorate his faith and courage by recalling to his memory the visit of the Lord under the oak, the words of mighty cheer which were spoken there, and above all the light of that Eye which was so over-poweringly upon him at the instant when the mysterious Man pronounced the words, "Go in THIS thy might."

The Lord has not discontinued these visits to His chosen, nor has the glance of His eye lost its trans-forming power. To strengthen the faithful in the hour of temptation, to cheer them in dark days of dejection, to give them nerve for trying duty, to fortify them against the blandishments of flattery or the seductions of wealth, He lifts up the light of His countenance upon them, saying, "It is I, be not afraid." Yonder is a trembling pastor, shrinking from the responsibility of the charge with which he has newly been entrusted. He wishes that he could be permitted to deliver back his commission into his Master's hands, fearing to become wretched through isolation, or chilled through neglect, or daunted through audacity. His fears are not less for himself than for the commission he has the honour to hold. He dreads becoming feeble and withered and useless amidst uncongenial scenes and unknown people. He feels that his past life has been unprofitably spent, and fears that the future will be more unprofitable than the past.   Like Elijah sitting down under the juniper tree, he wishes that he might die ; for his way is dark and his strength is broken.   But the Man with a staff in His hand still lives, to commission His servants for holy duty, and to renew their failing strength.   Jesus appears, and looks upon His feeble servant.   Eye meets eye ; heart meets heart.   It is a look of heartening cheer, of ineffable love, of super-human power.   It is enough.   Let but the eye of the Captain beam upon His humble soldier, and he will ask no more.   Able to do all things through Christ strengthening him, he will assume his post with cheerful confidence, and go forward, in the memory and might of that blessed visit, from strength to strength.

To return to Gideon and the scene under the oak. He is full of strange, conflicting emotions.   As yet he can but dimly perceive the magnitude of the change. An hour ago he was a plain farmer's son, intent upon getting his armful of wheat threshed without attracting the notice of the plunderers who were everywhere ravaging the country ; he is now in the presence of the mighty Angel who had appeared to Noah and to Abraham, to Moses and to Joshua of old, who has looked upon him, and appointed him to be the deliverer of Israel from the Midianites.   To him the whole thing appears incredible.   He is in utter amazement.   That a deliverer is needed, he sorrowfully knows : but that he should be that deliverer—he, an unknown young man, living in a poor district of the country—seems to him an utter impossibility. He cannot accept the commission without further re-monstrance. He exclaims, " *O my Lord, wherewith shall I save Israel? Behold, my thousand is poor in Manasseh, and I am the least in my father's house.*"

The territory of the tribe of Manasseh was sub-divided into ten districts, called " thousands,"—just as several English counties are sub-divided into districts called hundreds. These ten districts were inhabited by as many separate clans, each of which could trace its pedigree upward to Manasseh, Jacob's grandson, the father of the tribe, and preserved with equal jealousy its genealogy, its territory, and its independ-ence ;—reminding us of the Scottish clans of the Campbells and the Macdonalds, who have preserved their estates and their genealogies for centuries. The astonishment of Gideon found vent in the exclamation that the thousand to which he belonged, that of Abi-ezer,* was "the poor one in Manasseh." If a deliverer was to be raised up from their tribe, should he not rather be looked for among the richer thousand of the Helekites, or from the productive district of Shechem? —any one, indeed, rather than himself, whose family was poor in Manasseh, and himself the least in his father's house.

---

* Abi-ezer is called Jeezer, and his family Jeezerites, in the genealogy in Numbers (compare Josh. xvii. 2–6, with Num. xxvi. 29–33). Machir, the eldest son of Manasseh, had Gilead and Bashan (Josh. xvii. 1 ; Deut. iii. 15), on the other side of Jordan, constituting " the half tribe of Manasseh" (Num. xxxii. 33 ; xxxiv. 1, 4, 15), and not included in the ten mentioned above.

Great minds are usually humble ; and in this self-depreciation of the young Abi-ezrite we discover the same shrinking back from the Lord's work as was displayed by Moses and Isaiah and Jeremiah and other mighty men of faith.

> " How ready is the man to go,
>   Whom God hath never sent :
> How timorous, diffident, and slow,
>   God's chosen instrument."

Gideon's hesitation, however, arose from no ignoble motive.   It arose neither from a selfish shrinking from danger, nor from a captious unbelief, but from genuine humility ; and although in appearance there might be a momentary display of opposition to the Divine will, it was in appearance only, and not in reality—as the event decisively proved.

The mysterious Presence still continues sitting under the oak, with a staff in His hand.   To Gideon's timid, trembling expostulation, He replies, in words more significant and wonderful than before ;—words the full meaning of which it was impossible for him as yet to understand :—" *Surely I will be with thee, and thou shalt smite the Midianites as one man.*"

" I will be with thee."   What, then, will the Man seated under the oak be with Gideon ?   Will He be with him unseen ?   Will He attend him invisibly as certainly as He now converses with Him visibly ?   And is His mighty presence so potent as to ensure a certain and a rapid victory ?   If so, wherefore then do

we ask after His name,* when His words and His
works testify of Him? He who, not as a delegated
messenger, but in His own name and right could
thus speak, can be no other than the manifested
God!

In this second promise more is contained than in
the first. The first promise said, "I have sent thee;"
it referred him to the recollection of that wondrous
look, and encouraged him to fall back at all times
upon the consciousness of having been divinely commissioned. The second promise declares yet further
that the Lord will be with him—that the Divine
Presence, whether seen or unseen, will never forsake
him. It also specifies the kind of success he was to
achieve. He will not only overcome the Midianites,
but he will overcome them at a blow. Instead of
finding the enterprise beset with frightful hazards, he
will find it comparatively easy. Instead of having to
deal with the enemy in detail, in the tedious operations
of a guerilla war, he will be able to bring these wandering robbers to a focus, and strike them in a body
with one decisive stroke. Although it is improbable
that Gideon perceived all this at the moment—for it is
in the nature of prophecy to be more or less obscure
till the time of its fulfilment,—how completely did
the event verify the prediction of the Jehovah-
angel, that he should "smite the Midianites as one
man!"

---

* Gen. xxxii. 29.

One thing more, and one only, seems now to be required to complete Gideon's investiture with the commission, and to seal his acceptance of it. He desires a token :—a token that this strange and unexpected interview was not an illusion ;—a token to satisfy himself that he had not been deceived by a phantom or a dream. He therefore requests the Lord to afford him some assuring sign, which might remove all his doubts :—" *If now I have found grace in Thy sight, then show me a sign that Thou talkest with me :*" and begs Him to remain seated under the oak till he should have had time, according to the simple custom of those days, to prepare a present and set it before Him.

A simple meal was soon made ready. " *Gideon went in, and made ready a kid, and unleavened cakes of an ephah of flour : the flesh he put in a basket, and he put the broth in a pot, and brought it out to Him under the oak, and presented it.*" Of this provision the Stranger did not partake, but desired Gideon to spread it out upon the rock on which He was sitting, and to pour out the broth over it. The phenomenon which followed is best told in the words of the sacred narrator : " *Then the angel of the Lord put forth the end of the staff that was in his hand, and touched the flesh and the unleavened cakes ; and there rose up fire out of the rock, and consumed the flesh and the unleavened cakes. Then the angel of the Lord departed out of his sight*"—vanished, in an instant became invisible. This miraculous disappearance completed the demonstration. " *Gideon perceived that he was the angel of the Lord.*" *

If further assurance were wanting, it is supplied in the ashes of the kid consumed by the mystic fire, which still bestrew the rock. The token is indubitable; the sacramental seal has passed; the son of Joash is now a messenger of Jehovah, commissioned to smite the enemy, and deliver Israel. The absence of the mysterious One, now that He has vanished into invisibility, seems more oppressively awful than ever His presence had been. Gideon is overwhelmed. He can no longer contain himself. As he still stands by the winepress, the rocks which surround him re-echo his piercing outcry—"*Alas, O Lord God! for because I have seen the angel of the Lord face to face!*" A voice from the unseen—a voice like that which commanded Abram to sheathe the sacrificial knife—the same voice which he had just been hearing from the lips of the Lord made manifest to his bodily eye— calms his fears. " *The Lord said unto him, Peace be unto thee; fear not: thou shalt not die.*" Gideon believes, and is tranquil. But no time is to be lost. Having received his commission, he instantly commences preparations for the work to which the Man under the oak had called him.

---

* Not " an angel" as in our version ; but " the angel," as in the two preceding verses, where the noun is used anarthrously as here, and is rendered " the angel of the Lord."

14

HOME REFORMATION

TO the eventful day succeeded an equally eventful night. The sacred narrative relates that after the Lord had vanished, Gideon built an altar to Him "there :"—beside the winepress, upon the rock out of which the mystic fire had ascended and consumed the offering. In form, this altar may have resembled the altar of burnt sacrifice in the tabernacle at Shiloh—a square erection of planks of wood, five cubits in length, the same in breadth, and three cubits high, the top levelled for placing the sacrifice, and the hollow interior filled up with earth.* The altar thus hastily erected remained for ages afterwards : "unto this day," says the author of the Book of Judges, "it is yet in Ophrah of the Abi-ezrites."

The circumstances under which it was built are related in the verses which follow; and in the brief narrative we obtain such a glimpse of the religious condition of the Israelitish people, as enables us

---

* Exod. xxvii. The erection of altars elsewhere than in the tabernacle was forbidden (Lev. xvii. 8 ; Deut. xii. 13), but the prohibition was not in every case strictly enforced, as in the case of Samuel (1 Sam. vii. 9, 10) ; David (2 Sam. xxiv. 25) ; and Solomon (1 Kings iii. 4).

clearly to understand why such calamitous chastisements had befallen them. "The same night"—and
therefore probably before sunset, since, according to
Hebrew reckoning, the day begins at evening—Jehovah
spoke to Gideon once more. He commanded him to
throw down the altar of Baal which his father had,
and to cut down the grove, or shrine, which was by
it; and to build an altar to the Lord, on which a
particular bullock, described as "his father's young
bullock, the second of seven years old,"—whether in
reference to the seven years of the nation's distress,
or whether because his father's stock had been so
reduced by the Midianites that he had no other so
eligible for the purpose,—was to be offered as a burnt
sacrifice.

The altar thus marked out for demolition was
specifically connected with the service of Baal, the
supreme male divinity of the Phœnician and Canaanitish nations, and apparently also of the Midianites,
whose worship had already begun to prevail throughout Israel also.* In the "thousand" of the Abi-
ezrites, the altar of Baal stood in the grounds of Joash,
Gideon's father, the head of the clan. It was evidently
regarded, not as a private possession of Joash, but as
the public property of the towns-people of Ophrah.
It is not improbable that Joash himself was a sort of
priest of this idolatry. The veneration of the people

---

* On the worship of Baal by the Midianites, compare Numbers xxii. 41 with xxii. 4.

for their false god was shown by their clamouring for Gideon's death when they found that it was he who had overthrown his altar.   Not that they had as yet formally and openly rejected the Lord Jehovah : but, like some modern Romanists, whose devotion to Mary leads them practically to ignore Jesus, they had come to fancy that they wanted a lesser god and a less spiritual service ; and they soon found this forbidden worship so to fill their thoughts, that the God of their fathers was forgotten.

The first efforts of Gideon, therefore, after he had received his commission, were directed towards home reformation.   To a man of weaker faith the task would have appeared too perilous to be attempted. He knew that his life would be endangered by the attempt.   But ·as under the New Covenant, a man is declared unfit to rule the church of God unless he can keep his own household in subjection, so in those older times, before calling His servant to more public duty, the Lord animated his faith and zeal to become a reformer in his own family, and an example for all ecclesiastical critics and church reformers to the end of time.

" *He feared his father's household, and the men of the city.*" *   He knew their spirit, and tempered his zeal with discretion.   Before the visit of the Man under the oak, he would not have dared to provoke their anger.   He had mourned in secret over the sins

---

* Jud. vi. 27.

of his father and his family, but had not felt equal, younger son that he was, to undertake to rebuke and reform them. Now, however, he had become a new man, and was inspired with a courage equal to the duty. He would not rush blindly into danger, yet he would execute the Divine command. In the course of the evening, he intrusted some of his father's workmen with the secret of his purpose ; and it is a singular instance of the way in which the hearts of men are in God's hand, and also of the ascendency which Gideon must have acquired over the servants of his father, that he succeeded in persuading no less than ten of them to help him in the work. *" Then Gideon took ten men of his father's servants, and did as the Lord had said unto him : and so it was, because he feared his father's household, and the men of the city, that he could not do it by day, that he did it by night."*

At the dawn, as the men of Ophrah one by one left their houses, or the caves where they had passed the night, the demolished altar and shrine met their view. It was Gideon, the son of Joash, who had done it, and Gideon must die. " Bring out thy son," the impatient crowd clamoured to their chief—*" bring out thy son, that he may die."* In their resentment at the affront which had been offered to their god, they would have sacrificed the young iconoclast upon the spot. But " the Lord preserveth the faithful ; " and the son was shielded by the affection of his father, although that father, we may presume, had hitherto been the principal patron of the idol worship. Nothing could exceed the coolness and judgment with which the old man reasoned with the excited mob. If Baal were really a god, he could surely vindicate himself. If he were really a god, it would be impossible for a destroyer of his altar to escape vengeance. It would be absurd for the people to attempt to take the god's cause into their own hands ; for if he could not defend himself, of what use was it to serve him ? " *Will ye plead for Baal ? will* YE *save him ? he that will plead for him, let him be put to death while it is yet morning : if he is a god, let him plead for himself, because one hath cast down his altar.*"

The destruction of Baal's altar had been the work of the night ; a burnt sacrifice to the Lord Jehovah, reminding the people of the true worship which had been supplanted by a base idolatry, was also offered, as Gideon had been commanded. The devil's paraphernalia having been demolished, with what gratitude and joy would he offer sacrifice to the Lord ! The building of this altar was like the first ecstasies of a new-born soul ; or like the first efforts of one who, in a wicked neighbourhood, having himself found mercy, announces to all his determination to serve God, and exhorts them to repent and seek salvation. As Gideon with his ten assistants sawed the planks, and fitted them to each other, he may be imagined uttering in the words of Deborah, a lamentation for the idolatry and the dishonour of his country ;—" They chose new gods ; then was war in the gates : was there a shield or a spear seen among forty thousand in Israel ? " But his feelings were not those of lamentation only ; we can imagine him uttering words of holy decision, like Joshua, " Choose ye this day whom ye will serve ; as for me and my house, we will serve the Lord : "—words of adoring praise, in the language of the sea-baptized Israelites, "the Lord is my strength and my song ; He is my God and I will prepare Him a habitation :"—words of triumphant expectation, like Moses, " Rejoice, O ye nations with His people, for He will avenge the blood of His servants, and will render vengeance to His adversaries, and will be merciful to His land and to His people."* Reformation was beginning where it should always begin—at home. The Lord turned towards him at once the heart of his father, and of his father's servants ; and the deliverance of Israel began with the erection of a family altar.

Nothing can more clearly attest the faith and hope of Gideon than the name which he gave to the altar. He called it " *Jehovah-shalom* "—" the Lord [will give] peace." On the previous morning he had complained to the Stranger at the winepress, " *Jehovah-natash*,"— " the Lord hath forsaken us." But a change had taken place. The Lord had visited him, commissioned him, given him a promise, turned the heart of his kindred, and saved him from the fury of his enemies : so that the altar " *Jehovah-shalom* " was at once an expression of adoring gratitude and of believing hope.

---

* Jud. v. 8 ; Josh. xxiv. 15 ; Exod. xvii. 2 ; Deut. xxxii. 43.

15

SUMMONING THE HOSTS

THE die was cast. By demolishing the altar of Baal, and by publicly offering sacrifice to Jehovah, Gideon had proclaimed himself a servant of God, and had assumed a public position. His courage and self-denial received an immediate reward. In accordance with the words of our Saviour, "To him that hath shall more be given," he was blessed with a more plentiful effusion of the spirit of faith and power. In his own home and in his own city he had "endured as seeing Him who is invisible, not fearing the wrath of" his father or of Baal. He was now to be qualified for action in a wider sphere.

"*The spirit of the Lord clothed* * *Gideon*," says the history ; "*and he blew a trumpet, and Abi-ezer was gathered after him.*" Not that he was invested, like the high-priest, with robes of office ; nor did any mantle of a predecessor fall outwardly upon him, as when the mantle of Elijah fell upon Elisha. Apparel

---

* Jud. vi. 34, marginal reading : compare 1 Chron. xii. 18, and 2 Chron. xxiv. 20, where the same word is used, and in the margin is rendered " clothed."

is for protection, for convenience, for ornament ; but when a man is clothed with the Spirit, something more than any outward protection or adornment is bestowed. It is not an outward but an inward investiture. For it is not the corporeal man, it is the inner man, the true self, which alone can hold communion with God. It was not Gideon's bodily person which the Spirit clothed ; the Spirit of God pervaded, interpenetrated, quickened, and energised his whole being. It is in this way that we speak of being "baptized" with the Spirit. Baptism, as an outward ordinance, is an application of water to the surface of the body ; but the influences of the blessed Spirit are not superficial ; they are pervasive and permanent ; they enter into our inmost being, vivifying and cleansing and recreating the whole. It was thus that "*the Spirit of the Lord came upon Gideon.*"

The time had now arrived for him to enter upon a wider sphere of action. With the call of the trumpet, he summoned the men of Manasseh, and even the men of distant tribes, to rally round his standard. The Midianites were collecting their hosts, as if for some decisive and crowning engagement. No longer spread over the country in wandering parties, they "were gathered together and pitched in the valley of Jezreel." Gideon summoned the men of Israel to assemble also. He "*blew a trumpet, and Abi-ezer was gathered after him : and he sent messengers throughout all Manasseh who also was gathered to him : and he sent messengers unto Asher, and unto*

Zebulun, and unto Naphtali, and they came up to meet them." *

Mighty are the memories connected with the sound of the trumpet.   In every age it has been associated with the clang of arms, the evolutions of troops, the "pomp and circumstance of war."   Again and again has its shrill and piercing blast, re-echoing from hoary crag or castellated tower, kindled heroic enthusiasm, shamed the timorous into boldness, and awakened the torpid to activity.   The call of the trumpet has aroused the slumbering energies of patriotism ; it has rallied the courage of those who have conducted the attack, and it has animated the resolution of those who have stood on the defence.   Its heart-piercing language has been understood alike on the walls of Troy, at the gates of Rome, among the hosts of the Crusaders, and on the fields of Waterloo and Inkermann ; and stolid and passionless indeed must be the man, who, especially in times of public danger, can view the gallant rider all equipped for the fight, and hear the shrill trumpet resounding through the air, without feeling his heart to throb more vehemently, and a thrill of patriotic emotion to quiver through his frame.

To an Israelite the sound of the trumpet was associated not more with war than with religion.   When the fathers were journeying through the wilderness, the sound of the silver trumpets blown by the priests,

* Jud. vi. 33–35.

was the signal for their marches and for their convocations. The advent of the new year was celebrated by "the feast of trumpets," and in every religious ceremony it had been a familiar sound: "In the day of your gladness," said Moses, "and in your solemn days, and in the beginnings of your months, ye shall blow with the trumpets over your burnt offerings, and over the sacrifices of your peace offerings, that they may be to you for a memorial before the Lord your God." The majesty of the law given on Sinai was attested by "the voice of the trumpet which sounded long, and waxed louder and louder;" the walls of Jericho fell flat, when on the seventh day the trumpets of ram's horn were blown by the priests; and the Midianites themselves, when, two centuries before, they had troubled Israel, had been dispersed at the sound of the trumpet, when Moses detached for the fight a thousand men from each tribe, and sent "Phinehas the priest," to accompany them, "with the holy instruments, and with the trumpets to blow in his hand."*

We cannot doubt that these instances were in the mind of Gideon; and while the blast of his trumpet called his countrymen to war, it declared at the same time his own faith in the Divine calling of the chosen nation, and reminded them of the worship which they had wickedly forsaken. For years the trumpet had been silent in Israel. God's ordinances and His

---

* Num. x. 2–10; Exod. xix. 16; Josh. vi. 20; Num. xxxi. 6.

sabbaths had been disregarded; the memories of
Sinai and of Jericho had slumbered ; the orgies of
Baal had usurped the place of the holy convocations ;
and now that its sound was once more heard, it spoke
to the people of Him whose covenant they had long
forgotten, but whom they had at last invoked in the
hour of their anguish. Gideon himself was inspired
with superhuman energy.   Such are the men who
are clothed with the Holy Ghost in the acceptable day
of the Lord.   Power is in their word.   Like the war-
horse, their neck is clothed with thunder.   Their
trumpet voice recalls faithless deserters to the ranks,
and the scattered multitudes of the enemy disperse
and dissolve before them.

As the first efforts of Gideon were directed to home
reformation, so his first adherents were the men of his
own clan. "*Abi-ezer was gathered after him.*" A
prophet is usually without honour in his own country,
but it is often otherwise with a military hero ; for
courage and daring and confidence are qualities which
men can readily appreciate.   Gideon had dared to
throw down the altar and the grove.   He had risked
the displeasure of his father, and braved the anger of
his fellow-townsmen.   He had shown such heroism
and decision, that the people, anxious for a leader,
rallied with confidence around him.   The other nine
"thousands" of Manasseh soon heard the news, and
followed the example of Abi-ezer.   On the other side
of the plain of Esdraelon, his messengers went
throughout the northern tribes, and the people re-

sponded to the call. Asher came from the utmost north, Zebulun came from his "haven of ships," the men of Naphtali left their wooded hills ; and with the exception of the "ass couching between the two burdens," who "bowed his shoulder to bear, and became a servant to tribute,"* the ever selfish and time-serving Issachar,—for in every age and nation there are sordid souls who prefer money-making and inglorious ease to patriotic self-sacrifice—all the northern tribes furnished his army with recruits, to the number of more than thirty thousand. The southern and midland tribes were not summoned ; an omission which was deeply resented afterwards by the tribe of Ephraim.

The host of Israel and the host of Midian were now in close contiguity, the Midianites in the valley of Jezreel, the Israelites, not one-fourth of their number, on high ground to the south of them. The crisis has arrived ; a terrible battle seems inevitable ; and once more Gideon asks a sign from the Lord.

The story of Gideon and his fleece is one of those which a certain class of Christians would desire to see expunged from the sacred volume. The remarks of a pious Frenchman upon another portion of the Holy Writ are peculiarly applicable to this. "The whole character of Scripture is altogether different, according as we regard it with the eyes of human wisdom, or with those of faith. For my part, I remember a

---

* Gen. xlix. 13–15.

time when I never met with this narrative without a species of humiliation for my own understanding, and almost for the word of God ; whilst now, I turn to it over and over again, as to a favourite passage where my soul finds nourishment both delightful and abundant. This is because this narrative is as full of wholesome instructions for the little child who simply trusts to God's testimony, as it is replete with mysteries for the philosopher who assumes to judge the Scriptures instead of consenting to be judged by them." *

The young farmer's son must have been either less or more than man, not to have keenly felt the responsibilities of his situation. When he overthrew the altar of Baal, he did but risk his own life ; whereas now a vast multitude, thousands on thousands of his countrymen, had put their lives into his hands, and were looking to him to direct their movements against the enemy. And who was he, that he should be a captain of thirty thousand soldiers ? He had been accustomed to the flail and the plough, not to the spear and the sword ; he knew nothing of the manœuvring of troops, and probably had never seen a battle. Moreover the Midianites had concentrated all their strength ; their sentries guarded the outposts of their position ; and within sight of where Gideon stood, their innumerable tents covered the valley of Jezreel. No wonder that, in the extremity of his conscious weakness, he appealed once more to a

---

* Adolphe Monod's " Jesus Tempted," p. 3.

merciful God to give him an assuring sign that he was still in the path of duty. "*If Thou really wilt,*"—there is a Hebrew particle which our version leaves untranslated, and which perhaps it is not easy to render exactly into English—'if Thou *really* wilt save Israel by mine hand, as Thou hast said—if after all it is no delusion—if I am still Thy chosen instrument—if my calling has not been forfeited by an error—if Thy purpose still holds good as at the first,—then condescend, I beseech Thee, to give me a sign that it is so.'

Gideon's boldness in not merely asking for a sign, but in himself choosing what the sign should be, is perhaps rather to be excused on the ground of the unparalleled emergency, than commended as an example for imitation. The sign he requested was in appearance simple enough, yet it involved a miracle. He would take a fleece of wool, and lay it all night on the threshing-floor—a levelled place, open to the sky and to the breezes: "*and if,*" said he, "*the dew be on the fleece only, and it be dry upon all the earth beside, then shall I know that Thou wilt save Israel by mine hand as Thou hast said.*" The next night, with many expressions of humility, he requested the phenomenon to be reversed: "*Let not Thine anger be hot against me, and I will speak but this once: let me prove, I pray Thee, but this once with the fleece: let it now be dry only upon the fleece, and upon all the ground let there be dew.*"

In Palestine, as in many warm countries, the dew

in the summer is exceedingly copious. With the Hebrew poets it is an image of abundance and fertility ; the " dew of heaven " and the "fatness of the earth " are associated as cause and effect.* Nebuchadnezzar, exposed during his seven years' insanity to the variations of the weather, is described as having " his body wet with the dew of heaven ;" and the Bridegroom in the mystic Song exclaims, " My head is filled with the dew, and my locks with the drops of the night." † A description by a recent traveller, of the dews in the southern hemisphere, may help us to imagine its abundance in Palestine. " Our inland journeys," says the Rev. Thomas West, " were commenced before sunrise, and pursued during the cool of the evening ; but whilst thus avoiding one evil, another was encountered, equally great, if not worse. The roads in most places were no better than footpaths through the long grass and brushwood ; and everything being saturated with the heavy dew of the previous night, one could not proceed far on a journey before being thoroughly drenched. Indeed, it would have been quite as comfortable, in some instances, to have waded through a river as to push a way through the long grass, laden with glistening dew." ‡ With this the description of an old traveller perfectly agrees when he says of the Syrian roads in summer that

---

* Gen. xxvii. 28 ; Deut. xxxiii. 13 ; Zech. viii. 12 ; Hag. i. 10.
† Dan. iv. 23 ; Cant. v. 2.
‡ West's " Ten Years in Polynesia," p. 172.

" in the mornings the earth is saturated as much as if a shower of rain had fallen, and the paths are so slippery that it is difficult to stand."*

In both instances Gideon's request was granted. After the first night " *he rose up early on the morrow, and thrust the fleece togther, and wringed the dew out of the fleece, a bowl full of water.*" But as a woolly substance of this kind easily becomes saturated, he requested the sign to be reversed ; and the next night also the event was in accordance with his prayer, " *for it was dry upon the fleece only, and there was dew on all the ground.*" Thus his faith is confirmed. He no longer fears lest, deluded by a phantom, he should be leading his trusting countrymen into the jaws of death, as the mock-fire of the swamp dances before the traveller till he plunges headlong into destruction. Before actually engaging in the mighty contest he has betaken himself to prayer ; he has been alone with God ; he has wrestled and prevailed. Former promises have been renewed, and further assurances have been granted. Like Abraham pleading for Sodom, his importunity has been forgiven ; and the Almighty, remembering that he is but dust, has condescended to His servant's infirmity, and has " not denied the request of his lips."

---

* Eugene Roger, "Voyage de Syrie," liv. i. ch. ii. Virgil thus describes the abundance and value of the dew in Italy :—

" Et quantum longis carpent armenta diebus
Exiguâ tantum gelidus ros nocte reponet."

Georg. ii. 201.

It is maintained by several learned expositors that this sign was requested not for his own sake but for the sake of the people who were with him. We cannot concur in this view. There is no intimation that the fleece was publicly exhibited ; and had Gideon desired a sign for the encouragement of the multitudes around him, he would probably have chosen some more public and striking prodigy. Besides, the request of a token for his own confirmation* at this critical moment was precisely in accordance with his conduct when the Lord first met with him under the oak, when he implored Him, " Show me a sign, I pray Thee, that Thou talkest with me," and ventured to indicate the particular sign which would satisfy his faith.

In another view, however, this sign of the fleece is for all the faithful. Among the early Christians, Jerome, Augustine, and Ambrose beheld in it a mystical picture of the Incarnation—the Divine Word descending into the Virgin's womb, as the dew silently filled the fleece. Others in the double sign beheld a twofold picture of the Jewish race : first, before the time of our Lord, when Israel alone was refreshed with the dew of God's presence and truth, while the Gentile nations around were suffering the drought of a deep and awful ignorance ; and secondly, after the Lord had appeared and been rejected, when the Jewish fleece lost its moisture and became dry, while

* Ps. lxxxvi. 17.

the dews of the gospel were fertilizing the Gentile nations around. Modern commentators have pointed out from it how God could distinguish between Israel, small as a fleece of wool, and Midian, vast as the threshing-floor on which it lay ; and how He was able to bestow the dew of His grace, either on Gideon in particular, like the moistened fleece, or upon all his countrymen assembled, like the dew refreshing the earth all around. The poet of Methodism sees in the fleece " unwatered still and dry," while on every side the fruitful moisture was descending—a touching image of the soul of the penitent, all mournful and forlorn, while believers around are rejoicing in their Saviour.

16

THE DAY OF MIDIAN

WE come now to view the events of the day of Midian—one of the most memorable days in the history of the chosen people, and an emblem of a yet greater day of the Lord afterwards to appear.* Thirty-two thousand men of Israel had flocked to Gideon's standard ; and his first movement on this eventful day was to advance his army to a position " beside the well," or spring, " of Harod," which was probably lower down the declivity and nearer to the enemy. Scarcely had this movement been effected, when he received from the Jehovah-angel, a new and most startling intimation. His army, miserably equipped and poorly fed, was far outnumbered by that of the enemy. He might have deemed, not unreasonably, their number to be too few. But " *the Lord said unto Gideon, The people that are with thee are too many.*"

This intimation was not given without a reason being assigned. The majority of the men who had come together were not in a prepared state to receive a victory over the Midianites. They would not know

_____

* Isa. ix. 4.

how to appreciate it ; that evil tendency of universal man, to glorify self, and to rob God of His praise, existed in full force in them ; and they were unworthy of the honours of a victory which was to be achieved through faith. Besides, many of them were cowards at heart, and their presence was a source of weakness rather than strength ; yet these very men were the likeliest, in the event of a victory, to return home glorifying their own prowess, and forgetting the God who had interposed for them. Therefore " the Lord said unto Gideon, The people that are with thee are too many for Me to give the Midianites into *their* hands, lest Israel vaunt themselves against Me, saying, Mine own hand hath saved me."

The trumpet therefore sounds again, but no longer to swell the concourse of gathering thousands. Proclamation is made, " *Whosoever is fearful and afraid, let him depart early from Mount Gilead* "—a name, apparently, of the district in which they were encamped, and which must not be confounded with the Gilead on the other side Jordan. This proclamation was in exact conformity with the law of Moses ; which required that at the approach of a battle, the officers should " speak unto the people, what man is there that is fearful and fainthearted ? let him go and return to his house, lest his brethren's heart faint as well as his heart."* The enactment was framed in wisdom ; for cowardice is infectious, as the history of

---

* Deut. xx. 2, 8.

panics in the armies of ancient and modern times abundantly proves. Scipio the Roman being about to invade Carthage, was informed that among his forces there were some Sicilian horsemen who were terrified at what lay before them. He ordered them into his presence and demanded of them to speak the truth. Three hundred of them confessed that their hearts palpitated with terror. "Then," said the general, "you are dismissed ; go where you please, but you shall not be permitted to go with me to Carthage."

No less than twenty-two thousand availed them-selves of Gideon's proclamation. In behalf of these deserters it has been pleaded that "If the best ap-pointed armies in Europe had the same address from their generals, *bonâ fide,* as these Israelites had, at least an equal proportion would return home."* It is more to the purpose to remark with the same writer, that "a state of slavery debases the mind." It is likely that many of these homeward-bound poltroons had been the foremost in boasting ; for the courage which blusters most noisily at a distance evaporates most quickly when danger is at hand. What must have been the feelings of their commander as he watched his shrinking legions, two-thirds of whom might have been seen, on the morning of the day of Midian, rushing along every avenue of retreat, far more eager to escape than ever they had been to

---

* Adam Clarke, " Comm. on Jud." vii. 3.

enlist? Like the stony-ground hearers in our Lord's parable, they had heard the word, and anon with joy received it, but having no root in themselves, they endured but for a while, and when danger really threatened them, they turned aside. In all ages, the testing periods of the Church have yielded similar results; and it is for each reader to examine his own heart.

Ten thousand men however remained; but Gideon's faith was to be yet more severely tried. Another Divine message was revealed to him: "*The people are yet too many; bring them down unto the water, and I will try them for thee there.*" The ten thousand troops were accordingly moved to the pool of Harod, that they might drink. Arrived at the water side, the vast majority went down on their knees, and, putting their face to the water, sucked it up in a long satisfying draught; while a few,—three hundred only —remained upon their feet and took up the water by handfuls, lapping it hastily out of the hand with their tongues: a mode of drinking water which is still common in India and other parts of the east, where men can drink in this way with a rapidity which astonishes a European.

Such was the sign. The three hundred who lapped with the tongue, these, and these only, were to accompany Gideon against the innumerable host whose tents and camels covered all the plain; while the remainder of the ten thousand were to return, not indeed to their homes, as the twenty-two thousand cowards had done, but "*every man unto his place*" in the encampment :—for although these were not to occupy the principal post of hazard and of glory, a useful and honourable "place" was reserved for them in the pursuit of the morrow.   But the victory itself was to be achieved by the three hundred. "*By the three hundred men that lapped will I save you, and deliver the Midianites into thine hand.*"

What was the meaning of this sign ?   Wherein did the three hundred chosen ones differ from their comrades ?   The explanation suggested by Josephus— that Gideon was " to esteem those that bent down on their knees, and so drank, to be men of courage, but for all those that drank tumultuously, that he should esteem them to do it out of fear and in dread of their enemies," *—seems to us to be exactly the opposite to the true one.   It is absurd to suppose, after what had happened, that the most timorous and most faint-hearted should be selected to follow their commander in an exploit, to the performance of which a cool and steady courage was indispensable.   The remark of a modern poet that "it is not those who bow down on their knees to drink of the streams that water life, but those who take sparingly, as from the palm of the hand, who are destined to overcome and overthrow," † suggests the true explanation. We may conceive of the multitude who flung themselves down at the

---

* Josephus, "Antiq.," cap. V. vi. 3.
† Longfellow, preface to " Poems."

water's brink, so that they might imbibe a long and hearty draught, as being more or less self-indulgent; while the three hundred who, without laying down their weapons or putting themselves for a moment off their guard, were content with a hasty draught from the palm of the hand, were men of unusual energy and power of self-restraint,—men of a patriotic and resolute spirit, whose souls, in that hour when victory or defeat trembled in the balance, were too much absorbed in the work lying before them to allow of the slightest unnecessary indulgence; men whom not even the urgent call of thirst in the heat of the day could induce to lie down at their ease in so critical a moment. Though not fully agreeing with Tertullian, who finds in these three hundred chosen warriors a mystic symbol of the cross of Christ,* we may believe that they were men of the same spirit indicated by St. Paul, "striving for the mastery," and "temperate in all things,"—men of faith, like Gideon their commander; men in whom dwelt the spirit of Him who, beside Jacob's well, declined the refreshment which was offered Him with the memorable words, "My meat is to do the will of Him that hath sent Me, and to finish His work." †

"*Let all the other people go*," said the Lord, "*every man unto his place.*" Unlike the twenty-two thousand who had retired, who had no "place" in this

---

* Tertul., Carm. adv. Marcion, l. 3.
† I Cor. ix. 25 ; John iv. 34.

contest, these ten thousand had a place, every man of them. The distribution of Gideon's hosts may remind us of the varied future of the multitudes who hear the gospel call. Of these multitudes a great proportion offer no response, like the men of Issachar and of the other tribes, who refused even to leave their homes at the blast of Gideon's trumpet. Of those who respond to the call a large majority, like the twenty-two thousand who returned to their homes, having been moved only by a momentary impulse, speedily fall away and return to sloth and carelessness, proving that they had in reality no part nor lot in the matter. A goodly number, however, like the ten thousand who remained, continue more or less steadfast, and are employed in honourable service; while a few, like the three hundred chosen ones, advance to the highest posts of faith and labour. To these chosen ones is accorded the victory of the night; but let not their comrades despair, for they will find full employment on the morrow. In the Lord's service some are to be foremost and some are to come afterwards; some are to strike the decisive blow, while others are to complete the victory; some, as pioneers, are to venture first upon the perilous way, while others are called to follow up, to expand, and to complete their labours.

The ten thousand men who had been left beside the pool of Harod were expecting, it would appear, to be led into engagement with the enemy. But it had been willed otherwise; and, with the exception of the three hundred, their moment of action was not till the dawn of the next morning. The sun was now sinking in the west—the day of Midian was closing; and as the valley of Jezreel below him became wrapped in darkness, and the distant tents of the Bedouin became lost to the view, an anxious inquiry might arise in the mind of Gideon: What, after all, had been the result of the day when two-thirds of the host which the morning had beheld collected had retired to their homes, and the remainder, except a mere handful, were remanded to their tents? David before Goliath was less helpless than Gideon with his little band before the numberless hosts of the Midianites; but he has God's promise on his side, and that is enough. The three hundred remained at their advanced position, and lay down for rest. In the darkness Jehovah once more speaks to His servant: "*And it came to pass the same night, that the Lord said unto him, Arise, get thee down unto the host; for I have delivered it into thine hand.*"

In the incident which followed some will refuse to see anything more than a singular coincidence, while others, more enlightened, will recognise in it an instance of the ever-watchful care of an omnipresent Father. "*Arise, get thee down unto the host; but if thou fear to go down, take with thee Phurah thy servant down to the host; and thou shalt hear what they say.*" In accordance with this command, Gideon and his officer commenced without delay their dark and perilous descent. The Midianites who "lay along in the valley like grasshoppers for multitude" were sound in their first sleep; and the hazard of the enterprise consisted in the difficulty of eluding the vigilance of the armed watchers, whose fivefold ranks the two now stealthily approached. Creeping cautiously nearer and nearer, they at length were able to hear two sentries engaged in conversation. One of them was repeating to his comrade a dream of his—how he had seen a barley-cake roll through the camp and overturn the royal tent. "*Behold, I dreamed a dream, and, lo, a cake of barley-bread tumbled into the host of Midian, and came unto a (the) tent, and smote it that it fell, and overturned it, that the tent lay along.*" The other sentry was ready in a moment with his interpretation. The cake of barley-bread— a humble kind of food, considered fit chiefly for horses and dromedaries*—could only signify Gideon, the man of humble origin, at whose trumpet-call the Israelites were assembling. A secret terror was inspired by the mention of his name. The memory of former interpositions of the God of Israel on behalf of His people had not perished; and the fear of him had spread, doubtless, far and wide among the multitudes of Midian; so that the watchman only expressed their general sentiment, when he gave his explanation of the barley-cake, "*This is nothing else save the sword of Gideon the son of Joash, a man of Israel: for into his hand hath God delivered Midian,*"

---

* 1 Kings iv. 28.

and all the host." Gideon and his little band might
of themselves be as unable to cope with them as a
cake of barley was to overthrow the tent of their
principal sheikh, but if Jehovah-Elohim interpose,
Midian cannot stand !

Nothing could be better calculated to fortify the
courage and cheer the faith of Gideon and his men.
He plainly saw fear was pervading the ranks of the
enemy ; and the first act of the devout soldier of
Israel after overhearing this conversation—reminding
us of the Havelocks and Stonewall Jacksons of our
own times—was to render thanks to the God of
Israel.

" *And it was so, when Gideon heard the telling
of the dream, and the interpretation thereof, that he
worshipped.*" We here perceive that he was a man
of faith and prayer,—a man who walked with God,—
a man whose thoughts, even amidst the engrossing
cares of that momentous hour, were towards his
Maker,—a man who held communion with his God
even amidst the perils of a nocturnal sally and the
stratagems of war. Having worshipped, with light
and nimble steps he climbed the mountain-side, and
roused his little band with the words full of hearty
cheer, " *Arise ; for the Lord hath delivered into your
hand the host of Midian.*"

In the dead of the night the chosen three hundred
arose from their grassy bed to receive their captain's
orders. He divided them into three companies of a
hundred each, and directed these companies to advance

separately and take up their positions on the hill-side, above the encampment of the enemy.   Each man carried under his left arm an earthen jar or pitcher, such as was commonly used for drawing water : within the pitcher was placed what our version calls a " lamp," but which the margin more accurately renders a " torch "—a flambeau of some kind, made probably of resinous wood, and covered with some pitchy substance, like the " links " which are carried at night in a dense London fog.   The torch was probably already lighted, the flame being concealed within the pitcher. In his right hand each man carried a trumpet, ready to blow at the appointed signal.   Thus equipped, the three companies took up their several positions above the enemy's lines, every man in his place, motionless and silent in the midnight darkness.   In an instant, at the appointed signal, the three hundred earthen jars, dashed to pieces, were heard clattering upon the ground ; three hundred torches were seen blazing in the air ; and the resounding blast of three hundred trumpets was followed by the thrilling warshout, " *For Jehovah and Gideon !* "

The Midianites awoke in terror and confusion. The stillness of the night had been broken by the blast of innumerable trumpets ; the two names they most dreaded, Jehovah and Gideon, were being shouted by triumphant hosts on the heights above them.   Looking toward those heights they could see nothing but the fearful blaze of what they would imagine to be thousands of flaming torches, whose lurid light, flaring in their half-opened eyes, dazzled them, and rendered them incapable of judging of the number and strength of the armament above them, which their panic would magnify into an army consisting of hundreds of thousands, of which they imagined these to be merely the torch-bearers and trumpeters leading the way.

It was but the work of a few moments. A panic arose, which the sacred narrator has vividly described in three words, which recall the famed *Veni, vidi, vici* of Julius Cæsar—" all the host *ran, and cried, and fled.*" The trumpets still sounded on the hill-side ; confusion and consternation reigned among the terrified hosts of Midian, who, in the surprise and darkness, were unable to distinguish between friend and foe. The terrible name of Jehovah, which now rang in their ears from the heights above, recalled confusedly to their memory how His enemies had been scattered,— how thunder and earthquakes, hailstones and coals of fire had been at His command, in bygone ages ; a magic terror also was associated in their minds with the name of Gideon. Flying in indiscriminate retreat, they trampled on and put each other to the sword in their blind and helpless confusion. The same unseen Power which had previously sent a spirit of fear, now sent a spirit of frenzy, among them ; " *the Lord set every man's sword against his fellow, even throughout all the host.*" The rising sun beheld them turned into a rabble of fugitives, rushing in the wildest terror down the valley of Jezreel, towards the fords of the

Jordan and their native wilderness ; and so fearful was the slaughter, that before Gideon and his men could overtake them, out of a hundred and thirty-five thousand " men that drew the sword," a hundred and twenty thousand had fallen.*

---

* Jud. viii. 10.

17

PURSUIT OF THE MORROW

THE greatest soldier of France is said to have maintained that the skill of a consummate general is never so critically tested as in deciding how to turn a victory to the best advantage. We know not whether Napoleon I. was acquainted with the book of Judges; if he was, he would find in the narrative of Gideon's pursuit of the flying enemy a confirmation of his maxim. It was not enough that the hosts of the Midianites should be put to flight in the panic of a midnight surprise; the faith of Gideon was not satisfied so long as a single man of their number remained within the borders of the tribes of Israel. Rushing on "to Beth-shittah"—the 'house of the acacia'—and "to the border" (or brink) "of Abelmeholah, on* Tabbath"—probably the same as the "terrace of Fahil, a bank six hundred feet in height, with a flat horizontal top, which descends with a very steep front to the Jordan"†—the terror-stricken children of the desert were making the best of their way to secure the passage of the river. To

---

* So the Hebrew *al* signifies, rather than "unto."
† Robinson, iii. 325; Smith's Dictionary, "*Tabbath.*"

intercept their retreat, Gideon sent in pursuit not only the ten thousand men who had been reserved by Divine direction on the preceding day, but he also *" sent messengers throughout all mount Ephraim, saying, Come down against the Midianites, and take before them the waters unto Beth-barah * and Jordan."* The men of Ephraim responded to the call ; and while their brethren out of Naphtali and Asher pursued after those divisions of the foe which were taking a more northerly course, they took the wadys and torrent-beds which descend towards the Jordan from the highlands of Ephraim. Every avenue of retreat by which it was possible for the enemy to escape was thus occupied ; and as the Midianites, encumbered with their flocks and herds, could not make very swift progress, they found, at most points where they wished to cross the river, the men of Israel arrived before them, ready to contest their retreat.

Between one of these sections of the flying enemy and the men of Ephraim a second contest took place, which resulted in the two principal sheikhs, Oreb ("the raven") and Zeeb ("the wolf") being slain— the one at a rock, the other beside a winepress, which from that day forward bore the respective names of those desert chieftains. This conflict, although little is said of it by the author of the book of Judges, was

---

* "The house of passage," or "of the ford ;" probably not the same place mentioned John i. 28. None of these places have yet been satisfactorily identified.

so awful and terrible that the memory of it descended to following ages, together with the memory of the vengeance inflicted on Egypt ; and " the slaughter at Oreb " became, for prophet and psalmist, an expressive image of the most terrific outbursts of God's vengeance.* This fearful slaughter took place, probably, on the eastern or farther side of the Jordan, while Gideon, about the same time, had crossed at a point farther to the north, in pursuit of another division of the enemy ; and to him, after their battle, the Ephraimites repaired as to the acknowledged captain of all the Israelitish hosts, and " *brought the heads of Oreb and Zeeb to Gideon on the other side Jordan.*" †

The progress of Gideon in pursuit is related with minuteness and circumstantiality of detail. " *Faint, yet pursuing*," he and his little band of three hundred men crossed the Jordan in pursuit of that division of the Midianites which accompanied the flight of two principal chieftains, or " kings," Zebah and Zalmunnah. These men, when coming up from the desert at the head of their hordes into the luxuriant pastures of the plain of Esdraelon, had given as a cry to their followers, " *Seize these goodly pastures !*" ‡ They had also captured and put to death two § or more of the

---

* Isa. x. 26 ; Ps. lxxxiii. 9, 11.   † Jud. vii. 25.

‡ Ps. lxxxiii. 12.   Our version renders the Hebrew *naoth* " houses ;" " pastures," however, is the better rendering : comp. in the Hebrew, Ps. xxiii. 2 ; lxv. 43 ; Joel i. 19 ; ii. 22.

§ Jud. viii. 19.

brothers of Gideon ; so that, in addition to his great duty as the Lord's chosen captain, he was also pursuing after them as the nearest of kin—the avenger of blood.* They had succeeded in crossing the Jordan before the passes could be secured, followed by fifteen thousand men, who were probably better provided than the rest, and were making towards the desert with all haste. Vain were their struggles to escape ; for "the fear of the wicked, it shall come upon him ; and they that think to run from the sword of the Lord and of Gideon, do but run upon it." †

Arrived at Succoth on his way, Gideon asked for provisions for his little band, acquainting the men of Succoth, at the same time, with his object. The sympathies of these men were with might rather than with right ; and, characteristically enough, they asked him: "*Are the hands of Zebah and Zalmunnah now in thine hand, that we should give bread to thine army ?*" They probably considered the inadequacy of a little company of three hundred men to cope with an army of fifteen thousand ; unlike the man of faith, whose request they refused, who had more confidence in three hundred men, supported by a promise of Jehovah, than in as many thousands relying only on their own valour. They added jeering insult to their refusal. Thus the deliverer of Israel met with discouragement from his own people ; nor

---

* Num. xxxv. 19.   † Matthew Henry.

did he meet with a better reception when, mounting the hills that rise from the Jordan plain, he reached Penuel, where he made the same request as had been made to the men of Succoth, and received the same answer in return. How often have God's messengers had to encounter the selfishness and unbelief of " a gainsaying people " within the borders of their own Israel ! But retribution was in store for these people. Gideon, whose faith remained unshaken through all these discouragements of his journey, did not stay to argue with them, or even to repeat his request for provisions. He merely told them that when he returned victorious he would chastise them with thorns of the wilderness, and break down the tower of Penuel.

Still pursuing, Gideon ascended from the Ghor, by one of the numerous torrent-beds, to the downs of the higher level. He *" went up by the way of them that dwelt in tents "* *— the pastoral people, who avoided the district of the towns—not so much, probably, " because he hoped to find them kinder than the men of Succoth and Penuel," † as because he had received information of the road which the kings of Midian had taken. " In Karkor " he found them ; and on his arrival, which was by night, " *the host was secure.*" They had taken an unfrequented path, and did not expect to be so hotly pursued. The chosen three hundred, who had exchanged their lanterns

---

* Jud. viii. 8, 11.   † Matthew Henry.

and torches for swords and spears, though the host of the enemy outnumbered them by fifty to one, again put them to flight. The Midianites were utterly routed, and their two kings, the murderers of Gideon's brethren, were taken alive. The whole was the work of one eventful night ; "*and Gideon the son of Joash returned from battle before the sun was up.*" *

The day which followed was a day of triumph and of retribution. He brought the captive kings to Succoth, where yesterday he had been taunted with the hopelessness of his undertaking. "*Behold Zebah and Zalmunnah,*" he triumphantly exclaimed, "*with whom ye did upbraid me, saying, Are the hands of Zebah and Zalmunnah now in thine hand, that we should give bread unto thy men that are weary?*" True to his promise, "*He took the elders of the city, and thorns of the wilderness and briers, and with them he taught the men of Succoth,*" also "*beat down the tower of Penuel, and slew the men of the city.*" Having done this, the Midianite chieftains themselves, who had killed Gideon's brothers at Tabor, fell at sunrise by his own sword. Their fate was viewed by the Jewish Church in after-ages as a type of the destruction of other enemies of the Lord ;† and Christian expositors have seen in it an emblem of the victories of the Son of God over the powers of evil.

A few general reflections may bring to a close this sketch of Gideon.

---

* Jud. viii. 13.   † Ps. lxxxiii. 11, 12.

1. We have an illustration of the inherent weakness of the forces of evil. How imposing that array of the sons of the desert, with their tents covering all the plain, as locusts for multitude, while the heirs of God's promises crawled into thickets, or shivered in mountain caves! How thoroughly they succeeded in persuading Israel they were invincible, as Sisera had done before them! Yet in reality they were wanting in every element of strength. They succeeded, it is true, in domineering over the Israelites for seven years; but the most cowardly of curs will bark valiantly at one who is running away from him. The instant one resolute man appears to confront them in the name of the Lord, a secret chill, a paralysing terror, diffuses itself throughout the tents of Midian. And how cowardly and disgraceful was their panic-stricken flight, disclosing an utter want of confidence in themselves or in each other!

The history illustrates an important truth. The forces of evil may be of inconceivable magnitude and strength. We look at them through the mist of fear and unbelief, which causes ordinary proportions to appear colossal. Because some public abuse has long been tolerated, until those who have fattened upon it look down upon their fellow-countrymen with disdain; because some monarchy founded in injustice surrounds itself with a million bayonets, and affects to laugh at opposition which is only that of opinion; because (to view the subject on its widest scale) the devil and the powers of darkness have established among mankind a dominion so extensive, so subtle, intrenched behind the customs of immemorial ages, and fortified by every defence of superstition, of selfishness, of lust, of avarice, of infidelity ; because (to narrow our view to the case of the individual man) we ourselves may have had long and sad experience of the force of evil within our own breast, its obstinacy, its subtlety, its endless forms of disguise ;—on all these accounts it is easy to foster unbelief and to acquire an exaggerated idea of the potency of evil. Yet we know, from the sure word of revelation, not only that these forces will eventually be overthrown, but that the great Prince of Evil himself is conscious of his own weakness.   There is a Name before which he cannot stand.   Amid all the activity of his invisible hosts they are a prey to secret terrors : they know their doom ; they " believe and tremble."

Great is the encouragement, then, to follow that which is right, and to oppose steadily whatever is wrong.   " Resist the devil, and he will flee from you." Whoever would be courageous must first be honest and true, for a deceiver is a coward by the very necessity of his position.   Let us then not be afraid of attacking evil ; it is not bold at heart ; the thief's heart sinks within him when a policeman taps him on the shoulder.   Let us enter into no compromise with fraud or falsehood in any form, for it will make cowards of us.   We shall dread exposure ; we shall fear retribution, even that awful day when unfaithful souls shall be driven by a resistless Hand across life's

Jordan into that dreary wilderness where the guilty and the miserable wander to and fro for ever.

2. In the victory achieved by Gideon there is a further illustration of the truth already deduced from the history of· Barak, that *faith is the highest reason.* This truth may be perverted and abused, as in the case of the Romish Church, whose notion of faith is that of blind and unreasoning submission to its own dogmas ; hence the necessity of stating it clearly.

Gideon was a man of faith. He had within himself the evidence and conviction of things not seen. He believed in the Divine calling of the Hebrew people, in the theocracy, in the wonders of the Pentateuch, in the LIVING GOD. Faith lay at the foundation of all he undertook. It was in faith that he dared his father's displeasure and the anger of his fellow-citizens when he cut down the idol they worshipped. It was in faith that he blew the trumpet when the public distress was so extreme that it seemed improbable that a hundred men would be found desperate enough to obey the summons. It was in faith that he submitted to the reduction of his army, first by two-thirds, then to three hundred men. It was in faith that, with this little company, he plunged into the enemy's camp, as if into the jaws of death.

And his action throughout was vindicated by the result as being in the highest degree reasonable. He saw farther than others, because he trusted in God, the film of unbelief and of self-sufficiency being removed from· his eyes. Faith allies itself with the

Infinite Wisdom : he who will believe in nothing beyond himself, exercises only the lower reason, leaving the higher faculty dormant. Faith links our feeble intellect with the Supreme Reason. By it we enter a higher sphere, from which the unbeliever, whatever his erudition or eminence, is, and must ever remain, excluded. And judging of things only by what himself can see, it is as natural that he should pronounce the realities of faith to be unreal and visionary, as it is for a fish in mid-ocean to be unaware of the existence of a more highly organized world than his own on the dry land above the waters. How excellent that grace which pierces the otherwise impenetrable veil which conceals the Unseen from mortal eyes! And how salutary the rebuke to human self-sufficiency that "God hath chosen the foolish things of the world to confound the wise ; and God hath chosen the weak things of the world to confound the things that are mighty ; and base things of the world, and things which are despised, hath God chosen, yea, and things which are not, to bring to nought things that are : that no flesh should glory in His presence." *

3. Lest, however, we should exalt even faith too highly, we are reminded, by the subsequent history, of an error into which Gideon fell. After the victory by which the Israelites had been delivered, they offered to Gideon the hereditary monarchy ; but this,

---

* I Cor. i. 27–29.

as a believer in the theocracy, he declined.* So far well; but at this point human frailty appeared, even in the man of faith. Having declined the offered throne, he requested the people, out of the uncounted booty they had secured, to give him "*every man the earrings of his prey*," that he might make a trophy to be set up in his native city.

They consented: earrings to the weight of seventeen hundred golden shekels, or about sixty-six pounds weight of gold, were offered. With this he made an ephod—a sacred vestment like that worn by the high-priest,† and put it in his city; an action contrary to the law of Moses, which provided that the ephod was to be worn by the priest alone. Gideon may have designed, by exhibiting such a monument of his victory, to remind his countrymen of that worship of Jehovah which they were too prone to forsake; but although his end may have been commendable, he used unlawful means for its attainment. Or it may be that he was irritated at the degeneracy of the priesthood of his day: and being "exalted above measure through the abundance of the revelation" with which he had been favoured, he was tempted to vary from the priesthood ritual that he might shame the priests into greater attention. The result was deplorable. The ephod became an object of idolatry. "*All Israel went a whoring after it; which thing became a snare unto Gideon, and to his*

---

house ;" nor had he the moral courage which Hezekiah afterwards displayed, when he tore down the brazen serpent because it had become an instrument of idolatry.

The victory, however, was complete. " *Midian,*" says the sacred writer, " *was subdued, so that they lifted up their heads no more."* For forty years he lived in quietness among his people, died in a good old age, and was gathered to his fathers.

Part 4
JEPHTHAH

JEPHTHAH

IN one respect Jephthah the Gildeadite stands alone among the judges of Israel. He is not mentioned as belonging to any of the tribes of Israel. His investiture with office was not the result of a Divine intimation or interposition, but of popular suffrage. Unlike his predecessor Ehud, whom the Lord raised up in answer to the nation's prayers,—or Barak, to whom the Divine announcement was conveyed through a prophetess,—or Gideon, who beheld the angel of the Lord face to face,—or Samson, whose designation was foretold to his parents by the same angel before his birth,—Jephthah was a leader of the people's choice. Their nomination was approved and ratified by the Spirit of the Lord coming upon him after his election ; and although, in comparison with Gideon, he be as the moon compared with the sun, yet, in that kingdom where "there is one glory of the sun, and another glory of the moon, and another glory of the stars," he has obtained a place ; and is numbered amongst the men who " through faith have subdued kingdoms and wrought righteousness."* His

---

* Heb. xi. 33.

acts are those of one who does mighty deeds in an irregular manner, and "may be compared," as Bishop Wordsworth observes, "to that which has been done by the Wesleys and Whitefields in the Christian Church, at a time when bishops and clergy were deficient in zeal and faithfulness in the execution of their trust."

18

DOMINATION OF THE AMMONITES

" *THE children of Israel did evil again in the sight of the Lord.*"* Their repentances, though general, and perhaps at the moment sincere, were only transient. The complaint uttered by the prophet Hosea four hundred years later might have been uttered with equal justice in the days of Jephthah : "Your goodness is as the morning cloud, and as the early dew it goeth away."† They not merely returned to their own ways, but addicted themselves to new and various forms of idolatry.‡ They exceeded the folly of the neighbouring heathen, who contented themselves with worshipping their own national divinities. Blacksliders in heart, the Lord's people " overpassed the deeds of the wicked," and went beyond their former selves in the voracity of their appetite for shameful and forbidden indulgences. They " *served Baalim and Ashtaroth,*" which are perhaps to be here understood as general names—male and female divinities of all kinds. The inexor-

---

* Jud. x. 6.   † Hos. vi. 4.
‡ " Peccatis veteribus jungentes nova."—*Vulg.*

able Bel of Syria, the lewd Astarte of Zidon, the
relentless Moloch of Ammon, and Dagon the fish-
god of Philistia, each found a niche in Israel's pan-
theon of abominations. They did not so much as
allow to the Most High a place amongst the other
objects of their worship. The tabernacle at Shiloh
was left unvisited, and God's holy name was unheard
amidst the jargon of heathenish incantations. They
"*forsook the Lord, and served not Him.*" Had it not
been for the covenant of Abraham, the Almighty
might have left them, as He left the other nations, to
fulfil the imagination of their hearts, and to perish
in their sins.

Instead of this, mixing judgment with mercy, "*He
sold them into the hands of the Philistines, and into
the hands of the children of Ammon.*"* It is with
the latter exclusively that we are concerned in the
life of Jephthah. The Ammonites and the Moabites,
descendants of Lot, were tribes of a very different
character from the Midianites, whom Gideon had
driven out. From the eastern side of the Jordan
valley the mountains of Moab rise to the height of
from two to three thousand feet, and are seen from
every elevated part of Judah and of Ephraim, closing
the eastward view with their long horizontal outline,
their overshadowing height, their deep purple shade.
On a nearer approach, however, "the horizontal
outline which they always wear when seen from a

---

* Jud. x. 7.

distance is broken. A wide table-land appears tossed about in wild confusion of undulating downs, clothed with rich grass throughout ; in the southern parts trees are thinly scattered here and there, aged trees covered with lichen, as if the relics of a primeval forest long since cleared away ; the northern parts still abound in magnificent woods of sycamore, beech, terebinth, ilex, and enormous fig-trees."* It was from these wooded heights that Abraham must have caught his first glimpse of the land of promise, as it rose before his eyes on the other side of the Jordan ; that Balaam viewed the goodly country which was then in store for the people coming up from the wilderness ; and that Moses surveyed the land, to whose borders he had conducted the people of the covenant, but which he was not himself permitted to enter. " The whole range," says Dr. Stanley, " is one vast Pisgah, with the deep shades of the Jordan valley beneath, the land of promise beyond." In this vast forest land were the " oaks of Bashan," the chief glory of the vegetation of the country ; through those enormous woods vast herds of wild cattle wandered,—" the strong bulls of Bashan," such as may still be seen, together with countless herds of sheep, moving on like troops of soldiers, descending at sunset to drink of the springs.

It was not the first time that the men of Ammon had troubled Israel. They had conspired with other

---

* Stanley's " Sinai and Palestine," ch. viii.

tribes to prevent the passage of the Israelites through that country on their emerging from the desert. They had been accessory to the hiring of Balaam. After the settlement of the Israelites in Palestine, they had joined with Moab and Amalek in the occupation of Jericho.* And now, emboldened by the demoralised and feeble condition of the tribes of Reuben, Gad, and Manasseh, they had descended from their upland downs and their mountain forests, and "*vexed and oppressed the children of Israel eighteen years,*"† reckoning backwards from the date of Jephthah's assumption of the command. Nor were their ravages confined to the tribes who lived on their own side of the Jordan. They "*passed over Jordan to fight also against Judah, and against Benjamin, and against the house of Ephraim.*" Although they neither made a conquest of the country, nor brought it under regular military occupation, they kept the inhabitants in constant terror through their outrages, so that the land became a scene of violence and of dismay. The threat uttered through Moses was accomplished: "Ye shall sow your seed in vain, for your enemies shall eat it; and I will set My face against you, and ye shall be slain before your enemies: they that hate you shall reign over you; and ye shall flee when none pursueth you."‡

The ravages of the Ammonites were extended over a wider surface than those of the Midianites a genera-

---

* Deut. xxiii. 3, 4 ; Jud. iii. 13.   † Jud. x. 8.
‡ Lev. xxvi. 16, 17.

tion or two before, as the defection of Israel had become more general. Judah and Benjamin, which had for the most part escaped the miseries inflicted by the sons of the desert, now shared in the miseries inflicted by the sons of the mountains. "*Israel*," we read, "*was sore distressed;*" the gods they had chosen could afford them no succour in the day of their calamity, and, as of old, they "*cried unto the Lord.*" In the public distress, the shrines of Moloch and of Ashtaroth were deserted; altar and grove were demolished; the horrid butcheries of innocent children ceased. Ashamed of the orgies of their idolatry, and brought to the lowest depths of wretchedness through the remorseless tyranny which afflicted them, the men of Israel were brought to a public acknowledgment of their sin, and the long-neglected altar of God was thronged by penitents, saying, "*We have sinned against Thee, both because we have forsaken our God, and also served Baalim.*"

We cannot doubt that conscience was really at work, that many among the Israelites were stung with a sincere remorse. Yet they were a fickle and uncertain people. So long as prosperity lasted, they never gave themselves to repentance. It was only under the pressure of calamity that they sought the Lord; and as soon as He had removed the plague, they returned, like Pharaoh, to their old ways. "When He slew them, then they sought Him; and they returned and inquired early after God, and they remembered that God was their rock, and the high God their redeemer.

Nevertheless they did flatter Him with their mouth, and they lied unto Him with their tongues. For their heart was not right with Him, neither were they sted-fast in His covenant. But He, being full of compassion, forgave their iniquity, and destroyed them not : yea, many a time turned He His anger away, and did not stir up all His wrath." *   How is it that some writers can find nothing in the Old Testament but terror and severity ?   How can they justify their representation of the Jewish history, as a gloomy and terror-stricken scene, over which impends everywhere and always the dark shadow of the Hebrew God ? How can they shut their eyes to those incessant manifestations of the Divine forbearance, upon which the rebellious nation presumed so largely, and which never failed them when they humbled themselves before their God ?   Our blessed Lord's lamentation over Jerusalem was scarcely more applicable to the city and to the men of His own day, than it was to the Jewish nation of all previous ages since their departure out of Egypt.

On this, as on former occasions, their confessions were not unheard ; though, as when Gideon arose, the Lord's answer to them was not at first an answer of peace, but of rebuke.†   Whether it was given from the Urim on the high priest's breastplate, or whether, as in the time of Gideon, a prophet was raised up to proclaim it, is not stated ; but it was well calculated

---

* Ps. lxxviii. 34–38.   † Jud. vi. 7–10.

to deepen the repentance of Israel. The Lord reminded them, not only of their exodus from Egypt and of their deliverance from the Amorite kings who had disputed their entrance into Canaan ; He reminded them also of four signal instances in which, during the period of their residence in the land, they had cried to Him for deliverance from public oppressors, with promises of amendment, and had not been suffered to cry in vain. The children of Ammon and of Moab had oppressed them soon after the death of Joshua, and had been defeated by Ehud ; the incursions of the Philistines had been repelled with the ox-goad of Shamgar ; the Zidonians under "kings of Canaan" had been routed by Barak ; the Amalekites and Maonites, together with the innumerable hordes of the Arabian desert, had been driven away by Gideon.* Yet in spite of all these deliverances, in spite of their own often repeated promises, they had not only fallen into idolatry again, but into more grievous idolatry than at any former period. *" Did not I deliver you from the Egyptians, and from the Amorites, from the children of Ammon, and from the Philistines? The Zidonians also, and the Amalekites, and the Maonites, did oppress you ; and ye cried unto Me, and I delivered you out of their*

---

* The Amorites, Num. xxi. 21–35 ; Ammonites, Jud. iii. 12, 13 ; Philistines, iii. 31 ; Zidonians, v. 19 ; Amalekites and Maonites, vi. 3, and compare 2 Chron. xxvi. 6, 7. Maonites was probably the name of one of the Arab hordes which were confederate with Midian.

hand.   Yet ye have forsaken Me, and served other gods: wherefore I will deliver you no more.   Go and cry unto the gods which ye have chosen; let them deliver you in the time of your tribulation." *

Bitter as was this taunt, it had been richly merited. The prophet or priest who was commissioned to deliver this message, appears to have received no instructions to utter a word which might excite a hope of deliverance; in order that the nation might have time to feel its sin more deeply, and to "bring forth fruits meet for repentance." †   Such repulse is but intended to quicken and to deepen repentance. As every promise of blessing is conditional, so every threatening contains, whether it is expressed or not, a reserve of mercy to the penitent. ‡

That the Israelites understood this, is evident.   The Divine message was couched in severer terms than the corresponding message in the days of Gideon; yet notwithstanding the keen irony of its language, reminding us of Elijah when he mocked the worshippers of Baal, they did not abandon themselves to despair, but encouraged each other in promoting public reformation.   "For the deeper humiliation of

---

* Jud. x. 11–14.

† Deus non statim confitentibus peccata remittit, sed pœnam suam alicujus temporis patientiâ approbantibus, et facta edentibus contraria.—*Grotius.*

‡ This is laid down as a general principle in the Divine government of nations, Jer. xviii. 7–10.   The same applies, doubtless, to individuals.

those who are but superficially convinced, and to quicken those who are not truly in earnest, the Lord often seems to 'shut up His lovingkindness in displeasure.' He upbraids them with their sins, pursues them with awful threatenings, and almost brings them to conclude that their case is hopeless. He will, however, keep them from desperation : and when their prayers are rendered more fervent, their confessions more ingenuous, their self-examination more diligent, their submission to His justice and dependence on His mercy more entire, and their forsaking of sin more unreserved,—it may be certainly concluded that comfort and deliverance are at hand." *

Such appear to have been the effects which were produced upon the people by the announcement of these words of reproof. They confessed their just liability to whatever punishment the Almighty might see fit to inflict upon them ; they deprecated His wrath, banished the idols from house and gate and grove, and returned to the pure and simple worship of the one God. Nor was this a mere transient amendment. Their return to the worship of God seems to have been more permanent than previous repentances had been ; for we do not find that they relapsed into idolatry under the subsequent judges.

Indeed, the threat of being left to groan helplessly under the miseries of servitude to a race so

---

* Thomas Scott.

relentless as the sons of Ammon, must have been in itself sufficient to arouse them to repentance. Wherever these fierce denizens of the forest made their way, massacres, conflagrations, and devastation of every kind would attend their steps. A race whose chosen deity demanded little children to be roasted alive, was not likely to treat vanquished enemies with compassion. Their march might be tracked by hillocks of dead bodies and pyramids of human heads, by burning villages and desolate homesteads. In vain might the Hebrew virgin plead or the wife resist ; mercy and justice, charity and law, property and life, childhood and grey hairs, were alike disregarded. The stories of the Mahometan rule in Hindostan, of the massacres by the Druse fanatics in the Lebanon, and of the atrocities perpetrated by the Taepings in China, may assist the imagination to form some conception of the desolations occasioned in the land of Israel by the Ammonite ascendency. It is true, the Israelites had brought all upon themselves. Yet a tender father, while hating the vices of his dissolute son, cannot help pitying his wretchedness when sharp misery has brought him in penitence to his door. And of the Father of all it is recorded, that when they cried to Him in their distress, "*His soul was grieved for the misery of Israel.*"*

Matters were now coming to a crisis, and the total subjugation of Israel seemed inevitable. The Am-

---

* Jud. x. 16.

monites raised a war-cry, and formed an encampment
in the pasture grounds of Gilead. The Israelites had
been strengthened by repentance. The effort to
demolish their idols, and to re-establish the worship
of God, while it had relieved their consciences, had
also braced their energies; in accordance with the
invariable law, that a man's moral strength is increased
the moment he has abandoned the wrong, and reso-
lutely set himself to do what is right. They no longer
abandoned themselves to despair, but commenced
active preparations against the enemy. They formed
a camp at Mizpeh, the ancient landmark of Jacob.
The tribes of Palestine proper were not summoned to
this encampment, because the two tribes and a half
who dwelt "beyond Jordan" deemed themselves
numerous enough to repel the threatening invaders.
But there was a great perplexity. No man would
"*begin to fight.*" They were without a leader. No
divinely commissioned minister appeared, as in former
days, to lead the people on to victory. Then again,
as in a past generation, "in the divisions of Reuben
there were great searchings of heart." * The want of
a commander was felt throughout all the host. If
only a qualified man could be found, in the presence
of so formidable an enemy they would sink all petty
mutual jealousies, and would at once proclaim him
head of all the trans-Jordanic tribes. But where
could he be found ? "*The people and princes of*

---

* Jud. v. 15.

Gilead said one to another, What man is he that will begin to fight against the children of Ammon? he shall be head over all the inhabitants of Gilead." *

---

* Jud. x. 18.

19

APPEARANCE OF JEPHTHAH

IN these circumstances, the thoughts of the people turned towards a man of singular history and character, the fame of whose exploits had filled the country. He commanded a company of freebooters, who were not subject in any way to the Israelitish authorities, but, living in a pleasant region just upon the northern confines of Palestine, acted under his direction;—"not the most discreditable profession in those early ages of barbarous manners."* The course of sending for Jephthah, with an offer of the supreme command, must have appeared, at first, to be attended with serious difficulties. In the first place, he was not living in the country, but beyond its bounds, in the land of Tob, which belonged, apparently, to Syria;† and how could they elect, as leader

---

* Warburton's "Divine Legation," ii. 697.

† Most expositors, following Josephus, place "the land of Tob" in Syria, northwards of Manasseh, towards the eastern deserts. "Tob" in Hebrew signifies good. In 2 Samuel x. 8, we read of the Syrians of Ish-tob joining with the Ammonites. So late as the days of Judas Maccabæus, the Ammonites were still a powerful people, and acted with great cruelty towards some Jews who lived "in the places of Tobie" (1 Macc. v. 13). These Jews were called Tubiani (2 Macc. xii. 17).

of the national cause, a man who was not resident within their country? The company which he led was composed of men who, like himself, lived by free-booting, and were not subject to the laws. Further, it was well known that Jephthah had a complaint against the authorities of his country, who, he alleged, had treated him with injustice, and had driven him into involuntary exile. But the greatness and the imminence of the danger overbore all these considerations; and a deputation, consisting of the principal sheikhs of the tribes of Gad and Manasseh, was sent from their encampment to the land of Tob,—not more than two days' journey,—"*to fetch Jephthah.*" Their instructions were, to give him the unconditional offer of the command, and even to implore him to undertake it. "*They said unto Jephthah, Come, and be our captain, that we may fight with the children of Ammon.*" *

It has been questioned how far, in taking this step, they acted under the direct counsel of God. On the one hand it has been supposed that they sought Divine counsel, and obtained a public and authoritative answer, either from the high-priest or from a prophet; on the other hand, that they were only secretly directed by the Spirit of God. This at least we know, that their choice was approved. In this instance the voice of the people was the voice of God. Other judges had been specially sent to them;

---

* Jud. xi. 6.

Jephthah was the man of their own choice : reminding us that the Infinite God is not limited to any one method of operation, but has various ways of effecting His holy purposes ; that He works no less really and truly through the instrumentality of humanly contrived means than by direct operation ; and that when, in times of perplexity, we gain no evident answer to our prayers, we may use the best of our own judgment with the good hope that the Divine purpose concerning us will be accomplished thereby.

Jephthah's previous history and manner of life are related by the author of the Book of Judges in a few sentences. Rightly understood, they convey an idea of his character far from unfavourable. The circumstances of his birth were unpropitious; according to our version, *"he was the son of an harlot."* * His mother was probably a concubine residing in the house with Gilead his father ; † not an Israelitish woman, but of one of the surrounding nations. Had she been a Hebrew, Jewish custom would have permitted her son to share in the inheritance with the children lawfully born ; but the reason assigned by Jephthah's brothers for refusing him a share in the patrimony was, that he was the son of an alien. *"And Gilead's*

---

* Jud. xi. 1.

† "Quales concubinas etiam Abraham habuit ; i.e. solum uni viro addicta, sed citra vinculum matrimonii."—*Munsterus, in loc.* " Nullâ observatione ceremoniarum recipiebantur concubinæ e viris quæ in legitimâ uxore adhibebantur ; hôc excepto, erant uxores legitimæ."—*Vatablus.*

wife bare him sons ; and his wife's sons grew up, and they thrust out Jephthah, and said unto him, Thou shalt not inherit in our father's house ; for thou art the son of a strange woman." *

In our own age, when polygamy has vanished from all Christian countries, and when the honour of marriage has become universally understood, such conduct as that of Jephthah's brothers would be justified by public opinion.   But we must not judge of their proceedings by the standard of our own times.   Even now, nothing is more common than to profess zeal for the right, for the sake of pecuniary advantage ; and the zeal which Jephthah's brothers displayed in asserting the claims of legitimacy may have been inspired as much by self-interest as by concern for the honour of the law. †   Their treatment of him became at

---

* Jud. xi. 2.

† " A bastard shall not enter into the congregation of the Lord, even to his tenth generation " (Deut. xxiii. 2).   That is, one born of a stranger who is not an acknowledged wife.   But this is not to be understood as applying to " concubines " living in the house ; as is evident from the fact that of the twelve sons of Jacob, the heads of the tribes, four were thus born.   By his being forbidden to " enter the congregation," cannot be understood to be a prohibition from joining in any acts of religion, since this was permitted to all (Exod. xii. 48, 49 ; Num. xv. 14, 15). Yet it is evident, from the comforting words of Isaiah to such, that some sort of distinction was made, though they were not " utterly separated ; " see Isaiah lvi. 3, 6, 7.   Probably they were forbidden to celebrate the sacred feasts, as in the full communion of the congregation of the Lord, but must be contented to worship without, as uncircumcised Gentiles were wont to do.

length unbearable. It is not improbable that, like Joseph's brethren, they were "moved with envy" of his superior abilities. Jephthah himself resented their conduct as unjust, notwithstanding the sanction which it received from the magistrates, who encouraged the brothers in their persecution of him. For a time, their selfish and envious course appeared to prosper ; and as Joseph's brethren rejoiced that they were rid of the dreamer, so Jephthah's brethren rejoiced that they were rid of him whose superiority to themselves stirred up in their hearts the gall of envy. But in each case, jealousy was rebuked by the event ;—Joseph became Lord over his brethren and over all the land of Egypt, and Jephthah lived to see the very elders who had banished him bowing at his feet, and imploring that he would become their master.

The school of difficulty has produced many an illustrious pupil ; and to the hardships and mortifications which Jephthah endured in his youth may be traced that resolution and activity, that courage and judgment, which eventually raised him to the highest post of office in his native country. To be out of the reach of his brethren he retired into " *the good land*," " the land of Tob." He did not remain there in solitude, but was accompanied by a number of men who had resolved to share his fortunes. " *There were gathered vain men to Jephthah, and went out with him.*"

The band of men who thus followed him into exile were probably of the same class as those who, some

ages later, followed David to the cave Adullam—
" Every one that was in distress, and every one that
was in debt, and every one that was discontented." *
But it must be recollected, that in the reign of Saul
there were many reasons why a good man might be
in distress, an honest man in debt, and a peaceable
man discontented.† It is true that there were among
David's followers " wicked men, men of Belial," ‡ but
he evidently kept them firmly in check; and that
they were not altogether a worthless crew may be
inferred from the facts that his own family connected
themselves with them, and that instead of being
dreaded as a gang of plunderers, they were acknowledged to be a protection to persons and property,
" a wall unto us both by night and day," § in the
neighbourhood of their encampment.

In their estimate of Jephthah's followers, our English
version, rather than the Hebrew original, seems to
have guided some of our commentators. Thus an
amiable writer speaks of them as " rogues and rakes ;" ‖
but neither the original text, nor the ancient versions,
oblige us to suppose that these so-called " vain men "
were all persons of infamous character. The idea
conveyed is that they were poor men.¶ Among them

---

* 1 Sam. xxii. 2.

† " Illis temporibus interdum oppressa innocentia ad tales
præsidia decurrebat."—*Grotius*.

‡ 1 Sam. xxx. 22–25.   § 1 Sam. xxv. 16, 17.

‖ Sutcliffe's Commentary ; Stanley's " Sinai and Palestine,"
chap. viii.

¶ So the ἄνδρες κένοι of the Septuagint; the Vulgate gives both

were worthless characters, no doubt; but it will be
easy to see how, in those times, a band of men might
be collected who had no settled occupation, or who
had suffered injustice, and who in default of regular
means of subsistence, betook themselves to a free-
booting life. Probably they had signalised themselves,
before the elders of Gilead sent to fetch their captain,
by successful reprisals against the Ammonites. Probably, like David in a later age, Jephthah instructed
them in such Divine knowledge as he himself possessed. Of two things the sacred narrative clearly
assures us : first, that the life which Jephthah led was
not such as to quench the light of Divine knowledge
which was in him, as may be seen by his ready and
conclusive answer, full of Scripture knowledge, to the
message of the king of Ammon ; and secondly, that
the life which he had led was not such as had induced
his countrymen to question his patriotic devotedness
to the cause of his country ; for, in an emergency so
appalling, they would not have urged the chief command upon a man in whose personal fidelity they
could not repose the utmost confidence. The outlaws
of the land of Tob may even have led a better life,
and have held the faith and hope of the covenant
more firmly, than the dwellers in the limits of the

---

views, "viri inopes, et latrocinantes." The Hebrew *rik* occurs,
e.g. in Jud. vii. 16, "*empty* pitchers." Gen. xxxvii. 24, "the
pit was *empty*." Neh. v. 13, "*emptied*." Deut. xxxii. 47, "it is
not a *vain* thing," *i.e.* unimportant. Sometimes, undoubtedly,
as in 2 Chron. xiii. 7, it bears the sense of "loose, worthless."

twelve tribes : just as, in some periods of the history of the Christian Church, the faith has been more purely held and more virtuously illustrated by despised sects without, than by the torpid mass within, the recognised ecclesiastical pale.

This hardship and banishment was doubtless a discipline by which Jephthah was being prepared for the position which Providence designed him to occupy. Like Moses in the land of Midian, his soul expanded and his energies grew while absent from his brethren. Men are never to be despised merely because they are obscure or in a minority. The splendour of the sun is never so dazzling as when he emerges from behind an impenetrable cloud ; a great and true man never appears so noble as when his detractors and opponents come crawling to his feet ; and the Church of Christ never appears so worthy to be the bride of the Eternal Son as when, having survived calumny and the wrath of men, Isaiah's prediction is fulfilled : " The sons of them that afflicted thee shall come bending unto thee ; and all they that despised thee shall bow themselves down at the soles of thy feet, and shall call thee, The city of the Lord." *

By universal consent the exile of Tob was summoned to the head of his countrymen. " *The elders of Gilead went to fetch Jephthah out of the land of Tob : and they said unto Jephthah, Come and be our captain, that we may fight against the children of*

---

* Isa. lx. 14 ; Rev. iii. 9.

Ammon." In receiving this deputation, he doubtless recognised the faces of the very men before whom he had vainly pleaded his cause in bygone years,—perhaps the faces of some of his own brothers, themselves now numbered among the elders. He was not so overcome by the unexpected honour as to forget the events of the past ; and the stinging pungency of his questions, and the abjectness of their replies, go far to confirm the view already taken, that his expulsion had not been an act which their law would justify. Surely, if the elders had acted rightly and legally in that matter, they would not have been so mute as not to offer a word in justification of themselves. Indeed, he seems not to have had entire confidence in the deputation before him,—not to have been altogether free from the suspicion of treachery : " Did ye not hate me, and expel me out of my father's house ? and why are ye come unto me now, when ye are in distress ? And the elders of Gilead said unto Jephthah, Therefore we turn again to thee now, that thou mayest go with us and fight against the children of Ammon, and be our head over all the inhabitants of Gilead. And Jephthah said unto the elders of Gilead, If ye bring me home again to fight against the children of Ammon, and the Lord deliver them before me, shall I be your head ?"* That is (according to a learned modern Jew), 'It would be no great privilege for you to confer the headship on me, if I should gain the

---

* Jud. xi. 7–9.

victory first, for then I should be your head as a matter of right; but, make me your head at once, whether I may gain the victory or not.'* Nor would he accompany them until they had first bound themselves by solemn oath—and an oath before JEHOVAH, showing that they had now forsaken Baalim and Ashtaroth, and were calling upon the name of the God of their fathers—that on his arriving amongst his countrymen, they would at once invest him with the chief dignity; a promise which was punctually performed in the presence of the whole host encamped at Mizpeh. His election was confirmed by popular acclamation; not only the 'elders,' but "the people made him head and captain over them."

Thus a backsliding but penitent people received proof once again that the Lord regardeth the prayer of the humble! Their anxious suspense was at an end, for God had given them the desire of their heart. They were no longer as orphans. A captain was amongst them, under whom they could march confidently to the engagement with their mountain foe; for "the Lord will fulfil the desire of them that fear Him: He also will hear their cry, and will save them." †

---

* Sinyanki's " Notes on Difficult Passages," p. 63.
† Ps. cxlv. 19.

20

HIS MEASURES AND VICTORY

PLACED in command, the first act of Jephthah was to offer public homage, in the presence of those who had elected him, to the Lord Jehovah. He "*uttered all his words before the Lord in Mizpeh*"* Some learned labour has been expended in ascertaining why Mizpeh should have been the scene of this religious act : but the simple and sufficient reason is that the encampment was there. What those "words" of his may have been, it is not difficult to conjecture. He explained to the people the circumstances under which he had appeared amongst them ; he solemnly engaged himself to them, and received their oath of obedience to himself as judge and general ; he laid before them the means which he proposed to employ for the termination of the war. All these words were uttered "before the Lord." The high-priest, according to some, was invited to Mizpeh for the occasion, and answers of peace issued from the sacred breastplate. At least, we know that the Lord was in their midst ; and we can imagine how, on that day of

---

* Jud. xi. 11.

grace, some of the men would repeat the prophecy of Balaam, which had been uttered from the summit of those very mountains which overhung their camp : " He hath not beheld iniquity in Jacob, neither hath He seen perverseness in Israel : Jehovah his God is with him, and the shout of a king is among them." * In the joyful assurance of success which filled their hearts on that day of holy solemnity,—an assurance which was justified by the result,—they began to taste that comfort which is promised to all that mourn, and to rejoice because, although the Lord had been angry with them as a nation, yet now His anger was turned away.   To Jephthah himself it would be a day of prayer rather than of praise.   The people might rejoice because the Lord had given them a captain ; the captain himself sought direction and blessing from on high.

Jephthah's first act was not to rush into battle, but to send to the enemy a message of inquiry and expostulation.   In doing so, he assumes without hesitation the prerogative which has been conferred upon him.   He is not encumbered by his honours, like David in Saul's armour, but rises to the proper level of his position with the ease of true greatness : *"And Jephthah sent messengers unto the king of Ammon, saying, What hast thou to do with me, that thou art come against me to fight in my land ?"*† Thus the soldier restrains his ardour till the judge is satisfied

---

* Num. xxiii. 21   † Jud. xi. 12.

of the justice of the cause. He may also have been
guided by the express injunction in the law of Moses,
to make an offer of peace before proceeding to actual
fight.* A certain class of expositors maintain further
that he did this in his capacity as a type of Christ,
who proclaims peace and offers pardon to His enemies
before taking vengeance upon them.†

The Ammonite was not at a loss for an answer to
Jephthah's challenge. He alleged the right arising
from a prior occupation of the country ;—that Israel,
an intruder and a usurper, had wrested their lands
from his forefathers : "Israel took away my land,
when they came up out of Egypt, from Arnon even
unto Jabbok, and unto Jordan : now therefore restore
those lands again peaceably." ‡

In Jephthah's rejoinder we have an admirable specimen of historical and political reasoning. § He commences by denying the truth of his opponent's statement. The Israelites could not have taken away the
land from the Ammonites, for at the period in question
the Ammonites were not in possession of it ; it had
been wrested from them,‖ and was at that time held in
possession by the Amorite kings. It was not by Israel
that their ancestors had been dispossessed, but by the
Amorites, who in their turn, Sihon and his host coming

---

* Deut. xx. 10. And yet, singularly enough, Stanley speaks of
him as in his "wild rashness resembling a Bedouin chief rather
than an Israelitish judge."—"*Sinai and Palestine,*" chap. viii.

† So Augustine, Quæst. de Judic., xlix.

‡ Jud. xi. 13.   § Jud. xi. 15–28.   ‖ Num. xxi. 26–32.

out to attack the Israelites, were defeated and dispossessed; so that the main accusation, "Israel took
away *my* land," was untrue. It was not *his* land at
all when Israel obtained it. In the next place,
Jephthah pleads the right of conquest. "The Lord
God of Israel hath dispossessed the Amorites from
before His people Israel, and shouldest thou possess
it? Wilt not thou possess that which Chemosh thy
god giveth thee to possess? So whomsoever the
Lord our God shall drive out from before us, them
will we possess." As if he had said,—'Supposing
even that your statement was true, which it is not,
even then the title by which Israel holds possession
of the land is at least as good as the title by which
your ancestors held possession of it. You Ammonites
were not the original inhabitants of the soil; the
Emims inhabited it before you, * but you drove them
out in past ages, and secured possession, which good
fortune you would attribute to the favour of Chemosh
your god; and as Jehovah, the God of Israel, has
been pleased to give His people success in obtaining
the land, can you expect us to give it up?' In this
argument, Jephthah reasons with the heathen king
upon his own principles. If he would consider conquest, obtained through the favour of his god, a sufficient ground of possession, why should not Israel do
the same? Having thus appealed to history and to
reason, Jephthah concludes his despatch with an

---

* Deut. ii. 10.

appeal to precedent and prescription, not without a significant hint of the impossibility of overcoming God's people, Israel : "And now art thou anything better than Balak, the son of Zippor, king of Moab ? Did he ever strive against Israel, or did he ever fight against them, while Israel dwelt in Heshbon and her towns, and in Aroer and her towns, and in all the cities that be along the coast of Arnon, three hundred years? Why therefore did ye not recover them within that time ? " As if he had asked—' How is it that this question has been allowed to slumber for three hundred years ? * How is it, especially, that when Israel's occupancy of this country was yet a new thing, Balak, that powerful prince and your near ally, allowed our fathers to settle upon these lands without resistance, and never demanded their restoration, though he wished us ill, and hired the most famous necromancer of the East to procure a malediction upon us ? '

Thus Jephthah disposed of his antagonist's argument ; and appealing to the Most High as to the justice of his nation's cause, left its decision with Him.† The document is in every view remarkable. It shows how full and exact was the information which Jephthah possessed of the history of his people ; which

---

* The figure is only stated here approximately, in round numbers.

† " . . . Jephthah, who by argument,
Not worse than by his shield and spear,
Defended Israel from the Ammonite."—*Milton.*

is the more worthy of note, remembering how, for many years previously, the worship of God had been banished from Israel. It illustrates the excellence of his judgment, in selecting from the history such points as were suited to his purpose ; his readiness, for this answer must have been given upon short notice, as both armies were waiting in their encampments, and he could have had no knowledge of the line of argument he might be required to take ; and above all, his faith in God. He believed the records. He believed in the covenant, and in the Divine call of Israel. He was ready not only to avow his faith in God, but to stake all upon His truth. He staggered not through unbelief, but believed in a glorious destiny yet before the sons of Abraham. He " saw the promises afar. off, was persuaded of them, embraced them, and obtained them."* Thus, in those early times, there was more faith outside the borders of Israel than within them.†

Although Jephthah failed to convince the Ammonite king, the preparation of this reply seems to have had a blessed effect upon his own mind. It is at this point that we read of the Spirit of the Lord coming upon him. He was previously a person of capacity, courage, and faith; he now arrived at so full and living a persuasion of God's truth, as to become under its influence a new man. The Spirit of God did not, indeed, come upon him as mightily as upon

---

* Heb. xi. 13, 33.   † Luke vii. 9.

Gideon *—not in such extraordinary, all-pervading power. Gideon had sent messengers round the country to summon followers to his standard; Jephthah went in person. † *"He passed over Gideon and Manasseh, and passed over Mizpeh of Gilead,"*— where the Israelitish encampment was; and having mustered all his army there, *"from Mizpeh of Gilead he passed over unto the children of Ammon."* No details are given of the battle: it is only said that *"the Lord delivered them into his hands."* From Aroer, probably the place where the battle was fought, the broken and flying Ammonites were pursued as far as Minnith. Twenty cities were passed in the pursuit; but Minnith has not as yet been identified by eastern explorers, though it may be concluded from Ezekiel's allusion to its "market wheat," that it lay in the midst of a cultivated arable country. ‡ The success was decisive; *"the children of Ammon were subdued before the children of Israel;"* yet it was not so complete as the success of Gideon, after whose rout of the Midianites, they lifted up their heads no more.

In our own day there are various degrees in which Christians are filled with the Spirit of God. There

---

❊ The distinction in the Hebrew is partially lost in our version. In regard to Gideon, the word *"clothed"* (Jud. vi. 34), has been already explained; in regard to Jephthah it is merely " *was.*"

† It seems, however, that he sent messengers across the Jordan to invite the men of Ephraim (Jud. xii. 2).

‡ Ezek. xxvii. 17.

are victories over the devil's kingdom whose results endure for ages; and there are victories whose effect soon vanishes away. After their rout by Jephthah, the children of Ammon so far rallied as to become the most formidable of David's enemies ; and even the terrible retribution with which David visited them did not prevent them from becoming formidable again in succeeding ages. It was not a little thing for Jephthah to have effectually humbled, even for a time, the strongest and the most persistent of all the enemies of Israel.

21

THE VOW

THE subject of Jephthah's vow is in some respects one of the most difficult in all biblical history. Its intrinsic importance is not great, nor is its moral teaching particularly obvious ; but the tender and romantic interest of the story imprints it indelibly upon the imagination, and has served, unquestionably, to increase the keenness with which critics have discussed its issue. What Jephthah really intended by his vow,—in what sense he fulfilled it—and how far he was censurable either in uttering or in fulfilling it,— are questions upon which the opinions of the learned are so nicely balanced, that, if it were a question to be decided merely by the preponderance of authority, it is doubtful upon which side the scale would fall.

Among Jewish paraphrasts and commentators, the more ancient are mostly of opinion that Jephthah did actually sacrifice his daughter. They censure the rashness of his vow, but they do not appear to doubt that the sacrifice of the maiden was actually made. Some later Jewish writers, however, of great authority, have contended that Jephthah's daughter was not slain, but devoted to a life of virginity ; being shut up in a house which her father built for the purpose, and there visited four days in each year by the maidens of Israel, as long as she lived.

Among Christian writers, perhaps all during the first ten centuries—certainly the exceptions, if any, were few and far between—believed that the maiden was sacrificed. Chrysostom founds an eloquent homily against rash vows upon the two instances of Jephthah and Saul ; and argues, that although he had often heard pagans cast this in the teeth of Christians, yet it was an instance of the mercy rather than of the cruelty of the God of the Hebrews, by one such instance effectually to discourage rash vows for the future.* Augustine holds it as certain that she was sacrificed, her father being ignorant of the law. † Jerome says that as a punishment for his rashness in vowing, the Lord permitted him to immolate his child; ‡ and Ambrose, who in his writings frequently alludes to the subject, deplores the necessity which could only be solved by parricide; using the identical expression, "miserable necessity," which Cromwell is said to have uttered again and again as he paced his room the night before signing the warrant for the execution of the king. §

---

* Chrys. Hom. ad pop. Antioch, xiv. 3.

† Quæst. de Judic., xlix.

‡ "Ut qui improspecte voverat, errorem votorum in filiæ mortem sentiret."—*Cont. Jovinian*, lib. 1.

§ "Dura promissio, acerbior solutio, quam necesse habuit lugere etiam ipse qui fecit. Non possum accusare virum qui necesse habuit implere quod voverat, sed tamen miserabilis necessitas, quod solvitur parricidio."—*De Off. Minist.* iii. 12.

Later Christian writers have not been so unanimous.

Many, perhaps the majority, of those who have treated upon the subject, hold the opinion which, as we have seen, was universal in the early Church. Many others, of equal learning and eminence, have maintained that Jephthah's daughter was not offered by her father as a burnt-offering, but that she was permitted to live ; among these, there are some who believe with the modern Jews just mentioned, that she was shut up by her father and devoted to a life of seclusion ; while others suppose that she was devoted to the Lord's service in a life of celibacy, and was numbered during the remainder of her life with the " women who assemble at the door of the tabernacle of the congregation ;" * performing duties of sacred service in connection with the worship at Shiloh. † It

---

* I Sam. ii. 22 : Exod. xxxviii. 8.

† Possibly it may gratify the curiosity of the reader if I insert a list of commentators and others who have treated upon Jephthah's vow. This list does not pretend to be complete, but only so far as my own knowledge of the subject extends. Among those who believe that the virgin was spared are : Arias Montanus, Pagninus, Vatablus, Estius, Junius, Clarius, Munsterus, Drusius, Glassius, Grotius, Louis de Dieu, Pool, Patrick, Leclerc, Selden, Saurin, Bishop Hall, Waterland, Heinsius, Broughton, Perkins, John Wesley, Hales, Gleig, Gill, Adam Clarke, Benson, Gerlach, Auberlen, Bush, Stüder, Hengstenberg, and Kiel.

This may appear a formidable list. But on the other side of the question, viz. those who believe that Jephthah's daughter was sacrificed, are (without enumerating Jewish commentators) Justin, Tertullian, Origen, Chrysostom, Epiphanius, Jerome,

is impossible for opinions upon a historical subject to be more divided ; nor can we expect that absolute certainty will ever be arrived at.   Still, the inquirer need not be deterred from patiently examining the case, or from stating the results of such examination.

That Jephthah should have accompanied his prayer for victory with the promise of a votive offering in case the victory were gained, can occasion no surprise. It has, indeed, been objected to his conduct, that "the very idea of his vow, of his bargaining with God for assistance, has a heathenish savour."*   Undoubtedly, a similar practice obtained amongst heathens. Thus the mariners who were in the ship with Jonah added ' vows ' to their sacrifices in the hour of their terror ; among the Greeks, Callimachus made a vow upon the invasion by Darius, that if Minerva would grant him the victory, he would sacrifice upon her altars as many he-goats as should be equal to the slain among their enemies ; the well-known *votum* of the Romans was a prayer accompanied with a promise, that if the divinity complied with the petitioner's request, he would perform some service in grateful

---

Ambrose, Augustine, Gregory Nazianzen, Theodoret, Anselm, Aquinas, Prosper Aquitanus, P. Martyr, Luther, Salianus, Serarius, Menochius, Capellus, Lightfoot (who once defended the contrary opinion, but afterwards held that she was sacrificed), Isidorus, Tostatus, Bonfrere, Michaelis, Calmet, Henry, Spanheim, Warburton, Jurieu, Edwards, Jennings, Burder, Russell, Thomas Scott, Sutcliffe, Pfeiffer, Wouvers, Kitto, Havernick, Bullock, Wordsworth, and Stanley.

 * Kitto.

return ; and the walls of their temples were hung with votive pictures, which had been promised by the mariner or the passenger in the hour of danger, and were afterwards presented to the god in performance of his vow.*

But then such vows were by no means confined to heathens. On the contrary, they are the subject of explicit and frequent legislation in the code of Moses, showing that they were customary, and that it was taken for granted that such vows would be offered ; provision was made for legally annulling them, in specified cases ; while in other cases the offerer was held to his promise, and there are strict exhortations to punctuality in performing them.† Jacob vowed that if the Lord would be with him in his long journey, and would bring him back in peace to the spot where he was then standing, he would dedicate the tenth of his property ; the Israelites vowed that if the Lord would deliver Arad into their hands, they would utterly destroy his cities ; Hannah vowed that if the Lord would give her a son, he should be the Lord's for life, and a Nazarite ; and David speaks of paying the vows in the house of God which he had uttered in the day of trouble.‡ And thus Jephthah, trembling

---

* Jonah i. 16 ; Potter's Grecian Antiquities, ii. 69 ; Ramsay's Roman Antiquities, p. 338.

† Num. xxx. 2–8 ; Deut. xxiii. 21–23 ; Eccles. v. 4 ; Lev. xxvii. 7, 18–22.

‡ Gen. xxviii. 20 ; Num. xxi. 2, 3 ; 1 Sam. i. 11 ; Ps. lxvi. 13, 14.

under the heavy responsibility which lay upon him, vowed, in the excitement of the hour, that if he was permitted to return to his own house in peace, the first thing that met him coming out of his house should be the Lord's, and he would offer it for a burnt offering.   That, situated as he was, he should add to his fervent prayers a vow, was therefore not contrary either to the law of Moses, or to the practice of ancient believers.

The next inquiry is as to the meaning of his vow. Was it an utterly rash and ignorant engagement of a half-savage chief, the import of which he never considered till the moment when he was startled by the appearance of his child?   Or are we to conclude, with others, that being ignorant of the Mosaic law, and being too familiar with heathen customs, he supposed that a human victim offered upon God's altar,—if it should be a human being who first met him on his return,—would be an acceptable sacrifice?

That Jephthah was "hasty in opening his lips before God," is generally admitted ; although this rashness is singularly in contrast with his cautiousness and skill in negotiating and arguing with the Ammonite, and shows how elements the most opposite may exist in the same character.   That he deliberately contemplated as possible the sacrifice of a human being, is a supposition scarcely to be entertained of one who is spoken of in the New Testament as a man of faith.   Yet that human sacrifices were familiar to him cannot be doubted ; and it is possible that familiarity with the rites of the Ammonites, on whose borders he dwelt, and with whom human sacrifices, as is now the case in many parts of Africa, were religious rites of daily occurrence, may have blunted his feelings, and have caused him to forget how odious such offerings were in the sight of God. The excitement of the occasion, however, seems to have bewildered him, so that he forgot everything not immediately connected with his forthcoming expedition. His vow was utterly rash. He did not take time to consider, for example, that if an ass or a dog had first met him coming out of his house on his return, to offer it to the Lord would have been an abomination. Had he bestowed that thought upon the matter which reason itself would teach us to be necessary when we open our lips to our Maker, he could not have failed to reflect that it was possible, nay, likely, that his only and beloved child would be the first to greet him on his return. It was natural that he should offer a vow to the Lord ; strange that he should have done it with such impulsive rashness.

It is contended, however, by some, that there was no rashness in his vow ; that he foresaw the possibility of a human being, perhaps even of his daughter, coming out to meet him ; and that he expressly provided for its contingency. In support of this view, an alteration is suggested of a single word, the word "*or*" instead of "*and*" in our authorized version. The text will then read as follows ; " *Whatsoever cometh forth of the doors of my house to meet me, when I return in peace from the children of Ammon, shall surely be the Lord's, or I will offer it up for a burnt-offering."* * That is to say, whatever it was, he would dedicate it to Jehovah ; while if it were suitable for a burnt-offering, he would offer it up as such. But this explanation seems to be rather an ingenious escape from a difficulty than a straightforward interpretation of the text. We are thus shut up to the conclusion that the terms of Jephthah's rash vow were such as to require that a holocaust should be made of the living thing, whatsoever it might be, which should first come out to meet him.

His anguish upon meeting his daughter is described in the narrative with simple and touching vividness. Aware of his approach, the maiden, at the head of a band of female attendants, came out to meet her victorious father, heading the procession herself, and dancing to the beat of the timbrel, whose well-known sound was heard on all occasions of public or family rejoicing.† The instant he saw her, grief and dejection took possession of his heart, and he tore his clothes upon the spot, as was their manner of expressing grief ; while the tenderness of a loving father, and the stern resoluteness of a bandit chief, each found expression in the words with which he accosted his child. *"Alas, my daughter ! thou hast brought me very low, and thou art one of them that*

---

* Jud. xi. 31.

† See Exod. xv. 20 ; Job xxi. 12. "Sed quia sacerdotes eorum tibiâ tympanisque concinebant."—*Tacitus de Judæis.*

trouble me: for I have opened my mouth unto the Lord, and I cannot go back!" *   Thus, in this chequered life, sorrow treads upon the heels of mirth, our choicest comforts become our severest trials, the sound of the lute is exchanged for the moaning of the captive, and the pinnacle of exultation for the abyss of despair! That the light of his home should be removed, his expectation of posterity cut of, and his family become extinct among the families of his people,—these causes, added to the sorrow of a father at parting with an only child, would account for his distress: yet he seems never for a moment to have faltered in the determination to fulfil his vow.

We may well suppose that his grief was exquisitely embittered by his intense affection for his only daughter,—an affection of which she seems to have been altogether worthy. Her reply to her father reveals a character so noble and so beautiful, that it is difficult to find words with which to do it justice. *" My father, thou hast opened thy mouth unto the Lord, do to me according to that which hath proceeded out of thy mouth; forasmuch as the Lord hath taken vengeance for thee of thine enemies, even of the children of Ammon."* †

What amiable sweetness, what filial dutifulness, what ardent patriotism, what lofty sense of a father's honour, of a country's expectation, of the acknowledgment due

---

* Jud. xi. 35.

† Ver. 36. Our version introduces the word *if* unnecessarily.

to Jehovah for His interposition on their behalf, are here! How unselfish is this maiden of Israel! We know not what her prospects may have been, but at least she felt that her virginity was a thing to be " bewailed ; " yet with what cheerful readiness she sinks herself and all her hopes, rather than that her father, or her father's God should be dishonoured! Not that she had an unwomanly indifference to life's duties or prospects. On the contrary, although willing to be sacrificed for her father's sake, her request was to be permitted to live for two months, that she might bewail her virginity with the maidens her companions. At the expiration of that time her father was not put to the pain of sending for her. Probably she might have secreted herself, and have escaped her fate ; but the same nobility of character which had prompted her first utterance, led her to return of her own accord.* *" It came to pass at the end of two months that she returned to her father :"*—not earlier, for she

---

* Some of the Latin fathers have justly appreciated her heroism. Ambrose, for example, grows warm and eloquent in her praise : " Incantam patris oblationem sanguine suæ solvit," —*De Virg.* i. 8 ; and he proceeds to exhort young women, whose parents have vowed chastity for them, to respect parental authority. Again, in his treatise *De Off. Ministrorum*, iii. 12 : " Nec fletus æqualium movit puellam, nec dolor flexit, nec gemitus retardavit, nec dies præteriit, nec fefellit hora. Rediit ad patrem, quasi ad votum rediret, et voluntate propriâ cunctantem impulit, (this of course is imagination,) fecitque arbitrata spontaneo, ut quod erat impietatis fortuitum, fieret pietatis sacrificium."

was not sick of the world; not later, for she was honourable and true.

A more exquisitely painful scene is not presented in all history than that of this maiden of Gilead returning to her father, that his vow might be performed. Jephthah's sin was a sin of ignorance.* He lived in a time of great religious degeneracy. The priesthood was powerless for good, and the people had become familiar with the gods of Moab and of Ammon, who were worshipped with human sacrifices. He was separated by the misfortune of his birth from the congregation of the Lord, and had been driven from his own home, living amid scenes of plunder and bloodshed. Much charitable allowance must be made for such a man, and for the strong but mistaken sense of right, which led him, after having made a rash vow, to consider it his terrible duty to perform it.

But did he actually perform it? Did he sacrifice his child? Or may we not rather suppose that he gave her to the Lord, by devoting her to a life of celibacy?

It has been warmly contended that there is "no

---

* So Augustine: "Hic ejus error habet aliquam laudem fidei," while he admits the question of the immolation to be "magna et ad dijudicandum difficillima quæstio."—*Quæst.* xlix. Jerome, less cautious, thinks that he was rightly served for his rashness: "Ut qui improspecte voverat, errorem votorum in filiæ mortem sentiret."—*Cont. Jovin. I.* Ambrose admires his uprightness: "Etsi parricidium non probo, adverto prævericandæ matum et formidinem sponsionis."—*De Virg.* i. 2.

proof in the Old Testament that a single life was any branch or article of religion ; " * and one learned writer goes so far as to say that "to suppose that Jephthah devoted his daughter to perpetual virginity, is to suppose him acting as contrary to the law of God as if he had sacrificed her." † This view, how- ever, will not bear a close investigation.

There are traces in the Old Testament of the existence of an institution of holy women of a strictly religious order, who had relinquished worldly cares to give themselves wholly to God. In the account of the making the tabernacle, we read of the "female servants who served at the gate of the tabernacle of the congregation." ‡ They had given, in aid of its sacred service, their mirrors, indicating a renuncia- tion of the world ; or, as an old English writer puts it, they, "gave the instruments whereby they drest their bodies, to make the instrument whereby through faith they might sanctify their souls." § The word which is used to denote their assembling, denotes

---

* Matthew Henry.

† Jennings, "Hebrew Antiquities," i. 47. The story of Ido- meneus, *Æneid*, iii. 122, and *Ovid Met.*, xii., has been supposed to be borrowed from that of Jephthah. Idomeneus, King of Crete, being overtaken in a storm, vowed to Neptune that if he were saved, he would offer him in sacrifice the first object he should meet on entering his house. He met his son, and would have slain him ; or according to others, did slay him, and his subjects drove him out of the kingdom.

‡ Exod. xxxviii. 8.

§ Ainsworth on the Pentateuch, Exod. xxxviii. 8.

an assembling in rank, or for service ; and that they were understood to be a religious order, appears from the designation of them in the Septuagint version as "fasting women ;" and in the Chaldee, as "praying women." * That this order of women was in existence in the time of Jephthah, may be inferred from the fact, that we find it expressly mentioned within thirty years of his death, where it is recounted among the great crimes of the sons of Eli, that they committed sin "with the women that assembled at the door of the tabernacle of the congregation," † the sacred character of these women constituting an aggravation of their crime. And at the time of the birth of our Lord, Anna was one of those women, "which departed not from the temple, but served God with fastings and prayers night and day." ‡ Their services seem not to have been external, but of a strictly spiritual nature, combined, like the Nazarite males, with ascetic practices ; and that they were women of rank who thus devoted themselves, may be inferred from the mention of the brazen mirrors, which were expensive articles of luxury.

---

* Hengstenberg's "Egypt and Books of Moses," chap. vi. ; who remarks, עבא signifies military service. Figuratively, therefore, it stands for the *militia sacra* of the priests and Levites. In addition to the sacred host composed of men, there appears in our passage a corresponding one consisting of women ; and the manner in which it is spoken of, shows that it was a general, important, and formally recognised institution." Jephthah's daughter may have survived to the days of Eli. Compare 1 Tim. v. 5.

† 1 Sam. ii. 22.   ‡ Luke ii. 37.

It thus appears that there was, as a known institution in those times, an order of women who were mystically dead—who had renounced the world, and had given themselves to service connected with the tabernacle or temple. Yet for all this it is not proved that the daughter of Jephthah was thus consecrated. The peculiar expression of the sacred text, that " *her father did with her according to his vow which he vowed, and she knew no man*," may lend plausibility to the opinion, held, as we have seen, by many eminent and learned men, that she was devoted to a virgin life. But against this view there lie three objections, which, when taken together, compel us to adopt the opposite view. The first is, that a celibate life formed no part of her father's vow. The second is, that the great distance at which Jephthah was from Shiloh, where the tabernacle was, and the absence of any allusion in all his history to its existence, render the theory of his daughter being transferred thither improbable. The third is, that the misfortune of his birth would alone have prevented such an arrangement. If the sons of a bastard, according to the law of Moses, could not enter into the congregation of the Lord to the tenth generation, * it is scarcely probable that Jephthah's daughter could have secured admission among the privileged women who rendered service about the tabernacle.

We, therefore, look upon the maiden as having been

---

* Deut. xxiii. 2.

sacrificed. Upon the gloom of this painful history, however, an ethereal brightness shines. What can be more beautiful, more wonderful, than this pure and lovely maid, brought up among bandits, and far from the tabernacle of God, thus freely and sweetly giving up herself as a thank-offering for the victories of Israel?

And who can fail to see, in this story of the meek and self-sacrificing maid, "a marvellous and mysterious adumbration of a better sacrifice of another soul, of an only child, perfectly free and voluntary, and of virgin holiness and heavenly purity, the sacrifice of CHRIST, who gave His spotless soul to death for our sakes?" * Like Him, she offers herself a willing sacrifice, and in the full foresight of death, she comes down from her mountain liberty at the appointed time to offer up her virgin soul. Her life is given, the price, as it were, of Israel's victory over the enemy. Her suffering was not for her own sin, but through the error of another. Jephthah's daughter gave her body willingly as a sacrifice, yet she wept with her companions; Christ our Lord gave His soul willingly an offering for sin, yet He wept tears of blood.

As to the act of Jephthah, the brevity and obscurity of the record are full of significance. Let those who are most forward to condemn, look well to themselves. The subject is painful, but are there no immolations of children in our day, and within the borders of our

---

* Wordsworth, Pref. to Judges, p. 78.

Churches? On this point, one of the greatest living teachers of the Church expresses himself in words that are full of solemn interest:

"Is there not an immolation of children," says Bishop Wordsworth," worse than Jephthah's sacrifice of his daughter? She was a conscious and willing victim, offering herself to be sacrificed for the performance of her father's vow, because he had conquered the enemies of Israel. Her body was sacrificed, but her spirit was untouched. But there are moral immolations of children by their parents; immolations of their immortal souls to Mammon, to the god of money-getting; immolations to Belial, the spirit of licence and lust; and there are spiritual immolations of unconscious victims—immolations of young maidens in the flower of life and beauty to the solitude and seclusion of a cloister, into which they are beguiled with soft speeches, when they kneel before Christian altars crowned as victims, attired in pure white robes, as if they were brides of Christ. Therefore let Christian Churches meditate on the history of Jephthah, and let them apply it to themselves. Will it not be more tolerable for Jephthah in the day of judgment, than for those who offer such human sacrifices as these—sacrifices, it may be, not only of body, but of soul?" *

The celebrity of Jephthah, his singular vow, and the heroism of his child, invested the whole case with an extraordinary interest; and most especially, as

---

* Comm. on Judges.

was natural, for the young women of Israel, with whom it became an annual custom to go out for four days to commemorate their virgin sister. So popular, it appears, did this custom become, that it soon spread beyond the limits of Gilead, and crossed the Jordan; for we read that "it was a custom" not in Gilead merely, but "in *Israel*"—generally throughout the tribes—"*that the daughters of Israel went yearly to lament the daughter of Jephthah the Gileadite, four days in the year.*" *

The word rendered "to lament," our translators have rendered in the margin "to talk with;" and it has been the opinion of some that the young people devoted four days each year to visiting her and consoling her in her seclusion from the world. The most natural explanation is that the daughters of Israel held a commemoration, once a year, to *rehearse* the story, to bewail her virginity, and to celebrate her praise. How long this custom lasted it is impossible to say. A Greek writer, Epiphanius, relates that at Samaria and at Sychem they had made her into a goddess, and offered sacrifices yearly in her honour, † believing her to have been sacrificed. And it is possible, as most of the commentators remark, that the Greek fable of Iphigenia, daughter of Agamemnon, may have had its origin in a tradition of the chieftain, together with some confused tradition of Abraham's offering Isaac. ‡

---

* Jud. xi. 40.   † Epiph. Cent. Hæres., lv. 78.

‡ See this parallel traced in Adam Clarke's Comm., end of ch. xi., where he quotes at length from Lavour.

22

SHIBBOLETH

IT not seldom happens that men whom the course of events has raised to the pinnacle of fame are in themselves miserably dejected. It is perhaps too flattering to Jephthah to compare him with St. Paul, who, to keep him humble amidst the abundance of the revelations, was buffeted by a thorn in the flesh; but how often, in the order of Divine providence, are great achievements and proud successes accompanied by humiliating trials! Just as we were felicitating ourselves upon the accomplishment of some cherished purpose, and expecting pleasure in the enjoyment of our finished plan, misfortune dashed from our lips the cup, and left us to contemplate the instability of earthly hopes. The conqueror of the Ammonites, already dejected by the loss of his only child, soon found that to be elevated to the judgeship, was to be burdened with cares such as had never before perplexed him.

This trouble arose from the seditious turbulence of the tribe of Ephraim. As formerly in the time of Gideon, they were annoyed at not having been summoned to the battle with the children of Ammon;

and perhaps equally annoyed at not having been invited to share in the booty. Their reputation for courage, certainly was not the highest. " The children of Ephraim, being armed, and carrying bows, turned back in the day of battle." * They were numerous, haughty, and powerful. During the whole period of the Judges they were in possession of the precedency ; and the sanctuary of God at Shiloh was in the heart of their tribe. They did not disguise their jealousy when other tribes were preferred before them ; and now that a despised Gileadite had been raised to the supreme authority, and had succeeded in defeating a dreaded enemy without any help from their side of the Jordan, Ephraim could brook it no longer. A war-cry was raised : " *The men of Ephraim gathered themselves together, and went northward,*" to Mizpeh probably, and menacingly demanded of the judge the reason why they had not been sent for to assist in the defeat of the Ammonites ? The blame was even laid at Jephthah's door, and their exasperation was greater against him than it had been against Gideon. † Not satisfied with " chiding with him

---

* Ps. lxxviii. 9.

† " But what more oft, in nations grown corrupt,
    And by their vices brought to servitude,
    Than to love bondage more than liberty,
    Bondage with ease than strenuous liberty ;
    And to despise, or envy, or suspect
    Whom God hath of His special favour raised
    As their deliverer ? if he aught begin,
    How frequent to desert him, and at last
    To heap ingratitude on worthiest deeds ! "—*Milton.*

sharply," they threatened summary vengeance: "*We will burn thy house upon thee with fire,*" and offered battle; so that he appeared to have no alternative but to fight.* A discouraging recompense to a man who had just saved his country!

Before engaging with the army, he endeavoured to show them the justice of his cause. He denied the accusation that he had never summoned them to the enterprise; and told them plainly that they had refused to come to his assistance—true to their character of cowardly bowmen, as depicted in the 78th Psalm: "*I and my people were at great strife with the children of Ammon; and when I called you, ye delivered me not out of their hands. And when I saw that ye delivered me not, I put my life in my hands, and passed over against the children of Ammon, and the Lord delivered them into my hand: wherefore then are ye come up unto me this day, to fight against me?*"† There is a striking resemblance in general conception and in style between this reply and that to the Ammonites: nothing ideal or ingenious, but a plain, straightforward statement of the facts. It has often been contrasted with the felicitous reply of Gideon to the same tribe. But it has not so often been remembered, that the circumstances were widely different. Gideon's life was not threatened, nor was an army brought against him. Besides, insolence cannot always escape chastisement. The peace-

---

* Jud. xii. 1, 3.   † Jud. xii. 2, 3.

makers are indeed blessed: but "the haughty and quarrelsome will at length meet with those who are as ready to revenge, as others have been to endure, their affronts;"* and if the wrath, which a soft answer should have permanently turned away, re-appears with exacerbated bitterness, it is time that it should be dealt with in another way.

Jephthah had evidently no wish for this fratricidal contest. He did his best to prevent it. But being put upon self-defence, he found no difficulty in rallying the Gileadites around him. The scurrility of the men of Ephraim on former occasions, in calling the Gileadites runaways and deserters from Ephraim and Manasseh, had aroused in the men of Gilead a resentment so deep, that they evidently were not sorry to have this opportunity of taking their revenge. Where the precise point of this taunt lay, cannot now easily be ascertained; probably in some event not preserved in history. But cowards are ever the most ready to accuse others of cowardice; and it was perfectly in character for the mock-valiant bowmen, who had themselves "turned back in the day of battle," to reproach their neighbours across the Jordan as "*fugitives of Ephraim*," † as the worthless refuse of the descendants of Joseph, who had fled from justice and settled beyond the Jordan. Their fate illustrated the words of Solomon, that "the wicked is snared by the transgression of his lips." ‡ Their provoking

---

* Scott's Commentary.   † Jud. xii. 4.   ‡ Prov. xii. 13.

ribaldry cost them dear.   Even the best of men cannot always endure contemptuous taunts with perfect
equanimity ; and considering the state of society at
that day, it is not surprising that at length the
insolence of this hectoring tribe met with a fearful
revenge.

There appears to have been, first, a regular pitched
battle on a great scale, in which, under the command
of Jephthah, the Gileadites routed the men of
Ephraim ; * and after their defeat, the Ephraimites,
flying towards the Jordan and attempting to cross that
river, found themselves intercepted by strong parties
of the men of Gilead who had placed themselves so
as to command the fordable places.   Their better
knowledge of the practicable fords, and of the roads
leading to them, may easily account for their reaching
the river before the flying enemy could reach it.   The
rout of Ephraim may be inferred from the fact that
they did not reach the Jordan in anything like an
orderly march, but in a scramble—every man taking
care of himself.   It was under these circumstances
that the memorable test of "Shibboleth" was applied, with which, however, the name of Jephthah is
not connected.

"*The Gileadites took the passages of the Jordan
before the Ephraimites: and it was so, that when
those Ephraimites which were escaped*"—namely, from
being slain in the pitched battle, wherein Jephthah

---

* Jud. xii. 4.

had just defeated them—"*said, Let me go over, that the men of Gilead said unto him, Art thou an Ephraimite? If he said Nay, then said they unto him, Say now Shibboleth; and he said Sibboleth, for he could not frame to pronounce it right. Then they took him, and slew him at the passages of the Jordan; and there fell at that time of the Ephraimites forty and two thousand.*" *

Many illustrations have been collected of this variety of dialect in the same language, which it can scarcely be necessary to reproduce here. That the language of Palestine was diversely spoken in its different provinces in the days of Christ, is evident from the ready recognition of Peter by the high-priest's servant as a Galilean, his "speech betraying him." In the present day, the Arabic of one part of Syria is so different from that of another, that a person well able to understand the people of Smyrna finds great difficulty in understanding those of Aleppo; and even in the small island of Malta, where a corrupt Arabic is spoken, the peasants of the several villages are said to be nearly unintelligible to each other. Our own country affords ample illustration. A vanquished army of Northumbrians, retreating across the Tees, might with equal facility be detected by being required to say the word "River," as were the Ephraimites on the banks of the Jordan by being required to say the word "Shibboleth," or

---

* Jud. xii. 5, 6.

" stream." As our Northumbrians cannot pronounce the R, but utter instead of it a guttural sound resembling a W, the Ephraimites, unable to pronounce the Sh, discovered themselves at once by their saying Sibboleth for Shibboleth ; and so fierce was the revenge of those whom they had taunted, that the blood of forty-two thousand men mingled with the stream of the Jordan.

In this tragical scene, the vindictive fury of the men of Gilead cannot escape heavy censure. They had been irritated and exasperated by bitter words ; but in this, as in many other instances in history, we see the terrific madness of popular revenge.   No contentions are so bitter as those which arise among brethren : " A brother offended is harder to be won than a strong city."   Civil wars are usually carried on under greater exasperation of feeling than wars between nations of a different race ; nor is the breach, when once made, so readily healed.   As the sweetest wine, when acetous fermentation has set in, turns to the sourest vinegar, so it is in families and in Churches. How dismally protracted are some family feuds ! And how embittered against each other are the adherents of the two opposed parties in a riven Church ! Envy and variance set the world in flames, and the Church, too, alas ! from age to age.

How many " Shibboleths " have been invented to divide the Church of Christ ; to be watchwords of angry disputants, and pretexts for professed disciples of the same Lord abusing and excommunicating each

other! Let us not be too prodigal of our anathemas
upon these cruel Gileadites at the fords of the Jordan,
at least until we have taken leisure to compare the
mutual aspect of civilized nations, and the mutual
aspect of Christian Churches, in the later centuries,
when a conduct so much less violent might have been
expected Are there not Church parties in our own
day which set up Shibboleths of their own, and refuse
the interchanges of brotherhood to all who do not
pronounce the test-word in precisely the same manner
as themselves ? Does not the Established Church of
England, for example, insist on her Shibboleth of
Episcopal ordination with a rigour so relentless, that,
not to say a word of nonconforming Churches, the
ministers of her sister Established Church in these
realms,—that of Scotland,—because they have received Presbyterian ordination, are as jealously excluded from preaching in her pulpits and from minis-
tering at her altars, as if they were Mohammedans or
infidels ? The spirit of Jephthah's Gileadites has not
yet ceased to exist, nor is the common language of
all the tribes of the Lord's Israel as yet a passport
to brotherly recognition ; but one of the tribes, and
one, too, which more than any other, lives upon the
resources of the rest, presumes to treat as foreigners
and as aliens all the others, whose pronunciation of
the Shibboleth differs from its own ! Still, the spirit
of blessed charity is extending ; and surely we live in
the early dawn of that promised day when the tribes
shall no longer cherish their ancient discordances :

when "Ephraim shall not envy Judah, and Judah shall not vex Ephraim"; when all the divisive Shibboleths of sectarian warfare, having been forgotten, as childish quarrels are forgotten in the discretion of riper years, the Churches shall advance and act in concert in combined and successful invasion of every point of the devil's kingdom: "They shall fly upon the shoulders of the Philistines toward the west; they shall spoil them of the east together; they shall lay their hand upon Edom and Moab; and the children of Ammon shall obey them." *

After the massacre on the banks of the Jordan, we read of no other event during the administration of Jephthah.   The period of his elevation was only six years; and the Hebrew text informs us that he was buried "*in the cities of Gilead*," which our version interprets to mean, "in one of the cities of Gilead." †
Jewish ingenuity, however, as usual, has invented more than one fable to account for this peculiar mode of expression.   According to one account, he died of a slow disease, which caused his limbs to drop off, one after the other, in the course of his official journeyings, and that each limb was buried where it dropped off; so that it was literally true, that he was buried "in the cities of Gilead."   Another account states that his body was cut up after his death, and the several portions buried in different places.   It is a presumption in favour of the manner of his adminis-

---

* Isa. xi. 13.   † Jud. xii. 7.

tration, that no traces occur of a public relapse into idolatry, either during his own time, or that of his successors in office to the commencement of the period of the kings.

23

RESEMBLANCES

THE greatest writer of Christian antiquity has expatiated at some length upon the typical character of Jephthah.* He sees, in various parts of the history of the Gileadite chieftain, marked resemblances to Him of whom Moses and the prophets spoke. Few modern writers have alluded to these resemblances. Indeed, the whole tendency of modern religious thought has been, with some few exceptions, so opposed to the spiritualizing of Old Testament histories, that the undeniably appointed types of the Levitical economy, as they are unfolded in the New Testament, are referred to in these days but sparingly; and secondary resemblances are seldom brought under consideration.

It cannot be maintained that, in the strict theological sense, Jephthah was a type of Christ. For, " to constitute one thing the type of another, something more is wanted than mere resemblance. The former must not only resemble the latter, but must have been *designed* to resemble the latter. The type as well as the anti-type must have been pre-ordained ;

---

* Augustine, Quæst. de Judic., xlix.

and they must have been pre-ordained as constituent parts of the same general scheme of Divine providence." *   And therefore (to quote a living divine) "it must not be *any* character, action, or institution, occurring in Old Testament Scripture, but such only as had their ordination of God, and were designed by Him to foreshadow and prepare for the better things of the gospel."†   That the life and acts of Jephthah were so designed and planned by Divine providence, can scarcely be affirmed.   Bearing this duly in mind, it may not be unprofitable to close this sketch of his history with a brief view of those resemblances which it has been supposed to exhibit to the history and work of our blessed Lord.   And although such endeavour to approach Him who is the End of the Law and of the Prophets, be only like an attempt to touch the outermost fringe of His garment, it may not be in vain.

Did the brethren of Jephthah cast him out, alleging that his remaining amongst them would dishonour the law ?   So it is recorded of Jesus ; that "He came unto His own, and His own received Him not."   His own nation rejected Him, and for dishonouring the law.   "This man," they said, "is not of God because He keepeth not the Sabbath-day."   It is true He kept it fully, but not according to their tradition. They who trusted in the privileges of their nativity,

---

* Bishop Marsh's Lectures, p. 371.
† Fairbairn's " Typology of Scripture," i. 59.

and boasted—"We be not born of fornication," combined together with one consent, to do "against the holy child Jesus," whatsoever the hand and counsel of God "determined before to be done;" and deceived themselves into supposing that they honoured God in so doing.* And as, when Jephthah's brethren saw him driven out and fleeing, they little dreamed of the glory of his return ; so, when the Jews saw the Lord rejected and put to death, they little dreamed of the majesty of His resurrection and session at the right hand of God : "for had they known it, they would not have crucified the Lord of glory."

Did Jephthah consort with "vain men"—the poor and the despised amongst his countrymen ? Jesus ate and drank with publicans and sinners, was resorted to by the needy and the sorrowful, was heard gladly by the common people, was numbered with the transgressors, was crucified between two thieves, and took one of them with Him to paradise.

Was Jephthah sought for by the Gileadites who had cast him out ? So it is those who know they have rejected and grieved the Saviour, who afterwards turn unto Him for mercy. The nation which rejected Him will one day turn unto Him with weeping and supplication. And in "the land of Tob"—that "good land" whither He is gone up on high, He is ready

---

* "Isti, veluti legis observatores eum qui contra præcepta legis facere videbatur, tamquam legitimi non legitimum, jure sibi visi sunt ejecisse."—Augustine, *Quæst. de Judic.*, xlix. 17.

to be entreated even by His enemies and His murderers ; for He has gifts to bestow, even upon the rebellious.

Did Jephthah return and become head over those who had rejected him, conquering and driving away their enemies ? So Christ is become " head over all things to His Church ; " conqueror of Satan, sin, and hell, whose domination He overthrows for those who submit themselves to His headship. Nothing can withstand His victorious power. He is the chosen servant of the Lord, the Judge and Captain, through whom His brethren the Church—those very brethren who once cast Him out—shall be delivered from the yoke of the enemy and made triumphant for evermore.*

---

* I cannot go all lengths with St. Augustine, in his spiritualizing of this history. Take the following curious parallel between Jephthah's daughter and the Church, in which, nevertheless, there are one or two beautiful touches :—" Sed quoniam tunc fiat cùm completa fuerit sexta ætas sæculi, ideo sexaginta dierum a virginitate dilatio postulata est. Ex omnibus quippe ætatibus Ecclesia congregatur. Quarum prima est, ab Adam usque ad diluvium : secunda à diluvio, id est a Noe, usque ad Abraham : tertia ab Abrahæ usque ad David : quarta à David usque ad transmigrationem in Babyloniam : quinta ab hâc transmigratione usque ad virginis partum : sexta inde usque in hujus sæculi finem. Per quas sex ætates tamquam per sexaginta dies flevit sancta virgo Ecclesia virginalia sua ; quia licet virginalia tamen fuerant peccata deflenda, propter quæ universa ipsa virgo toto orbe diffusa quotidie dicit, Dimitte nobis debita nostra."—Augustine, *Quæst. de Judic.*, xlix. 17.

Part 5
SAMSON

24

GENERAL VIEWS

FOLLOWING the order of time, the last of the judges of Israel who in the epistle to the Hebrews are singled out as men of faith, was Samson. His life and acts are recorded by the sacred historian with an elaborate fulness which seems out of proportion to the measure of help and deliverance which he afforded to his people; nor is this by any means the only difficulty which we meet with in the study of the narrative.

The victory achieved by Jephthah, and his subsequent administration in north-eastern Palestine, seem to have been followed, as the victories and rule of Barak and of Gideon had been in previous ages, by a period of general tranquillity. Three judges are mentioned in succession after him—Ibzan of Bethlehem, Elon of Zebulon, and Abdon. Jewish tradition has identified the first of these with Boaz, the husband of Ruth, and ancestor of David; but it is more probable that the place of his birth was not Bethlehem in Judah, but Bethlehem in Zebulon.

The period during which these three judges successively ruled, was only twenty-five years; but that
their administration was peaceable and prosperous,
may be inferred from the fact that the history records
the burial of each of them in his own city, and also
from the very brevity of the record; for the happiest
state of the body politic, as of individuals, is often
that which affords the fewest remarkable events.   Yet
the leaven of idolatry was secretly working in the
community of Israel, and was preparing for them new
troubles, from enemies of whom we have scarcely as
yet heard in the course thus far of their history. *   The
struggle with the Philistines was destined to be more
protracted than any in which the Israelites had yet
engaged.   The Philistines were not, like the Canaanites, to be scattered by tempest; nor, like the
Midianites, to be driven by one decisive blow into
deserts no more to return; nor, like the Amorites, to
be dispossessed in a single campaign.   It was not
reserved for Samson to work as effectually as his
great predecessors for the salvation of his people.
His work, as foretold by the angel, was only to "*begin
to deliver Israel.*" †   No army was to assemble at his
command.   With his single arm, nerved with superhuman power, he was to engage in irregular and
spasmodic struggles, to perform prodigies in the sight
of the most persistent and powerful of all the enemies
of the elect people, and to commence a work of which

---

* Jud. x. 7.   † Jud. xiii. 5.

another and a greater Nazarite was destined to see
the completion.*   His mighty deeds served to show
the Israelites what wonders they might have performed if they would have laid hold of God's
strength ; while on the other hand, the manner in
which his powers were fooled away under the enslave-
ment of sensual lust, afforded a portraiture only too
striking and faithful of the moral condition of his
people.

Strange and bewildering as is this history in some
of its features, it bears indubitable internal marks of
truth. The story of Samson is not such as was likely
to be invented by a Jewish historian, anxious for the
honour of his nation. In the picture of the mighty
Nazarite there is a verisimilitude which it is impossible to gainsay. Although dissimilar from any other
character known in history, taken as a whole, Samson
is too evidently a real man to allow of any doubt as
to the authenticity of the strange and melancholy
tale. We seem to know this man more intimately
than any other of the judges of Israel. Of the
majority of them no characteristic personal traits
have been preserved ; and even of the few whose
story is related with more fulness of detail, there is
not one whose development, even from his birth to
his grave, we can so readily follow, whose portrait we
can form to ourselves so accurately, or into whose
inmost heart we are able to look with so certain an

---

* I Sam. vii. 10–13.

insight, as we can in the case of this hero of the Danites.

A first glance at this eccentric, yet most truly human, character, may perhaps convey the impression that it is altogether unlike that of any other man ; as if its possessor belonged to some other family of beings, and had strayed upon our planet by mistake; just as an Indian butterfly is to be seen, once or twice in a century, flying in Hyde Park, the question being unsolved as to the means by which it could have arrived there.   But deeper reflection will obliterate such an impression, and will lead us to the conclusion that the strangeness of the character of Samson arises not so much from its being unlike that of other men, as from its being cast in a more gigantic mould.   " That which chiefly strikes us in the character of this renowned Israelitish judge, is not so much any strange peculiarity in the kind or composition of it, as merely its vast strength and largeness ; he being, as it were, like Saul afterwards among the people, who was of the very same flesh and blood as they were, and only of far larger bone and muscle than they.   Just so was the character of Samson identical with that of very ordinary men, their character being only more diminutive than his—cast, as it were, in a much smaller mould—and so fashioned on a very reduced scale, that they perform no feats of any kind, and are never noticed and never known beyond the narrow circle of their own domestic relationships." *   Into his compo-

---

* Bruce's " Biography of Samson," p. 4.

sition there entered such marvellous and mighty energy of the passions, that both the good and the evil that were in him broke forth in flames that were irrepressible—flames by which he was himself consumed, almost before he had reached his prime.

The feats of prodigious strength and daring, which are almost all that perhaps the majority of readers connect in their own minds with the name of Samson, supply but a small fraction of the real interest of his life ; and indeed it is not till the astonishment excited by his wonderful and hazardous exploits has had time in some measure to subside, that we can really enter into the heart of the inspired story. There are writers whose study of his history has yielded no other conception of him, at least in the days before his captivity, than that of a rollicking Hercules, full of a grim and dangerous sportiveness. Others seem to view him as a malignant savage, ever restlessly rushing into broils and mortal combats, from the almost fiendish revengefulness of his nature. Others, again, viewing him less unfavourably, can see in him little beyond an intrepid and fiery mountaineer, possessing equally the vices and the virtues of the brigand or the outlaw. Without anticipating here what will be stated in a subsequent section, it may not be useless, at the outset of our inquiries, to point out how utterly unsatisfactory and inadequate are such conceptions. They mistake the accidents of the case for its essence. Samson's weakness is as wonderful as his strength. His moral picture is at least as remarkable as his physical. That which is chiefly remarkable in him is his intense humanness. He is (if I might so speak) a vastly enlarged specimen of our ordinary humanity, and especially of the ordinary Christian ; the Divine Spirit having placed him before us so that each one may see leading features of his own character portrayed as in a mirror, only that, being on a larger scale, they are more easily deciphered and discussed than in the case of ordinary men.

Another general view of the subject may not inopportunely be suggested here. Hitherto, in these sketches, we have contemplated the extraordinary results and triumphant victories of faith. We have seen men, with slender means at their command, becoming irresistible, both over their hesitating countrymen and over their enemies, through the faith that was in them. Out of weakness they were made strong, they waxed valiant in fight, and turned to flight the armies of the aliens. Their faith seemed to exalt their whole being, and to invest them with an indescribable nobility. But while holy writ abounds with declarations and facts illustrative of the mighty potency of faith, it is not entirely silent on the other side of the question : for after all, faith is not everything in the life of the servant of God, nor must it be disproportionately magnified. Faith is a great virtue, but it is not the greatest, and it is dead when alone.

In the New Testament we are not only reminded that charity is greater than faith, but we have the still more remarkable statement of Paul, " Though I have all faith so that I could remove mountains, and have not charity, I am nothing ;" a supposition which must not be regarded as introduced merely for rhetorical effect, but as indicating a condition actually possible. Just as it is possible that a man destitute of love, and acting under the force of inferior and selfish motive, might bestow all his property upon the poor, and give his body to be burned : so it is equally possible that a soul possessing even the faith which can remove mountains, may be without the "charity" that "never faileth."

In Samson we have the spectacle of a man in whom faith was mighty, but who, nevertheless, failed to subdue his own passions, and to keep his body under subjection. We see in him a living illustration of the warning of our Lord, that it is possible even to cast out devils and to do many wonderful works in His name, and yet to be strangers to His love. Not that this Israelite was always a stranger to Divine grace, or that there was no hope in his end ; yet his backslidings were so terrible, and his whole course was so marred through the ascendancy of base desires, notwithstanding his faith and his Nazaritish vow, that he stands a monument of the truth that faith when alone is dead,—a practical comment upon that solemn question of St. James, which Christians, following in this respect the mistake of Luther, are too apt to ignore—" Can faith save him ?" *

---

* Jas. ii. 14.

Even in asserting that there was hope in his end, we are going further than some devout and learned expositors will allow to be warranted by the narrative. The most recent English commentator on this part of holy writ speaks of Samson as a man who courted self-destruction, whose last act involved a refusal to leave God to work out His own vindication by lawful means, whose dying prayer stands in sad contrast to the dying prayer of our blessed Saviour, and who can only be spoken of as having come to "an unhappy end." *   Bishop Wordsworth has coloured the picture too darkly; yet on the other hand it cannot be affirmed that our satisfaction in contemplating the death scene is quite unalloyed. Samson is in this respect the representative of, it is to be feared, a numerous class in the Church of God. There are in the Church men of like passions with himself, and exposed to similar temptations, which they resist at times as he did, and possibly with the same faith; but whose resistance, like his, is fitful, so that they are frequently overcome, more and more frequently as life goes on. Like Samson, perhaps, they are children of many prayers and of great promise, but their sky has become overcast in the dawn; murky clouds have obscured their sun at noonday; no comfortable fulfilment of the promise, "At eventime it shall be light," has cheered their decline; their latter end seems worse than their beginning; and to many it

---

* Bishop Wordsworth.

must ever seem doubtful whether they " drew back to perdition," and perished, or whether, after all, through mercy unspeakable, they "believed to the saving of the soul." *

Such is a general view of the character of Samson, whose Divine mission it was to "*begin to deliver Israel out of the hand of the Philistines.*" † A brief reference to this remarkable people, who maintained a hostility so relentless and so protracted towards the Hebrew Church, may be not improperly introduced here, preparatory to a more extended review of Samson's exploits against them.

Of all the heathen nations mentioned in holy writ, the Philistines occupy the most conspicuous position. Other nations are seen to appear and disappear from the scene. Of the Philistine, the first notice appears previous to the confusion of tongues at Babel ; while the latest prophet except one in the Old Testament describes his cities as still proud and flourishing. ‡ It is not designed to enter here into a lengthened investigation of the origin and history of this people,— an inquiry of fascinating interest—but only to indicate as much as may be serviceable in connection with the following sketch.

" Have not I brought up Israel out of the land of Egypt, and the Philistines from Caphtor ? " § Such was the word of the Lord by the prophet Amos ; re-

---

* Heb. x. 39.   † Jud. xiii. 5.   ‡ Gen. x. 14 ; Zech. ix. 5-7.
§ Amos ix. 7.   Compare Jer. xlvii. 4.

calling the genealogical table of Moses just referred to, where Philistim and Caphtorim are mentioned as grandsons of Ham, the son of Noah. Caphtor, according to Jewish tradition and several ancient versions, was Cappadocia. * From that country the Caphtorim came forth, settling first, perhaps, in Crete, and afterwards in Palestine ; and in the time of Moses we find them dwelling in Gaza in the Philistian plain, having previously dispossessed the " Avims, which dwelt in Hazerim," or " in villages." † Long before this, there had been a Philistian kingdom, of which Gerar was the capital ; ‡ but from the time of the exodus, Gerar and the kingdom disappear from history, and the power of Philistia becomes concentrated in five great cities, each with its lord, as has been seen in a previous section.

It is probable that there were three distinct immigrations into Palestine which contributed to form the nation of the Philistines. The first may have been that of the " Casluhim, out of whom came Philistim," mentioned in the early part of Genesis. § The second may have been that of the Caphtorim, already mentioned, who were clearly a kindred clan. This migration may have occurred about the time of the exodus ; and it appears to have been so considerable, that the Mediterranean Sea, on whose shore they had settled, came to be called by

---

* Pusey, on the Minor Prophets, p. 221.
† Deut. ii. 23.   ‡ Gen. xx. 2.   § Gen. x. 14.

their name, " the sea of the Philistines ; "* while, at
the same time, the Israelites were led by the foot of
mount Sinai, in order not to expose them at once
to so powerful an enemy.† The third immigration
was probably that of the Cherethites, who are not
mentioned till the time of Saul, and are described as
a Philistian clan, enjoying at that time territory and
wealth. ‡ If we suppose that this third immigration
took place during the later period of the judges, it
will account for the accession of strength which the
Philistines had evidently received about that period.
Three centuries before the time of Samson, the Philistines had lost three, at least, out of their five great
cities, to Israel : § and, during the intervening period,
nothing is heard of their power, although the Moabites, Canaanites, Ammonites, Midianites, are described
as oppressors of Israel. There was clearly a revival
of their power toward the later period of the judges ;
and no other explanation seems so fully to meet all
the circumstances of the case, as that this revival was
promoted, partly, no doubt, by their growing prosperity, but partly also through an influx of the Cherethites, who at once amalgamated with the Philistines
already in the country.

It is thus that different, though kindred tribes,
arriving at periods separated by intervals of several
centuries, became united under the one name of

---

* Exod. xxiii. 31.   † Exod. xiii. 17.   ‡ I Sam. xxx. 14, 16.
§ Jud. i. 18.

Philistines; just as Saxons, Danes, and Normans, immigrating into our own island at different epochs, became gradually amalgamated, and united under the one name of English. And as the mixture of races is believed to be one of the chief causes of the strength and energy which mark the English people, a similar cause may have operated in more remote ages to produce the flexibility, vigour, and persistency, which distinguish the Philistine from all the other nations with whom Israel had to contend. Unlike the English, who took a united name, suggested by the shape of the island in which they finally settled, the Philistines took a united name—having the general signification of " emigrants," or "strangers"—suggested by their habits and history previous to their settlement. *

In one respect the Philistines resembled all the other hostile nations whom previous judges had subdued. They were superstitious idolaters. Each of their great cities seems to have been the seat of a special worship. At Ashdod and at Gaza were great temples to Dagon,† the fish god; Ekron was the seat of the worship of Baal-zebub and his oracle, whence he is called "the god of Ekron;"‡ at As-

---

* That the name "Philistine" was used by themselves, is clear from the challenge of Goliath (1 Sam. xvii. 8). On the etymology, see Smith's Dict., vol. ii. p. 843, note; where there is also an interesting view of the theories respecting the origin of this people which have been at different times propounded.

† 1 Sam. v. 3–5 ; Jud. xvi. 23.   ‡ 2 Kings i 2, 16

kelon was the far-famed temple of Ashtaroth, the Syrian Venus ; * and, in later times, of Derceto, the fish goddess, the symbol of the passive principle in reproduction. " Priests and diviners "† were attached to the various seats of worship ; and the people were so wedded to their superstitions, that in the times of peace they carried about with them charms which had been blessed by the idol-priest, and in war they conveyed their idols with them in their campaigns, and proclaimed their victories in their presence.‡ Between such a race and the covenant people of Jehovah, there could be no intimate and cordial friendship, so long as the latter remained faithful ; for " what agreement hath the temple of God with idols ? "§

In relating the youthful history of Samson, the author of the Book of Judges records that "*at that time the Philistines had dominion over Israel.*"‖ Each of their five cities had its own " lord," or petty king ; each had its own portion of territory adjacent, and its neighbouring dependent towns, or "daughters ;" but all together formed one state, and debated and acted together on any great occasion. Their territory formed part of the promised land, being in the allotment of the tribe of Judah,¶ but no portion of it was con-quered till after Joshua's death ; and the cities which,

---

* 1 Sam. xxxi. 10.   † 1 Sam. vi. 2.
‡ 2 Macc. xii. 40 ; 1 Sam. xxxi. 9.
§ 2 Cor. vi. 16.   ‖ Jud. xiv. 5.   ¶ Josh. xv. 2, 12, 45-47.

as we have seen, had been won from them by the
victorious arms of Judah and Simeon, had again
been lost. Not only had the Philistines succeeded in
recovering those cities, but they had carried on an
aggressive policy against the Israelites ; and, in the
time of Samson, had acquired so complete an
ascendancy over them, that the broken-spirited
Israelites reprobated any attempt at deliverance.*
An organized attempt at resistance was indeed made
under Eli the priest, when the Philistines had pene-
trated to the very centre of the country, but it was
unsuccessful; and the loss of the ark indicates a lower
depth of degradation and servitude than had been
previously reached.†

The Philistines were a far more powerful enemy
than any with whom the chosen people had yet contended. The plain in which they had settled is one
of the richest in the world, and in time of famine its
fields of corn were the hope of Palestine.‡   It was
also most favourably situated for commerce, being the
great highway between Phœnicia and Syria in the
north, and Egypt and Arabia in the south. A vast
slave trade was carried on, for which the unhappy
Israelites, during the times of their servitude, supplied
an abundance of victims.§   The Philistines were skil-
ful as smiths, as armourers, as builders ; and money
was plentiful among them.‖   They had ports attached

---

* Jud. xv. 12.   † 1 Sam iv. 2, 17.   ‡ 2 Kings viii. 2.
§ Joel iii. 4, 6 ;   Amos i. 6.
‖ 1 Sam. xiii. 20 ; xvii. 5, 6 ; Jud. xvi. 5, 18.

to Gaza and Askelon, and probably they possessed
a navy. Strong in weapons and in wealth, they
carried on a system of incursions which kept the
Israelites in a state of perpetual disquietude, destroyed the security of the roads, put an end to trade
and intercourse, enriched the invaders with plunder,
and resulted in a complete disarmament of the helpless Hebrews, that at length "there was no smith
found throughout all the land of Israel : for the Philistines said, Lest the Hebrews make them swords or
spears ;"* nor could an Israelite farmer so much as
sharpen his axe without the permission of these
tyrants.

Such was the intolerable yoke, toward the removal
of which from the necks of the elect people Samson
effected something, though less than he might have
done, had he not himself been enslaved by his passions.
With his death, the history of the Book of Judges
ends ; the subsequent chapters being, as it were, side
illustrations of the period, as is also the short Book of
Ruth. The deliverance from the Philistines which
Samson began to effect, was carried on by Samuel,
his great successor. The chronology of the period is
best fixed by comparing the statement in the Book
of Judges, that "the Lord delivered them into the
hands of the Philistines forty years,"† with the
account of the Philistines' subjugation, and of the
restoration of their cities to the Israelites by Samuel;

---

* 1 Sam. xiii. 19.   † Jud. xiii. 1.

after which it is said that "the Philistines came no more into the coast of Israel; and the hand of the Lord was against the Philistines all the days of Samuel."* This appears to mark the end of the forty years' usurpation; and as Samson is said to have "judged Israel in the days of the Philistines twenty years,"† it seems to follow that his death occurred not more than twenty years previous to the time just referred to, when the prophet Samuel erected his Ebenezer of triumph.   It follows, unless we imagine Samuel to have been less than twenty years of age at the time of this great victory, which seems improbable—that Samuel was born before Samson's death, and that the priesthood of Eli was contemporary with the judgeship of Samson.   Doubtless the wonderful stories of Samson's mighty deeds were listened to by the child Samuel while he ministered to the Lord in Shiloh; nor is it unreasonable to suppose that, while yet a youth, he felt himself stirred by an inward impulse to carry forward the work which the gigantic but unhappy Danite had begun.   The history of Samuel, however, lies beyond the limits of this volume.

---

* 1 Sam. vii. 13, 14.   † Jud. xv. 20.

25

THE YOUNG NAZARITE
Judges 13

THE tribe of Dan occupied the smallest allotment of any of the twelve tribes in the land of Canaan. It was the last of the tribes to receive its portion, which was surrounded by the three most powerful tribes of the Israelitish confederacy, Judah, Ephraim, and Benjamin. Small as was the territory, the Danites had succeeded but imperfectly in obtaining possession of it. In a previous section we have seen that they were less successful than most of their brethren in their operations against the heathen who had preceded them : "The Amorites forced the children of Dan into the mountain, for they would not suffer them to come down into the valley." * And even at a period long subsequent to those early struggles, "the tribe of the Danites sought them an inheritance to dwell in ; for unto that day all their inheritance had not fallen unto them among the tribes of Israel." †
The rich plain of the Shefelah, which, even in the present degenerate condition of Palestine, is enormously

---

* Jud. i. 35.   † Jud. xviii. 1.

productive, lay for the most part within the boundary of this tribe ; the remainder of its allotment consisting of the rugged and rent slopes of the ranges of hills by which the highlands of Judah and Benjamin descend to the maritime plain.   The extreme richness of this region rendered it a prize worth fighting for, and caused the history of the tribe to be a series of struggles, first with the Amorites and afterwards with the Philistines.   Time after time the Danites were forced up by their enemies from the cornfields of the plain, with their deep black soil, to the villages whose ruins still crown the hills that skirt the lowland.   A vivid and most characteristic picture of the manners of the men of this tribe is supplied in the narrative of Micah, in the eighteenth chapter of the Book of Judges—a most fresh and interesting story, from the study of which a clear insight may be gained into the social, political, and religious condition of the Danites at that time.

In a hollow, just below the brow of a sharp-pointed conical hill, overlooking the course of two mountain torrents, is the modern village of *Sur'ah*, which appears to be identical with Zorah, the birthplace of Samson.   It overlooks the whole Philistine plain, and most of the border land ; and the great hero must have been accustomed from childhood to the prospect of that Philistine country outstretched at the foot of his native hills.   He must have been familiar from childhood with border raids and border warfare ; and the stories which most fired his young imagination would be stories of the power and tyranny of the Philistines, who at that time had dominion not only over his own little tribe but over a great part of the land of Israel. Many a band of them, doubtless, did he see marching up the glen beneath his father's house, and returning again laden with the spoils of his brethren; many an act of rapine and cruel outrage and barbarous murder left an impress deep and lasting on his mind, stirring him in after years to revenge.

The circumstances attending the birth of Samson are related with great minuteness. Of Manoah, his father, nothing is known beyond what the sacred narrative supplies; nor can it now be determined whether Josephus had good authority for describing him as "without controversy the best and chiefest person of his country," and his wife as a woman of exceeding beauty.* She had no child; and "the angel of the Lord"—probably no other than the same Divine Person who had appeared to Gideon at Ophrah —appeared to her with the announcement that she would bear a son. The prediction was accompanied with a command that he should be separated to God from his birth as a Nazarite; that, accordingly, he was to drink no wine nor strong drink, nor to eat anything unclean, nor to allow a razor to come on his head; and the command was accompanied with the pro-mise—most seasonable and inspiring at that time of

---

* Jos. Ant. v. 8.

servitude and suffering—"*He shall begin to deliver Israel out of the hands of the Philistines.*" *

Manoah did not see the messenger, but he seems to have at once, in the spirit of humble faith, received the communication as from God ; and in the simplicity of his heart he entreated the Lord that the man of God might be sent again with yet further commands "*O my Lord, let the man of God which thou didst send come again unto us, and teach us what we shall do unto the child that shall be born.*" The simple faith here displayed is very instructive. We may repudiate as absurd the suggestion of Josephus, that jealousy prompted Manoah to offer this request ; and may accept the vindication of Ambrose, who maintains that the father of Samson was moved only by the desire to know the will of God more perfectly, and to participate in the grace with which his wife had been honoured.† It may be further noted that he displayed no doubt or hesitation on account of his wife's long barrenness, but at once believed the heavenly message and looked upon its fulfilment as certain.

His prayer was answered : "*The angel of God came again unto the woman as she sat in the field,*" and waited until she had brought her husband. No additional directions however were given. It was not to be supposed that the Messenger from the Ineffable Presence would have made an imperfect communi-

---

* Jud. xiii. 1–5.   † S. Ambr. Ep. 70.

cation ; but the humble man of Zorah did not think
of this, and the Great Father condescended, as in ten
thousand other instances, to the erring weakness of
His child. Like Gideon before him, Manoah entreated
the Stranger to remain until he had offered Him the
hospitality of a kid ; not knowing, as the narrative
expressly states, that He was an Angel of the Lord.
Even the mysterious reply of the Stranger to his offer
of hospitality did not suggest to Manoah that He was
any other than an ordinary prophet ; and in his
simplicity he asked the direct question, " *What is Thy
name, that when Thy sayings come to pass we may do
Thee honour ?* "—apparently having in his mind the
customary present which a prophet commissioned on
such an errand might expect, and of which instances
are not wanting in the Old Testament.*

It was at this point that the eyes of the simple
believing Danite began to be opened to perceive the
real character of his mysterious Visitor. To the inquiry after His name, the Angel-Jehovah replied, "*Why
askest thou thus after my name, seeing it is secret?*"
or "*wonderful ;*" the Hebrew word being the same,
with merely the variation of an adjectival suffix, as
that employed by Isaiah, when speaking of Christ, he
says, " His name shall be called *Wonderful.*"† It is
the more to be regretted that our authorized version
has not used the word *wonderful* here, instead of

---

* 1 Kings xiii. 9 ; 2 Kings v. 15 ; 1 Sam. ix. 7.
† Isa. ix. 6.

secret; because immediately afterwards, in speaking of the acceptance of Manoah's offering, it is said that " *the angel did wonderously* "—according to His name of *Wonderful.*

The kid which Manoah, like Gideon, had hastily fetched, was now, together with a meat-offering, laid upon a rock which served for an altar, and presented in sacrifice to the Lord. Manoah was not a priest, and therefore was not entitled, any more than Gideon was, according to the letter of the law, to offer a sacrifice; but he was constituted a priest for this special occasion by the Divine permission, though not, so far as we are aware, by express command. And the acceptance of his sacrifice, as well as of those offered by Gideon and by Samuel,* who were not of the sons of Aaron, proves that the Mosaic law allowed of some latitude of interpretation, and that the act of assuming the priest's office was sinful or otherwise according to the motive which prompted it and the exigency of the case. It is clear, at all events, that this sacrifice offered by an unconsecrated person was accepted. " *For it came to pass, when the flame went up toward heaven from off the altar, that the angel of the Lord ascended in the flame of the altar.*" In the flame of the burnt-offering the mysterious Presence vanished; having first brought fire out of the rock to consume the offering, and then ascending and vanishing in the flame.

---

* 1 Sam. vii. 9.

We are too little acquainted with the world of spirit, and with the laws which govern the manifestation of spiritual beings, to enable us to explain either the visibility of the Angel or His disappearance. We cannot explain, for example, or define the law according to which the body of our Saviour, after His resurrection, was sometimes visible and sometimes invisible ;—how It could enter a room, the door being shut, and this not by a miracle, but in accordance with the natural properties of that risen Body. Solutions of this kind are beyond our philosophy in this corporeal state. But there is nothing repugnant to reason in supposing that conditions may exist, whether of the object beheld, or of the beholder, under which a non-corporeal being may become manifest to us ; certainly there is no difficulty in believing this to be possible in the case of Him who, while Lord of all, has taken human nature into union with Himself.

The good man and his wife were overpowered by the wondrous sight. They "*looked on it, and fell on their faces to the ground.*" Lifting up their heads at length, all around them appeared no otherwise than as they had been accustomed to see it. The rock was there which had formed their altar, and the ashes of the sacrifice were upon it ; the conical rock towered above them, the plain of the Shefelah, with its corn-fields and the blue Mediterranean beyond, lay outstretched at their feet ; "*but the Angel of the Lord did no more appear to Manoah and to his wife.*" What were their feelings, as rising from the ground they glanced at each other? A legend maker would have filled them with transports of joy at having received the long-desired promise of a son, together with so wonderful a manifestation of the Divine favour; but in the sacred narrative the exquisite simplicity of truth appears. "*Manoah knew that he was an Angel of the Lord;*"—but instead of congratulating his wife upon the distinction conferred on them, and upon the satisfaction of their mutual hope so long delayed, "*Manoah said unto his wife, We shall surely die, because we have seen God.*" The interview had filled him with unutterable awe and fear. Like Jacob at the brook Jabbok, he had "seen God face to face;" could his life be preserved? * He was not so ignorant as to affirm that they had seen the *Jehovah*, All-sufficient and Ineffable One, whom "no man hath seen at any time;"† it was enough that, as he declared, they had seen *Elohim*, the Manifester, the Messenger; and, like Gideon, when the apparition had passed away, he supposed that he could no longer remain in this world. But he had "a help meet for him;" and in this instance the woman was wiser than the man. Her reply to her alarmed lord has in it such an exquisite naturalness, as to supply in itself no slight evidence of the authenticity of the entire story: "*If the Lord were pleased to kill us, He would not have received a burnt-offering and a meat-offering at our hands, neither would He have showed us all these*

---

* Gen. xxxii. 31.   † 1 John iv. 12.

things, nor would as at this time," that is, before they came to pass, *"have told us such things as these."*

In the most degenerate times, the Lord has always had His hidden ones, whom—like the seven thousand in Elijah's time who had kept themselves free from the Baal worship, or like Cornelius and his household amidst the corruptions of pagan Rome—He is pleased to "set apart for Himself."* Very beautiful and suggestive is the picture which the sacred writer here presents of a pious couple, true worshippers of God in an age of ignorance and idolatry, and true helpers of each other, notwithstanding the long disappointment of their early hopes in the holy bond of marriage. To such humble and faithful ones, who amidst prevailing corruption retained their integrity and adhered to the service of Jehovah, in a time when "the word of tne Lord was precious, and there was no open vision,"† He was pleased to manifest Himself, and openly to show His favour.

"The woman bare a son and called his name Samson," or *Shimshon,* as in the Hebrew ; a name to which several significations have been assigned. The most natural is that of *"little sun,"* or *"sunlike,"* as a derivative of *shemesh,* the Hebrew word for *"sun ;"* but some (as Josephus) refer it to another root, and understand it to mean *"strong ;"* while others again (as Gesenius) take it to allude to the awe and astonishment which Manoah felt at the appearance of the Angel.

---

* Ps. iv. 3.   † 1 Sam. iii. 1.

The childhood and youth of Samson are described in two short but quite beautiful verses, which the dividers of our Bible into chapters and verses have, with a discrimination not uniformly displayed by them, made to stand out prominently, separated, as it were, from the sad and polluting details which follow. "*The child grew, and Jehovah blessed him; and the Spirit of Jehovah began to move him at times in the camp of Dan between Zorah and Eshtaol.*"

The child was blessed in fulfilment of the vow by which his parents, on the bidding of the Angel, had consecrated him as "*a Nazarite to God from the womb.*" How religiously this vow was kept by his parents—how diligently they inculcated its nature and obligations upon their son—how all through his erratic manhood the remembrance of it never forsook him,— may be inferred from that sad and shameful scene of his latter days, when at last he allowed the harlot to extract from him the secret of his strength. To denote his vigorous observance of the law, it was enjoined, not only upon himself, but upon his mother before him, to "*eat no unclean thing.*" To show that his mission was not an ordinary but an extraordinary one, and that his wonderful acts of courage and strength were not due to any artificial stimulus, they were to "*drink no wine nor strong drink.*" And as an outward and visible sign of his separation to God, it was commanded, "*No razor shall come on his head.*" *

---

* Jud. xiii. 4, 5.

These were the usual conditions of the vow of a Nazarite, as laid down by the law of Moses. In addition to these, the Nazarite was forbidden not only to drink but to eat of the fruit of the vine in any form—the grapes, whether moist or dried, being as rigorously forbidden as the wine extracted from them. He was further prohibited from touching any dead body, and from performing the last offices even for his nearest kindred, being regarded, "all the days of his separation as holy unto the Lord." * The Nazarite vow is viewed in the Pentateuch only as temporary; provision being made in the law for a proper release from it at the expiration of the appointed period, which extended commonly to thirty or sixty days; although one instance is on record of the vow extending to twenty-one years.† The Apostle Paul appears to have once taken a modified Nazarite vow upon himself, probably only for the customary period of thirty days, and to disarm Jewish hostility. On another occasion, and with the same object, he paid the charges for four poor Jewish Christians, the term of whose vow had expired, and who probably were unable to provide the usual fees for their legal release. ‡ The vow, which involved only a very mild asceticism, seems to have been regarded usually as a kind of penance;

* Num. vi. 2–8.

† Smith's Dict. (vol. ii., p. 471–475), Art. "*Nazarite*," where the whole subject is fully discussed and explained.

‡ Conybeare and Howson's St. Paul, ii. 298–301.

and its performance, in ordinary cases and for limited periods, attracted little or no public attention.

It is not proposed to enter here into a disquisition on the history of the Nazaritish vow, an institution which clearly existed amongst the Hebrew people before the time of Moses, and whose origin is involved in obscurity. Samson is the earliest example on record of a Nazarite known as such by name, and he is also the earliest example of the Nazaritish vow being imposed not voluntarily, but by Divine appointment, and not for a limited period, but for life. Three Nazarites are mentioned in Scripture :—Samson, Samuel, and John the Baptist. To these an early Christian tradition adds James the Just. The Hebrew word *nazir*, is also used in three passages unconnected with what is elsewhere understood as the Nazarite vow, in the sense apparently of separation from others as a prince. * There can be no question that Samson was brought up a Nazarite in the strictest sense. The blessing of Jehovah which rested upon his childhood was at once a result and a reward of the care with which his parents instructed him in the law of the Lord, and, as he became able to understand it, in the special nature of that vow by which he had

---

* Gen. xlix. 26, where dying Jacob invokes blessings "on the head of Joseph, and on the crown of a Nazarite from his brethren."—Compare the authorized version : the other passages are Deut. xxxiii. 16, a repetition of the above, and Lam. iv. 7, which does not appear to refer to the ordinary Nazarite under a vow.

been separated for life as a witness for the covenant God of Israel.

Well may we linger upon the Eden-like picture of this youthful Nazarite, for in his chequered and aberrant after-history, we shall not meet again with anything so fair. The statement that "*the child grew, and the Lord blessed him,*" points to something more than development of physical strength. It may be doubted, indeed, whether the superhuman strength occasionally put forth by this singular hero was habitual to him ; whether it existed any otherwise than in sudden illapses, occurring at particular periods, when an extraordinary power possessed him. We imagine him at this tender age, not according to the fable of the infant Hercules, strangling monstrous serpents with his baby hands—a frightful prodigy of precocious strength and courage ; but rather according to the pattern of the child Samuel, of whom it is said that he " grew, and the Lord was with him ;"* or, allowing for the difference of the epoch, of that later Nazarite whose education "was in the deserts till the day of his showing to Israel," and of whose early days we read that "the child grew, and waxed strong in spirit."† Some, indeed, have not shrunk from suggesting a resemblance to another Holy Child, Who "increased in wisdom and stature and in favour with God and man ;"‡ and they have pointed to Samson as a prefiguration of Christ in a variety of

---

* 1 Sam. iii. 19. † Luke i. 80. ‡ Luke ii. 52.

particulars in which the two histories coincide ; as for example the announcement of his nativity by an angel—in the terms of which his mother was saluted —in the circumstance that it was not his father but his mother who gave him his name—in the signification of that name itself—and in the Divinely appointed vow by which he was consecrated to the Lord.

It was in his early youth, doubtless, that "*the Spirit of the Lord began to move him at times in the camp of Dan between Zorah and Eshtaol.*" The situation of the place suggests that he was yet an inmate of his father's house—in this respect unlike Samuel, his neighbour and successor, who was given up by his parents to reside with Eli, then the high-priest, at the sanctuary of Shiloh. "The camp of Dan," under another name, "*Mahaneh-dan,*"—which, however, is merely the Hebrew left untranslated—is mentioned elsewhere in the Book of Judges, where it is described as being "behind Kirjath-jearim," * the "city of forests." This place was situated higher up the mountain-slopes than Zorah, where the parents of Samson resided. It is described by a recent traveller, who viewed the circumjacent region from the heights of Mizpeh, as being "perched on the side of the hill where the ark of the Lord remained so long in the house of Abinadab," † Travellers by the road from Jaffa to Jerusalem pass the ravine

---

* Jud. xviii. 12.   † Porter, 171 ; Robinson, ii. 11.

known as *Wady Ady*, at the upper or eastern end of which is the modern village of *Kuriet-el-Enob*, believed to be the Kirjath-jearim of Scripture; a place of which a German tourist reports, in singular accordance with the signification of its ancient name, that "for real genuine woods, so thick and so solitary, he had seen nothing like them since he left Germany."*

In this uneven and densely wooded country, behind the "city of forests," was Mahaneh-dan, the encampment which the boy, who was destined to be afterwards chronicled by the prophet Samuel as "him of Dan,"† was accustomed to visit, climbing the rugged hills above his father's house. The position was an important one. Previous to Joshua's conquests it had been a sanctuary of Baal, and it had borne the name of that heathen god.‡ In or near Samson's time it had been the fortress of the six hundred men of Zorah and Eshtaol, who went forth to recover the lost possessions of their tribe;§ and it appears to have been a permanent encampment or military station of the Danites. His boyish days were spent within an hour's walk of the camp; and as David, when a shepherd lad, was directed by his father, a century later, to leave "his few sheep in the wilderness," while he carried messages and pro-

---

* Tohler, quoted in Smith, ii. 43.

† I Sam. xii. 11, *Bedan;* so at least some render this Hebrew name.

‡ Josh. xviii. 14. § Jud. xviii. 11, 12.

visions to his soldier-brothers in the encampment in the valley of Elah,* so doubtless it was with the full consent of his parents that Samson, while yet a boy, visited often "the camp between Zorah and Eshtaol."

His parents, doubtless, encouraged these repeated visits. Perhaps, like the father of Hannibal, they taught him to vow life-long hostility to the enemies of his country. He would hear, from the veterans of his own tribe, and from men of Judah and men of Benjamin, on the border of whose inheritance the Danites fixed their encampment, tales of Philistine violence and cruelty which would stir his youthful blood, and move him with compassion for his outraged countrymen, not only of his own little tribe, but of other tribes of Israel. He would hear of the blasphemies of the Philistines against Jehovah, whose covenanted servant and witness he already knew himself to be. He would learn from the fighting men in the encampment how fruitless had been all the resistance of the Israelites, how helpless they were to prevent their maidens being sold away into unknown lands by the Philistine slave-traders, and their cultivators of the soil from being plundered at every vintage and harvest. He would find despondency prevailing in the camp. There was a tyranny over Israel which could not be successfully resisted. The cruel bands of armed plunderers, whom he had often seen marching up the

---

* 1 Sam. xvii. 2, 17, 28.

glen beneath his father's house, and returning again laden with the spoils of his brethren, could not be suppressed. The courage of the chosen people was sinking beneath the inexorable oppression under which they groaned, and hope itself was beginning to expire. "Knowest thou not," said the men of Judah to Samson, "that the Philistines are rulers over us?" *

It was in these times of national dejection and disgrace that the spirit of indignation, of righteous impatience and scorn of intolerable wrong, began to display itself in the uncombed Nazarite lad who frequented the camp. It was Samson's special gift to feel and exhibit an inexpressible indignation and hatred on account of the tyranny of the Philistines; it was reserved for a holier Nazarite, brought up not in the camp but in the sanctuary, to subdue by his prayers the enemy whom Samson's might and Israel's armies had failed to subdue. †

" *The spirit of the Lord began to move him at times in the camp.*" The Hebrew word which describes the action of the spirit of Jehovah upon the youth, is one which seldom occurs, and the versions render it differently. "The Spirit of the Lord began to be with him," says the Vulgate ;—"began to go forth with him," say the Seventy ;—"began to sanctify him," says the Targum of Jonathan ;—"began to strike him like the iron on the anvil," is the gloss of an old

---

* Jud. xv. 11.   † 1 Sam. vii. 9-13.

French writer. Where the word occurs elsewhere in the Bible, our translators render it "*troubled.*" Thus the Psalmist exclaims, "I am so *troubled* that I cannot speak;" and Pharaoh and Nebuchadnezzar are, each of them, said to be *troubled* on the morrow after their dreams. * We may conceive, then, that Samson became "*at times*"—for this movement of the Spirit is represented as only occasional—filled with perturbation and distress. Indignation at the wrongs his countrymen were suffering, grief on account of their apparent helplessness, zeal for their deliverance and for the honour of Jehovah, filled his young soul, and wrought him up at times to an ecstatic fervour. A greater than Samson had "gone out unto his brethren," when they were slaves in Egypt, "and looked on their burdens." Indignant at the wrongs heaped upon the innocent, Moses yielded to the impulse of his indignation, slew an Egyptian, and hid his body in the sand. Such an act, committed under such circumstances, must not be estimated according to the standard of our civilized times, when every wrong may be righted by appeal to law. Nor were the times of Samson calculated for the display of the gentle graces, at least in public affairs; and his young soul was moved by the Spirit of Jehovah to the contemplation of deeds from which perhaps we should now recoil. "*At times*"—on certain occasions which might make known to his people that Jehovah was marking out the young Nazarite of Zorah for special

* Ps. lxxvii. 4: Gen. xli. 8; Dan. ii. 1; iv. 5.

service—he was filled, evidently to those around, with uncontrollable indignation at the bondage they suffered, and with mysterious anticipations of the future.

26

THE MARRIAGE AND ITS RESULTS
Judges 14:1—15:7

THE first recorded act of Samson is one which involved a violation of the law. Having gone "*down to Timnath*"—a place on the borders of the plain, which at that time was in possession of the Philistines—he "*saw a woman in Timnath of the daughters of the Philistines*," whom he resolved to solicit in marriage. Nothing can be more explicit than the prohibition in the Mosaic code of any such alliance between the chosen people and the idolaters inhabiting the land. * But in the times under review, the law on this point, though well known, appears to have been but little regarded ; † and in the absence of any authority able to enforce it, " every man did that which was right in his own eyes. ‡

The young man's wishes, however, were not to be gratified without remonstrance on the part of his parents. At what age he had arrived when he named his request to them, we are not informed ; among the

---

* Exod. xxxiv. 16 ; Deut. vii. 3, 4 ; Josh. xxiii. 12.
† Jud. iii. 6, 7. ‡ Jud. xxi. 25.

Jews a young man might be given in marriage after he had completed his thirteenth year and one day, and a virgin when she was twelve years old and one day; but the males were usually married at the age of eighteen. * The father and mother of Samson reminded their son of the claims of his own nation. They wished him to look round among the women of his own people; they reminded him that the Philistines were beyond the pale of the covenant; they expressed their amazement that he should select a wife from among the heathen. But all was of no avail. The impetuous ardour of the love-blinded youth overcame the remonstrances of a father and a mother who, excellent people as they were, seem to have thought that they had done their duty when they had stated their objections. "*Get her for me,*" said he, "*for she pleaseth me well;*" or, more literally, "*she is right in mine eyes.*"

Samson's conduct in consulting his parents before his betrothal to the maiden, has been extolled as a model of filial dutifulness. We fear, however, that no great praise must be accorded to him. Undoubtedly he acted rightly in consulting his parents, and undoubtedly it is the duty of children generally to do so. In his case, however, it was a matter of necessity, in order to accomplish his desire. There was no other way of obtaining the maiden, except through the request of some of the suitor's family. The choice of

---

* Paxton's " Illustrations of Scripture," i. 441.

the bride depended, according to the customs of the
time, not on the bridegroom himself, but on his rela-
tions or a friend appointed for the purpose, his personal solicitation being inadmissible.*　Samson, as a
youth living at home with his parents, could expect
success in his suit only through their intervention.　If
they persisted in refusing to negotiate with the girl's
family, his case was hopeless.　Hence his emphatic
assurance to them that his mind was made up, that
his judgment was satisfied, that she was right in his
eyes ; hence the passionate and imperative demand
which overbore the mother's and even the father's
opposition.　The self-will of the lad conquered the
resistance of his parents—with what bitter results to
himself the sequel will show.

" *Then went Samson down, and his father and his
mother to Timnath,*" to go through the formal ceremony of espousal ; a proceeding undertaken by a
friend or legal representative on the part of the bridegroom, and by the parents on the part of the bride ;
confirmed by oaths, and accompanied with presents to
the bride ; after which several months usually elapsed
before the celebration of the marriage.　The betrothal
increased his happiness ; he " *talked with the woman,
and she pleased Samson well.*"　No recollection of his
Nazarite vow appears to have marred his pleasure, as
he basked in the fascinating glances of the fair idol-
atress.　It was the hour of passion, reason and con-

---

* Paxton i. 442 ; Smith ii. 240.

science being lulled to sleep. "She is right in mine eyes," he may have exclaimed with intenser ardour than ever; forgetting that "there is a way which seemeth right unto a man, but the end thereof are the ways of death." *

And yet he ought not to have forgotten, for on his way down to Timnath, an incident had occurred which, had he rightly viewed it, would have reminded him of that high calling by which he was set apart for Jehovah. He had taken a route different from that by which his parents went. While among "the vineyards † of Timnath"—vineyards such as are still found in all the hamlets of that region, along the base of the hills and upon the mountain-sides, often in sequestered spots among rough wadies and wild cliffs, far from any human habitation—"*a young lion roared in meeting him.*" Lions are not now to be found in those solitudes, or indeed in any part of Palestine, though they are still to be met with in the desert to the south, and are found in abundance on the banks of the Euphrates, and in the jungles and marshes of Mesopotamia. ‡ But in ancient times they must have been numerous in Palestine itself, as is evident from the names of places, § and from the frequent mention

---

* Prov. xiv. 12.

† "Probably to eat grapes," says Matthew Henry ; forgetting that the fruit of the vine in any form was prohibited.

‡ Russell's "Aleppo," 61 ; Layard's "Nineveh," 566.

§ *Lebaoth*, Josh. xv. 32 ; *Beth-lebaoth*, Josh. xix. 6 ; *Arieh*, 2 Kings xv. 26 ; *Laish*, Jud. xviii. 7 ; 1 Sam. xxv. 44.

of them by the Hebrew writers, who describe them as attacking flocks, even in the presence of the shepherd,* as laying waste villages and towns,† and devouring men.‡

Samson, wandering by himself on his way down to Timnath, was encountered by one of these creatures. As the lion, with a roar, was about to spring upon him, " *The Spirit of the Lord came mightily upon him,*" and in a sudden illapse of superhuman energy, he received the beast upon his sinewy arms and "*rent him as he would have rent a kid,*" although "*there was nothing in his hand;*" much as David, while yet a shepherd boy, may be supposed to have killed the lion and the bear; § or as Benaiah, one of David's mighty men, who "slew a lion in the midst of a pit in time of snow." ‖ These examples, and especially the vivid figure employed by Amos, the herdman of Tekoa, where he depicts "the shepherd taking out of the mouth of the lion two legs, or a piece of an ear¶ —doubtless the transcript of a scene which he himself had witnessed while tending his cattle—may serve to show that the slaughter of a lion single-handed, though a prodigious feat, is scarcely to be deemed miraculous.

Yet, taking into account the entire history of Samson, and his peculiar calling, this killing of the

---

* 1 Sam. xvii. 34 ; Isa. xxxi. 4.   † 2 Kings xvii. 25.
‡ 1 Kings xiii. 24 ; xx. 36 ; 2 Kings xvii. 25 ; Ezek. xix. 3, 6.
§ 1 Sam. xvii. 34, 35.   ‖ 2 Sam. xxiii. 20.
¶ Amos iii. 12.

lion cannot be dismissed with mere astonishment at an unsurpassed feat of strength. Samson, as a Nazarite, was a living parable. The Nazarite was to be a living type and image of holiness, a symbol of entire consecration to the Lord. " It was no mere ascetical institution, as if the outward self-denial in meat and drink was in itself pleasing to the Lord ; such a spirit was as foreign to Judaism as it is to Christianity. The Nazarite was an actual symbolical lesson in a religious and moral respect "*—a kind of priest, by his manner of life, as the priests by the duties of their office, acting the part of a symbolical light and teacher to Israel. It is thus that Samson has been regarded as a type of Christ, and his victory over the lion as a figure of Him who goes forth conquering and to conquer ; who among the wild beasts in the wilderness in the power of the Spirit overcame the devil, that roaring lion ; and who, in the language of the Psalmist, treads upon the lion and the adder, and tramples the dragon under His feet.† We also, says St. Jerome, are Nazarites in Christ, and are able to conquer the lions through His power. ‡

But let us return to the narrative. The young Nazarite, on his way to Timnath, was placed in imminent danger, from which however he was

---

* Fairbairn's "Typology of Scripture," ii. 391.

† Mark i. 13 ; Ps. xci. 13.

‡ His expression is curious : " Nostrum Caput habet comam perpetuam ; et in Capite nostro, qui Christus est, fertitudinem possidemus ut interficiamus leonem."—(*Comm. in Amos* viii.)

rescued, strength being given him to rend the lion as he would have rent a kid. Yet he is not dissuaded from his purpose, nor do the mercies of God lead him to repentance. His downward course is begun, youthful passion prevails; and not even so remarkable a deliverance leads him to pause in his career. He keeps his adventure a secret, not even telling his father or his mother what he had done: his passionate desire to see the maiden absorbing every other feeling, even that of natural pride at his exploit, and of gratitude for his victory. His wonderful gift of strength has been exercised, but his weakness is equally wonderful.

A less unfavourable view, indeed, has been taken of his conduct. Many of the commentators excuse it, alleging either a Divine command, or at least a Divine dispensation authorizing him to take a heathen woman as his wife. This opinion is founded on the statement in the sacred narrative, that "*his father and his mother knew not that it was of the Lord that he sought an occasion against the Philistines.*" But the sin of Samson was not of the Lord, though the deliverance wrought thereby was. Not the evil, but the good elicited from it, was of the Lord. In Scripture language, God is frequently said to do that which He permits to be done; nor is it to be supposed that He would incite Samson to a direct violation of the law. "Would that he had been as careful," exclaims Ambrose, "in holding fast his grace, as he had been strong in

overcoming the beast ! " *   It looks," says a modern
writer, "almost as if the devil here entered into him,
for he stops to take counsel in this matter neither of
God nor man." †

Here then we see the first development of those
fleshly lusts in the future man, which did all but
drown him in destruction and perdition. His besetting sin led him, we may almost imagine, "to make
its own cunning use of what faith suggested ; taking
advantage of that, so as to encourage itself thereby,
in following out its own lawless purpose the more
resolvedly." Samson was undoubtedly moved " of
the Lord, to seek an occasion against the Philistines ;"
to break away from their yoke, and destroy their
power. But did he inquire of the Lord in what way
that occasion might best be found ? Do we find him,
like his successor Samuel, saying, even in this his
youth, " Speak, Lord, for Thy servant heareth " ?
Did he, when expostulated with by his parents, refer
at all to the will of God in the matter? Had he
any other reply than that the woman pleased him
well—as if *his* being pleased were all in heaven or
earth that had to be considered ?

It is thus that from the outset of his career,
Samson shows himself qualified only, as the angel
had foretold, to *begin* to deliver Israel. From the first
his great destinies appear marred by his vices and

---

* S. Amb. prol. i. de Spir. Sancto ; Ep. xix I.
† Bruce's " Samson," 24.

indiscretions, which incapacitated him from acting efficiently as the leader of a great people. " A mere slave of the senses, like him, who could repeatedly sacrifice or endanger the most important interests to a woman's sigh, was not one into whose hands the elders and warriors of Israel could intrust their lives and fortunes. Had he wrought out the possibilities of his destiny, and had his character been equal to his gifts, there is no knowing to what greatness he might have attained ; but, as it was, he left a name which is at once a miracle and a by-word, a glory and a shame." *

After a time, the nuptials were celebrated. A feast was prepared ; the usual customs were followed ; and to Samson thirty Philistine young men were allotted as "friends of the bridegroom" during the seven days of the festivities. On his way down to Timnath, Samson had turned aside to see the spot where he had killed the lion. The "carcase" was still lying there ; not in a putrid state, but the skeleton only and its integuments being left, all the soft and fleshy parts, doubtless, having been picked out and cleared away by vultures and ants immediately after the animal's death. In this domicile a swarm of bees had found a home. Samson took some of the honeycomb, and gave part of the honey to his parents when he rejoined them, without telling them how it had been obtained. The most unlikely agents may become instruments in

---

* Kitto, " Bible Readings," 399.

accomplishing the purposes of God, or in deciding our destiny ; and it was this swarm of bees which led to Samson's first open rupture with the Philistines— the commencement of an avowed enmity which never ceased but with his life. Riddles were then, as now, a common amusement on festive occasions. When it came to Samson's turn, he proposed one suggested by the honey he had found in the lion's carcase, accompanying it with a bet, that if they discovered the solution he would forfeit to each of them a dress of a superior description, but that if it remained unsolved, each of them should forfeit a similar dress to him. The Philistine young men guessed and tried in vain ; and so incensed were they at the idea of thirty of them being outwitted by this rough and long-haired Hebrew, that they persuaded the bride, under threat of setting her and her father's house on fire, to extract the secret from him. Men do not use threats with a woman until arguments have failed ; and it is only just to the maiden to suppose that she at first refused their request, perhaps indignantly, and only yielded under fear of a calamity which she saw, from their irritated temper, was only too likely to happen.

She pleaded, therefore, with Samson, as one pleading for life ; and not for her own life only, but for the lives of the whole family. At first she was sternly repulsed. To an Oriental, while yet young and newly married, his parents are first in his confidence, and his wife only second ; Samson accordingly replied, "*Behold I have not told my father nor my mother, and shall I tell it thee?*" But she had found her lord's weak point; "*She wept before him, and it came to pass that on the seventh day he told her, because she lay sore upon him.*" Few men perhaps, would have held out under such pressure; and his yielding on this occasion could be readily excused, if only he had remembered the error and fortified his soul for the future. His wife betrayed his secret— what else could a Nazarite to the Lord expect, who had married a Philistine?—and his companions, just at the last moment allowed by the wager, came forward with the solution of the riddle, "*What is sweeter than honey, and what is stronger than a lion?*" In reply, they heard only the bitter remark, in allusion to his wife's treachery,—"*If ye had not plowed with my heifer, ye had not found out my riddle.*" Samson left them, to provide for the payment of his forfeit; and the woman who had betrayed him he left at her father's house.

The slaughter of thirty Philistines at Ashkelon, furnished him with the changes of garments necessary for the discharge of his promise. These men he slew in one of those illapses of extraordinary strength which were connected, in a mysterious manner, with his Nazarite vow,* but no particulars are recorded such as would enable us to judge of the morality of the nation. It is clear, however, that he did not in-

---

* Jud. xiv. 19.

dulge in a promiscuous vengeance ; had this been his temper, he needed not to go so far as Ashkelon in order to find victims. He went, doubtless, in search of particular individuals,—men known to him, probably, as foremost among the oppressors of Israel, whose hands were red with the blood of murdered innocents, and whose houses were full of the spoils of his people. Not as an act of private revenge, but in his public character as a commissioned avenger and deliverer of his nation,—like his predecessor, "Shamgar the son of Anath, which slew of the Philistines six hundred men with an ox goad," *—Samson "*went down to Ashkelon and slew thirty men of them and took their spoil.*"

After this exploit, which must have struck terror into the hearts of the uncircumcised Ashkelonites, unaccustomed to see in the men of Israel anything but helpless subjection, Samson "went up to his father's house ; " his wife having been given by her father "to Samson's companion, whom he had used as his friend." After a time, unable to forget her, he revisited Timnath for the purpose of renewing the acquaintance. Being repulsed, he had his revenge—for mere revenge and cruelty on this occasion it was, unprompted by any motive but personal vindictiveness. Having caught three hundred jackals, animals which still abound in the glens † around Beth-shemesh, he tied

---

* Jud. iii. 31.

† "We lingered long amid the ruins of Beth-shemesh, pondering the incidents of sacred history which the places round us naturally suggested. The purple shadows of the wild glens

them in pairs, tail to tail, with a lighted torch between, and let them go into the cornfields and vineyards of the Philistines. For the loss of their property occasioned by the fires thus kindled, the Philistines in their turn exacted a retribution compared with which the trick of Samson was innocent. The bride who had been the unconscious occasion of all these troubles, and also her father, they "*burnt with fire*,"—an act, the malignity of which illustrates the character of the nation, and vindicates Samson's remark, that, although in this instance he had done the Philistines a displeasure, yet after all he was "*more blameless*" than they. Again he went forth, and "*smote them hip and thigh with a great slaughter*," avenging thus the memory of the cruelly injured dead.

In such strange and wild confusion was the deliverance of the chosen people from the Philistine yoke commenced. Yet amid all the perplexities of the time, the father and mother of the young Nazarite, and other like-minded and faithful ones in Israel, might see that their salvation was begun. Dimly and fitfully this truth may have appeared

---

gradually waxed darker and darker ; the bright stars came out one by one. Still we lingered, reluctant to turn away for ever from a place so strangely interesting. A long, low, plaintive wail suddenly broke the deep silence of the mountains over us. Another, like an echo, answered it from the valley. Then another and another, louder and clearer and nearer, until mountain, glen, and distant plain resounded with a ceaseless howl of jackals. They seem to be as numerous yet as they were in Samson's days."—Porter's " Giant Cities," 217.

to them, like broken patches of mountain seen through shifting mists of the morning; yet the truth neverthless it was. Single-handed, impelled by a potent force, the youth who had at times been moved in the camp of Dan by the Spirit of Jehovah, comes forward as a foe to the oppressors. The good is mingled with much evil. Still, not even moral weakness and headlong passion can obscure the fact that this youthful arm has struck a blow which causes the proud enemy to stagger. The lordly Philistines are constrained to ask, in anxiety if not in consternation, "*Who hath done this?*" A ray of hope brightens the dismal prospects of Israel.

27

TWENTY YEAR'S JUDGESHIP
Judges 15:8—16:3

O F the events of the twenty years during which
Samson judged Israel, none have been preserved except such as relate to his personal history ;
nor have we the means of ascertaining in what degree
his authority was recognised, or how far beyond the
bounds of his own tribe it extended. The narrator,
in sketches of the most vivid and picturesque
character, shows us the opening of his career, and its
termination, while the intervening period—the table-
land of his life—is hidden from our view. Between
the date of his retiring to the rock Etam after the
slaughter of the Philistines, and the disastrous day
some twenty years later, when he was enticed by
Delilah, two great exploits are related—the slaughter
of a thousand men by the jaw-bone, which took place
at the commencement of the period, and the carrying
away of the gates of Gaza, which occurred probably
towards its close. He had begun to deliver Israel.
His name and fame kept the Philistines in check,
and prevented them from completing their designs of
conquest. There was in the land a man of faith, and
the enemy was kept at bay. If it was not permitted

to Samson to lead the armies of the chosen nation to
victory, he was at least a shield and a defence to his
country during the twenty years of his administration.

After the events discussed in the previous section,
Samson went no more to his father's house, but
resided by himself in one of the caves of that wild
and rocky region. Of his parents nothing more is said,
except that his father died before him. * Although
at this time probably not more than twenty years
of age, he had already marked his name with eminence; and it was under the guidance, no doubt, of the
God of Israel that "*he went down and dwelt in the top
of the rock Etam,*" † or rather, in a cleft or cavern
of that rock; ‡ such a place, perhaps, as the cave
of Adullam, where David and his motley band of
followers found shelter; or as that cleft where Moses
stood when the glory of Jehovah passed by.

---

* Jud. xvi. 31.

† The situation of this rock is uncertain. It may probably be
the same as the Etam mentioned 2 Chron. xi. 6; only this
could not have been near Bethlehem as Wordsworth and the
article in Smith's Dictionary suppose; for the text shows it to
have been on lower ground than Zorah or Timnath, whereas
Bethlehem is much higher.

‡ Comp. Isa. ii. 21; lvii. 5, where the same Hebrew word,
siph, is used. The word occurs also 1 Kings xviii. 21, where
Elijah, standing before the multitude of Ahab's people on Carmel,
which is rent by innumerable cracks and fissures, appealed
to them, adopting a metaphor from the surrounding scenery,
"How long hesitate ye between two clefts:" between two
opinions, our version has it—correctly giving the sense, but
dropping the metaphor.

In this wild and lonely abode, what strange and conflicting memories must have haunted him! Is he to be compared, there in the rock-fissure at Etam, to the retreating tiger, gorged with his prey and returning sluggishly to his lair, to sleep and dream until recovered from that fit of cruel ravening? Or to the mountain robber returning to his impregnable dwelling to rest and to plan some new enterprise of plunder? More likely was it by far that Samson retired thither to bury himself in solitude, to meditate and pray, and to consider what way of escape was open to him from the complications in which he had become so ruinously entangled.

We can conceive of him here as reviewing the happy and innocent days of his childhood and youth, so recent, yet placed apparently so far in the distance, when the Spirit of God moved him at times in Mahaneh-dan; days which he could never forget so long as memory remained. That bright sunny morning had been overcast, and followed with ever-threatening gloom; but in the cave of Etam there appears a rending and parting of the leaden clouds, and a hopeful brightening of the sky. The backslidden spirit of this erring, yet not utterly lost Nazarite, was here recalled toward the path of obedience. His blind infatuation had been rebuked by the course of events. The maiden whom he had sought had perished in the flames. His unlawful love had brought not only upon her but upon her father an untimely end. True he had avenged their death, and had struck terror into the Philistines; but his own heart must have been pierced with poignant sorrow, and through sorrow his conscience, we may believe, was quickened. In the rocky cleft of Etam he may have repented of the sin whose sad consequences he had now time to reflect upon, and have experienced the stirrings of a spiritual resurrection, the dry bones being brought together and clothed, and the dead soul revived through the mighty working of the Spirit of the Lord.

It is in this state that we conceive him to have been when the next recorded incident, one of the most wonderful in his entire career, occurred. The Philistines had sent an army to search the land, and to take prisoner the Nazarite, who, single-handed, had inflicted upon their countrymen so terrible a chastisement. The doom which was in store for Samson, had they succeeded in their design, may be inferred from the treatment of him when, many years later, he actually fell into their hands. His quarrel with the inhabitants of Timnath became a general question, and was deemed by the Philistines a national wrong. An armament, therefore, was directed against Israel, to retaliate upon that nation the injuries which had been inflicted by an individual. Either the Israelites must deliver up Samson, or they must expect all the punishment which their tryants could inflict upon them.

Accordingly, "*the Philistines went up and pitched in Judah, and spread themselves in Lehi;*" a place, the situation of which has not yet been ascertained, but which, no doubt, was in the vicinity of the rock Etam.   To the men of Judah remonstrating against this invasion, the Philistines replied, " *To bind Samson are we come up, to do to him as he hath done to us ;*" and the reply was sufficient to awe them into submission, and to induce them to betray their national hero and defender into the hands of the enemy.   They knew where to find him.   Three thousand men of Judah went down to his hiding-place, and charged him with being a troubler of Israel.   They " *said to Samson, Knowest thou not that the Philistines are rulers over us ?   What is this that thou hast done unto us ?* "   Like the brethren of our Lord, who did not believe in Him, and like the Hebrews in Egypt, who did not understand that Moses was to be their deliverer, * these men of Judah either had not heard of the oracle respecting Samson, or, which is far more probable, they had not faith to believe it.   Nothing could be more abject than their spirit of servitude; nothing more utterly disgraceful than their language to the man who had begun to deliver them, " *We are come down to bind thee, that we may deliver thee into the hand of the Philistines.*"

It is here that Samson appears at his best; and his behaviour towards his base and cowardly countrymen confirms the view that there had been in his case a spiritual revival.   Forgetful of their high calling and of the covenant of God, absorbed in a mean and

---

* John vii. 5 ; Acts vii. 25.

timorous solicitude for their personal safety, the men of Judah purchased peace with their Philistine oppressors by betraying a brother, who ought to have been the pride of their country. What could be more degrading than their contented avowal that the Philistines were their rulers? Instead of recognising in Samson a deliverer whom the Lord had raised up for them, and rallying round him that they might smite their oppressors with his help and drive them out of the land, the men of Judah cast reproach upon him, and laid hands upon him to take him. And what could be more generous, more noble, more like Him who submitted for our sakes to the scourge and to the cross, than Samson's conduct? Did he exert his mighty strength to put to flight his contemptible countrymen, who came to take him and to deliver him bound into the hands of the enemy? On the contrary, he only stipulated with them that they should not themselves put him to death ; and having received their promise, he submitted himself to their hands ; "*and they bound him with two new cords, and brought him up from the rock.*" Is it possible to overlook the resemblance between these facts in Samson's history and those connected with the betrayal of our blessed Lord, who, after the Jews had mocked Him, declaring, " We have no king but Cæsar," instead of exerting His power and summoning legions of angels to His rescue, permitted Himself to be betrayed, bound with a cord, and delivered into the hands of those that sought His life ?

Bound with two new cords, the exulting Philistines brought Samson up from Etam, where, in a cleft of the rock, he had been communing with his God and recovering his spiritual strength, and carried him up to Lehi. The echoing valleys rang with their acclamations of triumph as they conveyed the mighty captive, now, as they thought, effectually pinioned and securely within their power. " *When he came unto Lehi, the Philistines shouted against him* " in savage and disdainful mockery, challenging him, perhaps, as the Jews afterwards challenged the Holy One of Israel, to deliver Himself, if it were in His power to do so, from His tormentors. Little did they know the power of his faith, the might of his vow. In their shouts of derision Samson felt the signal for action : " *The Spirit of the Lord came mightily upon him, and the cords that were upon his arms became as flax that was burnt with fire, and his bands loosed from off his hands.*" A rope of flax that has been burnt in the fire retains its form when taken out, but it has no strength ; it is a mere cinder, which falls to pieces at the slightest touch. Such, in point of strength, became the cords with which the hero was bound ; so easily did he free himself from them, so complete was his triumph in the power of the Spirit of Jehovah over the combined enmity of the heathen and of his own countrymen. Are we not again reminded of a mightier Samson, Who also submitted to bonds, and was delivered up through the combined malice of Jews and heathen, but Who, in the power of the

Spirit, burst the bands of death itself, "because it was not possible that He should be holden of it"?*

But Samson was not to be merely freed from the cords which had bound him. Risen, as it were, from threatened death, the Spirit of Jehovah was still mightily upon him. No sword was in his hand; but when the arm is nerved with strength, the most humble and unlikely of weapons will become effective. Casting his eyes rapidly around, he saw "*a new jaw-bone of an ass, and put forth his hand and took it.*" With this for a weapon, he fell upon the Philistines, who were filled with awe and fear at seeing him rend asunder the fetters which had bound him. They fled, and he pursued them, smiting one heap after another as he overtook them; nor did he stay his arm until a thousand men had fallen at his feet. He commemorated his victory in a short poetical strain—

> "With the jawbone of an ass, heaps upon heaps,
> With the jaw of an ass have I slain a thousand men;"

which has been censured by some as a strain of self-glorification, showing that Samson was not as modest in victory as he had been brave in fight. "He erected no altar, he offered no sacrifice; but forgetful of the duty of praise and thanksgiving, and assuming the honour of the conquest to himself, he chanted a hymn of victory and a poem of praise to himself, and consecrated the place to his own name, *and called that place Ramath-lehi.*"†

---

* Acts ii. 24.   † Wordsworth.

It is to be remembered, however, that it is by no means unusual in the East for a man to celebrate his own exploits ; and too much must not be inferred from the absence of the name of Jehovah from this brief couplet. The number, "a thousand," is doubtless used here as a round number, and there is in the original a play upon the words which cannot be reproduced in English. The name *Ramath-lehi*, or "jawbone height," contains no direct allusion to himself, but directs attention to the unlikely weapon with which he had scattered the enemies into whose hands he had been delivered as a captive.

The incident which followed confirms the view above expressed, that in the solitude of the cleft of Etam, Samson had experienced a spiritual revival. Exhausted by his efforts, "*he was sore athirst*," and he betook himself to prayer. He had not then altogether forgotten his God ; nor does he forget to ascribe his deliverance to Him in all humility. He "*called on the Lord, and said, Thou hast given this great deliverance into the hand of Thy servant ; and now shall I die for thirst, and fall into the hands of the uncircumcised?*" The prodigy of strength which he had just performed is ascribed not to the force of his own arm, but to the favour of his God ; and in the mercy of the past hour Samson finds encouragement to pray that, although ready to sink through exhaustion and to die of thirst, no succour apparently being near, Divine mercy may once more interpose for his relief. " It is a strong presumption," remarks Dr.

Kitto, "in favour of the genuineness and vitality of his faith that he did so. Not many would have had such strong persuasion of the Lord's providential care as would lead them to cry to Him for water to supply their personal wants in the like exigency. This therefore is one of the incidents which enabled the author of the Epistle to the Hebrews to put the name of Samson among the heroes of the faith. The incident shows what manner of man, essentially, he was, and indicates the kind of spirit in which his great operations were conducted."

In his hour of extremity the servant of God was not forsaken; but the correct view of his deliverance, as we conceive, is not that furnished in our authorized version. The Hebrew word *lehi*, or "jaw," is also a proper name. Some expositors, modern as well as ancient, take the word in the former sense, agreeing with our translators, that "*God clave a hollow place in the jaw, and there came water thereout*"; and many have been the edifying remarks founded on the miracle as thus represented. Not to quote from the patristic writers, who, as their manner is, have written copiously on the spiritual sense of the miracle, it may be sufficient to quote two bishops of the English Church. "God," says Bishop Hall, "who had fetched water out of the flint for Israel, fetched it out of a bone for Samson. He gave him honey from the mouth of the lion, and water from the mouth of an ass. Who will not cheerfully depend on Him who can bring moisture out of dryness, and life out of death ?"   Bishop Wordsworth remarks : " There is something of spiritual significance in the gushing forth of the fountain from the jawbone which Samson had cast away. God can make His grace to flow from the most despised instruments."

The other explanation of the word, however, is to be preferred.   It was about the time of wheat harvest, and therefore hot summer weather.   It was not an imaginary fear that, exhausted as he was, Samson might " die for thirst, and fall into the hands of the uncircumcised."   His prayer shows that he was fully conscious that he was fighting, not from personal ambition or revenge, but as the appointed champion for Jehovah ; and the Lord helped him out of his trouble by cleaving " a hollow place," not "*in the jaw*," as our version renders it, but "*in Lehi*," the name of the place where Samson then was.   Water flowed for him out of the hollow rock, as of old at Horeb and Kadesh, thus connecting the Nazarite of Dan, in the wonder of this deliverance, by a new link with God's people of a bygone age.   That this is the correct view is obvious from the statement that the fountain, which Samson in humble gratitude named *En-hakkore*,—" the fountain of the suppliant," was still in existence at the date when the Book of Judges was written.

Thus it was that at Etam and at Lehi there was a glorious revival of the gracious spirit of Samson's youth.   The light of the Lord's reconciled countenance was shining upon him, and a wonderful token

confirmed his faith.   Having cried to the Lord in his
fainting extremity, " *God clave a hollow place that was
in Lehi, and there came water thereout ; and when he
had drunk, his spirit came again, and he revived.*"   Is
it fanciful to suppose that the statement which immediately follows, that "*he judged Israel in the days of
the Philistines twenty years,*" is to be understood as
immediately connected with this ?   We have the history of his youth, and of the events leading to his
entrance on the judge's life, of which this is the closing one.   We have then narrated the sad story of the
events which led to his death.   These two sections of
his history are separated by the mention of twenty
years.   The inference is, that twenty years, or nearly
that period, elapsed, of the events of which no record
is preserved.   His fame and power were now established.   For a time, the Philistines dared not to lift
up their heads.   The exploit of the jawbone, and the
sudden outgushing of the fountain of En-hakkore in
answer to Samson's prayer—a fountain which did not
dry up, but remained as a witness for the God of
Israel and for His chosen servant—confirmed his
power, and convinced even his own countrymen that
he was called of God.   In the absence of any records of
the period, we may imagine him passing those twenty
years more or less in the spirit at once of power, of
humility, and of faith, which filled him at Lehi and
beside the fountain of En-hakkore.

28

THE END

AFTER a long interval, which is left a blank in the recorded history of Samson, he is introduced to us again, on his way to ruin. "*Then went Samson to Gaza, and saw there an harlot, and went in unto her.*" We are not to understand that this occurred immediately after his deliverance at Lehi. It was not all at once that he sunk into such a quagmire, the two events being carefully separated in the narrative by the insertion of a reference to the entire period of his judgeship for twenty years. In the interval he had doubtless performed many illustrious deeds ; and the mad festivities of the Philistines, when at length they made him prisoner, sufficiently show how formidable an antagonist he had been to them during that period. He was still observing his Nazarite vow, nor had his strength departed from him.

Of his journey to Gaza, it is not said that it was "of the Lord." Probably the impulse that led him to visit this stronghold of the Philistines was not a call of duty, but some such base motive as the temptations of great cities supply. He may have supposed that in Gaza, the remotest from his home of all the cities of Philistia, he might pass unrecognised among the ever-moving throng of traders, travellers, and pleasure seekers that continually crowded its busy streets, although his life-long growth of hair was certainly most unfavourable to a purpose of remaining unknown. It is possible that, as a consequence of long immunity from danger, he may have presumed upon his strength. In Gaza, however, he was found ; and the lodging which he selected in that city showed that, although a Nazarite, abstaining from wine and strong drink, he was nevertheless a victim of the lusts of the flesh. It is not enough to defend one part of the spiritual fortress against the enemy ; nor are we to imagine that safety lies in anything less than the guarding of the citadel at all points. Thrown off his guard by passion and by self-confidence, little did Samson imagine as he entered the harlot's house, how soon he was to be entrapped through this fatal snare ; remaining, notwithstanding his marvellous gifts, a monument for all ages of the truth of the warning, " Her house inclineth unto death."*

In his noonday prime—perhaps about the fortieth year of his age—having long kept in check the Philistines' power, being supposed personally invincible, and having acquired a name which of itself was a terror to them, Samson may have listened to the voice of other flatterers than women, and have begun by degrees to relax his efforts as the sworn scourge and destroyer of the Philistines for the deliverance of Israel. Pros-

---

* Prov. ii. 18.

perity and comparative ease may have relaxed his moral fibre and enervated his nature; suggesting to him that he had accomplished all, or nearly all, that he had to do, and that having well earned his nation's gratitude, he might now settle down and be at rest, without being at the pains of constantly occupying a position of watchful hostility toward the enemies of his country. It was probably in this spirit of contented ease and mistaken liberalism that he went down to Gaza. Being found on the devil's ground, he fell into the snare of his besetting sin; and although for this once he was delivered from the hands of his enemies, it was only for once. Failing to take warning, and yielding to his sin yet again, "*the Spirit of the Lord departed from him*," and disgrace and death were the penalty.

If Samson went to Gaza with a feeling of careless security, he had altogether mistaken the Philistine character. From the first his movements were watched. His entrance into the city had been observed. They compassed the house where he was, sleeping around it, so as to be ready to fall upon him when he should quit in the morning. Samson however arose at midnight, slipped quietly by the watchers, and reached the city gate unopposed. It was closed, but he soon effected an escape. Laying hold of the two valves of the gate, he tore up by his herculean strength the two side-posts upon which they swung, and placing them, together with the cross-bar by which they were fastened, upon his shoulders, he "*carried them up*

to the top of an hill that is before Hebron"—a height
about three-quarters of an hour's walk from the city,
from which the mountains that surround Hebron
may be distinctly seen.

Samson was thus once more out of the reach
of the Philistines. But although no longer in danger
from them, he was still in danger from that blinding
and debasing passion which possessed him. The mercies of God, instead of leading him to repentance,
appear rather to have promoted a feeling of false
security ; until at length, refusing to be warned, he fell
into a snare from which the Lord would not deliver
him. He "*loved a woman in the valley of Sorek,
whose name was Delilah.*" The place was not far from
his own abode, and the woman clearly was not his wife,
as some have supposed, for in that case she would have
been found at Samson's house, whereas Samson's repeated visits were made to her. A succession of such
visits clearly there was, although the inspired narrative
does not distinctly state this. The account, though
circumstantial, is brief, and "in the conversations between Samson and the woman, results only are stated,
without any notice of the little artifices of conversation
and dalliance, the watching for the favourable moments
and natural turns of thought and incident, which dis-
guised the wickedness of the design, and gave a seem-
ing indirectness to the woman's attempts to get possession of his secret."* There is every probability that

---

* Kitto, p. 431.

these attempts were made by her at different times, when she saw that she had a fair opportunity, and when a sufficient interval had passed to blunt the keenness of any suspicion that may have been awakened in his mind.

His visits to the house of Delilah supplied the Philistine leaders with just such an advantage as they desired ; for, as Bishop Hall has remarked, they "knew already where Samson's weakness lay, though not his strength ;" and it is not unlikely that they were familiar enough with the woman's extraordinary subtlety and power of fascination. The Philistines offered her a reward if she could discover the secret of his strength, enough in those days to enrich her for life—each of the five lords promising eleven hundred shekels of silver, a sum equal by computation to about six hundred pounds of our money, but equal in purchasing power to more than as many thousands. The magnificence of the promised present, therefore, attests how formidable a person Samson was considered ; and it confirms our belief that in the twenty years during which he judged Israel, he performed many mighty acts which the inspired record leaves unnoticed. "*Entice him*," they said to the woman, "and see wherein his great *strength lieth, and by what means we may prevail against him, that we may bind him to afflict him.*" The five lords of the Philistines left their several cities to come up to the harlot's house to arrange the plot ; showing Samson's visits there to have been become frequent and notorious.

The treacherous woman, whom Milton, in his Samson Agonistes, following many others, has without proof supposed to be a Philistine, set herself to extract from the mighty Nazarite the secret of his strength. At first he treated her importunity playfully, saying, "*If they bind me with seven green withs that were never dried, then shall I be weak, and be as another man,*" and allowed her actually to make the experiment. On another occasion he told her to bind him "*fast with new ropes that never were occupied;*" and on a third occasion to "*weave the seven locks of his head with the web,*"—an expression, the meaning of which has been variously explained. In all these he evaded her; for when she told him that there were Philistines lying in wait close at hand who were ready to fall upon him, he broke the withs and ropes like a thread, and on the last mentioned occasion, having gone to sleep, he "*went away with the pin of the beam and with the web,*" so that his strength was not known.

Several days probably elapsed between one of these experiments and another, and on each occasion spies were in attendance to take charge of the fettered giant, if it should prove that he had actually revealed the secret of his strength. That they should have renewed their attempt after three failures, shows the confidence of the harlot that she should be able to win him over, and to secure his destruction. And, indeed, on the third occasion, Samson had brought himself to the very brink of the precipice. In his presumptuous trifling with the Divine gift entrusted to him, he went so far as to suffer the hair of his head to be meddled with, though it was sanctified to the Lord.   It was at this time, probably, that "*the Spirit of the Lord departed from him*"—that the miraculous Divine gift which he had possessed was withdrawn, although, befooled by amorous passion, he knew it not.

And yet how could he imagine it to be otherwise ? It has been supposed that even from the first he saw the danger he was in, only that he had not energy to escape ;—that when he suggested to Delilah to bind him with seven green withs, there was a kind of hidden meaning, as if he had said "You could bind me with a straw—you could persuade me to anything."   "It was, in fact, the language of poetry, indicating both self-knowledge and a kind of strange presentiment, such as we have ourselves had opportunity to notice in the case of the wicked, who fell at last into the bloody hands of the executioner ; but in whom, as in Samson, there appeared a gleam of internal light, warning them beforehand of all their pitiable weakness, and of that retribution which they had the utmost reason to dread."*

However this may have been, it shows him to have been totally blinded by the woman's infatuation, when, after having allowed his hair, which was the pledge of his separation to the Lord, to be tampered

---

* Bruce's " Samson," p. 126.

with, he did not perceive that the end was near. After the manner of her accursed craft, the harlot reproached him with not returning the love she bore to him, pretending that she must either know from him the secret of his strength or die with the anguish of jealousy. Did he believe her ? No ; like Adam in the garden, he was not deceived. He knew that it was all over, and he gave himself up, having no power to return from that house of death which, with no excuse and with his eyes open, he had entered. Yet it was not for many days that he took the fatal step. How that step was taken can best be told in the simple and forcible language of our version : " *And it came to pass, when she pressed him daily with her words, and urged him, so that his soul was vexed unto death ; that he told her all his heart, and said unto her, There hath not come a razor upon mine head ; for I have been a Nazarite unto God from my mother's womb ; if I be shaven, then my strength will go from me, and I shall become weak, and be like any other man.*"

The die was cast. The harlot saw that she had succeeded. Beguiled by her sorcery, wearied with her importunity, entangled like a bird in her snare, Samson at length made in one moment that awful disclosure which, during all the years of his bygone life, he had anxiously hidden from the Philistines. He so far imposed upon himself as to imagine that neither Delilah, nor any one else, would be able to make use of the secret against him. He supposed that no one would dare to approach him so closely as to shave off those sacred locks ; or that if such an attempt were made, he would "*go out as at other times before, and shake himself*" free from his assailants. Vain supposition ! "*He wist not that the Lord was departed from him.*"

The crafty woman did not at once act upon the information she had extracted from her infatuated paramour whom she now perceived to be in her power, but allowed time to elapse, so as to allay any uneasy suspicion which a consciousness of his indiscretion might awaken in his mind. In the interval she sent down to Philistia, "*and called for the lords of the Philistines, saying, Come up this once, for he hath showed me all his heart.*" A genuine harlot, she remained unmoved by the proof her wretched dupe had given of his regard for her, and was willing to conspire to destroy him, provided she were paid for it, but not else. The lords of the Philistines, well understanding this, "*came up to her, and brought money in their hand,*" as they had agreed ; on receipt of which she was ready to proceed with her task of horrid treachery. Already, with the hellish witchery of her charms, she had drugged him into the sleep of spiritual death ; it was without difficulty, therefore, that on his next visit to her house, according to a common custom in the East, "*she made him sleep upon her knees;*" and sleep he did so profoundly, perhaps under the influence of some soporific drug, that he remained unconscious while the seven sacred locks of his head were being shaved off by a man hired for the purpose. As before, she awoke him with the cry, " *The Philistines be upon thee, Samson ;*" and as before, he thought to free himself in an instant from their grasp. It was in vain. He found himself "*weak as another man.*" His hair, the symbol and pledge of his consecration to Jehovah, had been shorn ; the crown of his glory had been sacrificed to a harlot ; and with the violation of his vow his mysterious strength had departed from him. To resist was of no avail. A party of Philistines, who had been lying in wait under Delilah's direction, fell upon him, and soon overpowered him, They held him fast ; savage operators at once put out his eyes, and having fettered his hands and feet with double brass chains, they brought him to Gaza. There, in the prison, blind and helpless, he was sentenced to grind at a handmill—the hardest and lowest kind of slave labour.

Nothing in all history is more affecting than the picture of this fallen hero of Israel ; blind, helpless, tortured with slavish taskwork in a loathsome dungeon, and apparently doomed to wear out the remnant of his life in unutterable and unrelieved wretchedness. Two of the noblest of sacred dramas, the one in the language of poetry, the other in that of music, depict with unequalled power the touching misery of the fallen hero, and the boundless exultation of the heathen over their illustrious captive.* "Ah ! Samson, mighty Samson : is it really Samson, that the slaves

---

* Milton's " Samson Agonistes," and Handel's "Samson, an Oratorio." Both of these works open with Samson already

and the rabble of Gaza now insult with impunity? Why breakest thou not thy bonds? Why dost thou not slay them in a moment? Why dost thou suffer the uncircumcised to insult thy God, and give all the glory to Dagon? Where is thy indignant soul which scattered armies, and made the earth to tremble at thy name? Is thy strength fled; are thy locks shorn? What! hast thou lost thy God in the house of adultery? Ah, thy strength is gone, thy glory departed. This is the fruit of despising thy parents' advice in marriage, of suffering thy concupiscence to lurk unmortified. Hadst thou fallen in battle for thy country, immortality would have attended thy name. But to fall by the worst of women—tell it not in Gath, publish it not in the streets of Ashkelon! Well, go in silence to the prison, grind at the mill, weep for thy sins, and thy hair shall yet grow, that God may have mercy on thy soul." *

It was as much in pity and for the recovery of His servant, as in anger to chastise and punish him, that the Lord departed from Samson, took away his gift of strength, and left him to grind, lone and miserable, in that cruel prison at Gaza. It was a proceeding which evidently he had not been prepared for. He had never really conceived that it would come to this;

---

blind, and in captivity. No less than three of Handel's oratorios are founded upon the Book of Judges—"Deborah," "Jephthah," and "Samson"; but the great musician gave the preference to his "Samson," and justly.

* Sutcliffe, vol. i., p. 226.

that he would fall helpless into the hands of the Philistines. He had presumed upon God's mercy, and "despised the riches of His forbearance and long-suffering,"* until at length, like the sudden flash in heavily-charged clouds, vengeance blazed forth, and all but consumed him. In one short day did he find himself landed as it were in hell itself, and left to linger there in "total eclipse;"† tormented by malignant devils in the shape of men besetting him; resentment burning within him as a fire; while fitful gusts of shame and remorse and utter unbelieving hopelessness swept ever and anon athwart him, rendering the flame of his torment yet hotter and more intolerable,—a type of thousands more, who lie spiritually blind and imprisoned, and bound in fetters of iron, the pains of hell laying hold on them; until, goaded on by their misery, all hope in themselves expires, and out of the depths they begin to cry to the Lord.

How long the untamed and savage fury of his wrath continued raging before it began to subside—how long he was in regaining a calm view of the covenant he had forgotten, and in beginning to yield himself to meditation and prayer—cannot be precisely stated. It is clear, however, that the return of his mysterious strength was connected with the second growth of his hair, which "*began to grow again after he was shaven.*" We can scarcely suppose that so

---

* Rom. ii. 4.   † Handel's "Samson."

obvious a circumstance would have been mentioned, unless it were intended to indicate, as Ambrose observes, that " the spiritual hair of his piety and faith began to grow again with the growth of his natural hair, when he was brought by suffering to a sense of dependence on God." It was better that he should be thus chastised, than that he should go on further in sin. " After all," says a writer already quoted, " we see mercy mixed with justice. Samson's eyes were now put out, a just requital for gazing on unhallowed beauty ; but that was better than the having eyes to gaze on sin. His feet were fettered in the mill ; but that was safer than to deviate from the paths of purity. His soul was assailed with anguish and remorse, with the insults of the heathen, and the horrors of the prison; but these were preferable to the caresses of Delilah. Here his hair grew with time, and his strength returned by repentance." *

Although the Philistines knew that Samson's strength had departed with the loss of his hair—that condition of Nazariteship with which it was inseparably connected—they probably did not expect that upon his repentance, upon his voluntarily renewing the vow of devotement to Jehovah, which he had so shamefully broken, his superhuman strength would return. Their festival of rejoicing over the hero's capture and fall was delayed, for some reason with which we are not acquainted—Divine providence

* Sutcliffe, i. 266.

ordering it so—so that his hair had time to grow again, and at the same time his spiritual strength had returned. At length the day arrived. A great sacrifice was offered to Dagon, and the blind prisoner was fetched out of his dungeon to endure the mocking insults of the Philistines. He was led into the house of Dagon, where some three thousand people were upon the roof, prepared to deride the fallen hero, while they shouted, " *Our god hath delivered into our hands our enemy, and the destroyer of our country.*"

We have no accurate acquaintance with the style of the architecture of Dagon's temple at Gaza. It may have resembled a Turkish kiosk, and have consisted of " a spacious hall, the roof of which rested in front upon four columns, two of them standing at the ends, and two close together in the centre. Under this hall the leading men of the Philistines celebrated a sacrificial meal, whilst the people were assembled above upon the top of the roof, which was surrounded by a balustrade." * At all events, there were spacious upper galleries, or perhaps seats arranged tier above tier upon the roof, from which the spectators could look down upon what was passing in the arena below.

And now came the closing scene. Samson, having requested the lad who guided him to place him so that he might lean upon one of the pillars, offered up

---

* Keil; and Faber, p. 444. Doré, in his great picture, the " Death of Samson," has depicted a totally wrong style of building. Some of his series of Samson-pictures, however, have a strange suggestiveness.

in the temple of the heathen idol a prayer to the living God. In this prayer we find no reference to himself as a private individual, but only as the recognised servant of Jehovah. Unless this be borne in mind, the prayer is scarcely intelligible. "*O Lord God, remember me, I pray Thee, and strengthen me, I pray Thee, only this once, O God, that I may be avenged of the Philistines for my two eyes.*" This was no utterance prompted by personal revenge, for it was Samson's commission from the beginning to deliver Israel from the Philistines. Weary of life it is likely he was, and impatient of his misery ; but in putting out his eyes the Philistines had insulted a servant of the God of Israel, and Samson had just heard them ascribing his fall and sufferings to the might of Dagon their god ; therefore he prays that in his capacity as a servant and representative of Jehovah, he may be avenged on them.

And now he feels himself clothed with power as of old. He has lifted up his heart to his God, and through his recovered hold upon the covenant, which in an evil hour he had let go, he now finds himself again in sympathy with the Mighty One of Israel, and is conscious of an illapse of even more than his former mysterious strength. "*Let me die,*" he exclaims, "*with the Philistines.*" Why should he desire to live, when life must be to him a lifelong shame ? Why desire to live, when to live was to carry about with him an ineffaceable mark, in his eyes put out, of his sad unfaithfulness and of the scorn of the enemies of

Jehovah? His life, in such a case, could only be to the Philistines a triumph; and now therefore, pardoned and restored, he prays that the shame of his sin may be taken from him for ever, and that the heathen might have no cause to triumph over him, or to mock through him the Holy One of Israel. With his sinewy arms he lays hold of two of the pillars supporting the roof. "He *bowed himself with all his might.*" The strain and pressure on the roof and galleries were probably such that the deflection, however slight, of a single prop, would bring the entire structure to the ground; Samson's mighty strength, applied to two of these props, produced this result; "*the house fell upon the lords, and upon all the people that were therein.*"

Thus the sons and daughters of the uncircumcised who had assembled to make sport of the fallen judge of Israel were crushed in one common destruction; their pæans to Dagon were exchanged for dying groans; and the Nazarite, in the moment of his own death, gained the greatest of his victories—a victory of Jehovah the God of Israel, against Dagon the idol of the Philistines. Being enticed, he had sinned; sinning, he had suffered; suffering, he had repented; repenting, he had prayed and waited upon the Lord; waiting upon the Lord, he had renewed his strength, and "*the dead which he slew at his death were more than they which he slew in his life.*"

Worthy then was he that his body should be tenderly borne away from among the mangled heaps of the uncircumcised, and carried by "*his brethren and all the house of his father*," as a prince and a great man in Israel, to the ancestral sepulchre, "*between Zorah and Eshtaol, in the burying-place of Manoah his father.*"   After all his sins, the All-merciful One, as we believe, gave him true repentance, and he died in faith.   The Philistines were not only plunged into grief at the loss of so many of the flower of their country as perished on that fatal day, but they were filled with consternation and terror.   Their triumph had been short.   The omnipotence of the God of Israel had been demonstrated.   The man of faith had suffered a woful eclipse, and had been sorely punished for his sin.   But in the end he had prevailed ; and his mighty exploit in death prepared the way for the victorious career of another Nazarite, already in training in the sanctuary at Shiloh, who was destined to overthrow the Philistine ascendancy, and to terminate the period of the judges by anointing a king to rule over the twelve tribes of Israel.